ography

Political Geography

An Introduction to Space and Power

Joe Painter and Alex Jeffrey

Los Angeles • London • New Delhi • Singapore • Washington DC

First published 2009

SAGE Publications Ltd
1 Oliver's Yard
55 City Road
London EC1Y 1SP

SAGE Publications Inc.
2455 Teller Road
Thousand Oaks, California 91320

SAGE Publications India Pvt Ltd
B1/I 1 Mohan Cooperative Industrial Area
Mathura Road, Post Bag 7
New Delhi 110 044

SAGE Publications Asia-Pacific Pte Ltd
33 Pekin Street #02-01
Far East Square
Singapore 048763

Library of Congress Control Number: 2008939921

British Library Cataloguing in Publication data

A catalogue record for this book is available from the British Library

ISBN 978-1-4129-0137-6
ISBN 978-1-4129-0138-3 (pbk)

Typeset by C&M Digitals Pvt Ltd, Chennai, India
Printed by TJ International Ltd, Padstow, Cornwall
Printed on paper from sustainable resources

FSC
Mixed Sources
Product group from well-managed
forests and other controlled sources
Cert no. SGS-COC-2482
www.fsc.org
© 1996 Forest Stewardship Council

To Rachel and Laura

Contents

Preface to the First Edition

The initial idea for this book arose while I was working at the University of Wales in Lampeter. I was teaching a course on Political Geography, which covered the usual topics of states, nations, territories and global and local power relations. Given the dramatic political changes that were going on in the world around me, this seemed highly topical, as well as allowing me to make good use of a long-standing academic and personal interest in politics. Casting round for ideas through which to interpret contemporary political change, I saw that many of the most interesting conceptual developments and theoretical debates in human geography seemed to be those associated with an upsurge of interest in social and cultural theory. The implications of these theories were widely regarded as highly political, and yet they seemed to be relatively little used by political geographers studying the kinds of substantive topics in which I was most interested. I'm delighted to say that four years on increasing numbers of geographers (and others) are drawing on the insights of social and cultural theory in explaining political-geographic change. The aim of this book is to show how some of these insights can help to make sense of the field of political geography.

There a number of people who have helped me along the way, and whom I would like to thank. Graham Smith first introduced me to Political Geography when I was a student and encouraged me to get this project off the ground in the first place. John Allen, Felix Driver and Miles Ogborn provided very constructive comments on a draft of Chapter 1. Although they did not always realize it at the time, I have had stimulating conversations on the subject-matter of the book with Parminder Bakshi, Paul Cloke, Mike Crang, Philip Crang, Mark Goodwin, Miles Ogborn, Isobel MacPhail, Chris Philo and Alan Southern. The Geography Departments at the University of Wales, Lampeter and the University of Durham have proved welcoming, stimulating and supportive environments in which to work. Laura McKelvie at Edward Arnold has been patient and supportive. I owe most of all to Rachel Woodward, who has helped with ideas, discussions, constructive criticisms and much else besides. None of these people bears any responsibility for the shortcomings of the finished product. Finally, I have dedicated the book to my parents, Beatrice and Desmond Painter, with much love and thanks for their support over the years. They first showed me the importance of politics. I hope this book will show them why geography may be important too.

Joe Painter
Gateshead

Preface to the Second Edition

The second edition of this book emerges into a dramatically different political and intellectual context from the first. Where the first edition charted a new world order marked by post-Cold War transformations and political movements, this edition is written in a geopolitical moment characterized by the US-led military intervention in Iraq, the rise of global concerns over climate change, new anxieties over the consequences of corporate-led globalization and the increasing prominence of China as a global superpower. In tandem with these global trends we can also observe new styles of political participation and agency on a micro-scale. New social movements and non-governmental organizations (NGOs) are changing the nature of state-society relations and creating new styles of citizenship based upon direct action. This edition provides an opportunity to reflect on this political context and how it has reshaped our understandings of space and power. In intellectual terms, the second edition finds Political Geography a much altered, expanded and, we would say, strengthened strand of human geography. The first edition argued for the incorporation of social and cultural theory into Political Geography. Over the last 13 years this theoretical turn has been embraced by many political geographers, establishing a body of sophisticated and empirically rich scholarship. In this edition, we review this work and chart further questions for research and discussion. In doing so we have expanded the range of topics under consideration, undertaken a complete revision of each chapter and expanded the number of chapters from six to nine.

We would like to offer thanks to a number of people who have assisted and supported this project from its inception. In particular, we would like to thank Robert Rojek at Sage for his support and patience through the writing process. Joe would also like to thank a wonderful group of colleagues and former colleagues at Durham University, including Ben Anderson, Luiza Bialasiewicz, Karen Bickerstaff, Harriet Bulkeley, David Campbell, Rachel Colls, Mike Crang, Stuart Elden, Steve Graham, Paul Harrison, Adam Holden, Kathrin Hörschelmann, Kurt Iveson, Gordon MacLeod, Cheryl McEwan and Colin McFarlane. Alex has benefited from a welcoming and stimulating working environment at Newcastle University School of Geography, Politics and Sociology, in particular from teaching political geography alongside Nick Megoran. Alex would also like to thank Colin McFarlane, Alex Vasudevan,

Matthew Bolton, Dan Swanton, Peter Thomas, Craig Jeffrey, Jane Dyson, Ewan Jeffrey and Sara Fregonese for advice and friendship. The new edition is dedicated to Rachel Woodward and Laura Jeffrey, with much love and thanks.

Joe Painter and Alex Jeffrey
Gateshead and Durham

Introduction

In recent years human geography has seen a considerable blurring of its constituent sub-disciplines. The traditional divisions between economic, social, political and cultural geography seem increasingly irrelevant as geographers focus more and more on the connections between them. It no longer makes sense (perhaps it never did) to think of separate economic, political and cultural 'spheres', each with distinctive geographical conditions and effects. Among others, Marxist geographers have charted the connections which make the economy 'political', feminist geographers have thought in new ways about the division between public and private which has undermined any essential distinction between the social and the economic and political, while environmental geographers have shown the importance of understanding the ways our use of, and impact on, the environment depends on particular cultural constructions of 'nature' and of our relationships to it.

One of the liveliest of these refashionings of the study of human geography has taken place in social and cultural geography. Among other things this has involved a focus on a range of new concerns, including:

(1) *The communication of meaning*. Drawing from work in cultural and media studies, geographers have become increasingly interested in the ways in which social life is rendered meaningful to people. The process of ascribing meaning ('signification') is seen as an unequal one, so that different meanings operate to advance the interests of different people or social groups. Meaning is not seen as transparent and clear, but as socially-produced and contested.

(2) *The production and effects of discourses*. Related to (1), the concept of discourse refers to a range of meanings, or meaningful statements, which come to be linked together in a broader framework. The framework, or discourse, provides a particular 'mode of thinking' which allows us to understand things in a certain way. For example, a discourse might identify some issues as more important than others, or some forms of behaviour as better than others. They aren't (necessarily) more important or better in any absolute sense, but they are made to seem so by the discourse.

(3) *Human subjectivity and identity*. Our 'subjectivity' is 'who we are', or rather 'who we feel ourselves to be' and 'who we are made to be' by society. Social and cultural geographers have been interested in the development of

different subjectivities and identities in different places and among different social groups, and the ways in which the construction of identities happens through the operation of different discourses. Many writers have suggested that as individuals we all have multiple identities: we are different people in different contexts.

(4) *Critique of geographical knowledge.* Geographical knowledge does not consist of transparent and value-free truths in the way that has often been assumed in the past. Like all knowledge, it is the product of partic- ular social and political contexts, and as such it advances certain inter- ests, often at the expense of others. One aspect of the 'cultural turn' in geography has involved investigating the process through which geo- graphical knowledge has been (and is) produced and uncovering the (often unequal) power relations which it serves.

(5) *The operation of human agency.* Human agency refers to the capacities of human beings and their role in producing social outcomes. While human beings are not able just to do anything they please, human agency does 'make a difference', even if its effects are not always intended. Human agency is always situated in and conditioned by particular geo- graphical contexts. Unequal access to resources and knowledge means that the capacity of some groups and individuals to 'make a difference' is greater than that of others.

Although first highlighted in social and cultural geography, interest in these issues has recently spread much more widely through the discipline of human geography as a whole (not least because of the blurring of boundaries between its constituent parts). The relationship between discourses, knowledge, mean- ing, agency have long been seen as political, though this has often been inter- preted as referring to informal politics, or 'politics with a small p'. Recent work by political geographers has begun to question this assumption and explore how these questions of human agency and thought can be applied to the for- mal institutions of politics, of 'Politics with a capital P'. That is, the institutions and processes of the state, government and formal political organizations which have in the past made up the subject-matter of the sub-discipline of 'Political Geography'.

The purpose of this book is both to present these new strands of political geography to a wider audience and to contribute in a small way to the further blurring of the various sub-disciplines. Our principal interest is in how we might best interpret and understand changes in the complex relationship between geography and politics. We are not concerned to present a full account of all the detailed shifts in the political geography (however defined) of the world around us. Rather, what we do want to do is to illustrate through selected examples what a Political Geography which is sensitive to Social and Cultural Geography might look like.

Wherever possible we draw on the ideas and research of those geographers who have shaped this field. Where necessary, though, we also refer to the work of those in other disciplines, such as anthropology, sociology, political science and critical international relations, if it illuminates the important issues. We hope the book will be useful and interesting not only to those taking courses in political and cultural geography, but also to all those concerned about the relationship between space, place and political processes.

The book is organized into nine chapters. Chapter 1 discusses the characteristics of politics and presents the approach to studying politics which we will be using in the remainder of the book. The remaining eight chapters deal in turn with some of the topics that have constituted the traditional subject-matter of 'Political Geography'. As we have suggested, while the topics are conventional, their treatment is intended to be less so.

Chapters 2 and 3 examine the state. Chapter 2 considers the rise of the system of nation-states and the process of state formation. Chapter 3 focuses on the transformation of many liberal-democratic countries from a welfare to a 'workfare' model of labour market and social regulation. Chapter 4 looks at the changing organization and role of the liberal-democratic state in the late twentieth century, examining how the expansion of the state has reshaped notions of political participation. We focus in particular on the changing geographies of citizenship and elections. In Chapter 5, we consider the politics of the city, focusing on the nature of contemporary urban change and the politics of urban infrastructures, gentrification and the public sphere. In Chapter 6, we examine the relationship between identity politics and the development of social movements, charting in particular the transition from organized labour movements centred on trade unions to the emergence of new forms of grass-roots political action. Chapter 7 explores the political geographies of nations, nationalism and regionalism. Like other concepts confronted in this book, we adopt a critical perspective that foregrounds the socially constructed nature of supposedly fixed identities and territorialization. Chapter 8 covers imperialism and the continuing implications of colonialism for the relations between the West, its former colonies and the people who live there. Finally, Chapter 9 explores the concepts of geopolitics and anti-geopolitics. Geopolitics is perhaps the area of political geography that has received the greatest attention since the first edition, and we assess the history of this term and the recent work by scholars in the fields of critical and feminist geopolitics to explore the hidden power/knowledge relations of geopolitical ideas.

ONE

Politics, Geography and Political Geography

What is this thing called politics?

Politics matters!

There is an ancient Chinese curse that runs: 'may you live in interesting times'. Cursed or not, from a political point of view life today is certainly interesting. Great political changes have swept the globe in the past 25 years. In 1984, when Joe began studying geography at university, the world was in the depths of the 'new cold war'. The hawkish Ronald Reagan had just been re-elected for a second term as President of the USA. In Moscow, it seemed to be business as usual. Konstantin Chernenko emerged as the latest in a succession of Soviet leaders determined to remain true to the traditions of Soviet state socialism. The global military order organized around NATO and the Warsaw Pact was intact, with the USA in the process of deploying nuclear-armed cruise missiles in Western Europe in the name of 'collective security'. The radical right-wing doctrines of monetarism and free-market economics that had been enthusiastically adopted by the Reagan and Thatcher governments in the USA and the UK had yet to generate much support in other industrialized capitalist countries. In China, just ten years on from the end of the Cultural Revolution, economic reform was well under way, but there was as yet no hint of the lengths to which the Communist Party would go to maintain political control. While Eastern Europe, including the then Yugoslavia, remained politically stable, in other parts of the world, civil unrest or civil war were much in evidence. In South Africa, with no sign that Nelson Mandela would be released from prison, the struggle against apartheid was intensifying. In central America the US-backed military campaign against the reformist Sandinista government in Nicaragua was in full swing.

By 1995, when the first edition of this book appeared[1] (and coincidentally when Alex began studying geography at university), it seemed as if the world had been turned upside down. Nelson Mandela had been elected President of South Africa following the dismantling of apartheid and the ending of white minority rule. The USSR no longer existed. In Eastern Europe, ethnic conflicts were dramatically fragmenting the political map. The Warsaw Pact had been dissolved. For a few brief months after the fall of the Berlin Wall in 1989 there was serious talk about the possibility of a 'New World Order'. The privatizing radicalism of the Thatcher governments caught on throughout Europe, despite the departure from office of Mrs Thatcher herself. Meanwhile, in Tiananmen Square it became dramatically clear that free-market reforms in China were emphatically not to be extended to the liberalization of political life. In Nicaragua, after years of conflict with the USA, the Sandinista government was voted out of office.

The political world of 2008 is dramatically different again and in ways quite unforeseen in 1995. On 11 September 2001 terrorist attacks instigated by radical Islamists associated with Osama bin Laden's 'Al-Qaeda' network killed an estimated 3,000 people in New York, Washington DC and Pennsylvania. The American government responded by launching a so-called 'war on terror'. Although there is no evidence of Iraqi government involvement in the 2001 attacks, the 'war on terror' included a full-scale US-led invasion of Iraq, the overthrow of the authoritarian regime of Saddam Hussein, and the American occupation of the country. Afghanistan, where bin Laden was based, was also attacked and occupied. Despite the installation of nominally democratic governments in both countries, at the time of writing the occupations are continuing. In Europe, most of the former state socialist countries have joined the European Union. Neo-liberal economics forms an international policy orthodoxy. China's hosting of the 2008 Olympics has galvanized opposition to its policies in Tibet. Human-induced climate change is widely recognized as the most urgent long-term political issue and a threat to the survival of the human species. Meanwhile, in Central America, Sandinista leader Daniel Ortega is once again President of Nicaragua.

Recent political change has certainly been profound and dramatic, but also paradoxical. Politics has never been so important, yet, at the same time it has never been so unpopular. Almost every week sees another newspaper article or television feature on the distrust and contempt with which the public in many countries regard their elected representatives. There seems to be an increasing perception, in the West at least, that governments simply no longer have the power to influence events in the way that they once did (or at least claimed to). Governments frequently claim that global economic forces are shaping their national economies, and there is relatively little that they can do to intervene. While this is partly used to explain the failure of policy, it is certainly the case that economic processes do flow across international boundaries as never before, limiting the capacity of any one government to affect their direction. This has led to new kinds of relationships between governments as they try to regain control. The growth of the European Union, for example, and the setting up of a North American Free Trade Area are, in part, attempts to exert political influence over economic affairs at a wider geographical scale than that of the nation-state.

At the same time, however, such 'supra-state' institutions raise political questions too. In a free trade area, not all regions or countries benefit equally, and the European Union has had to establish special funds to support those regions where exposure to international market forces would cause major social upheaval. In addition, larger political institutions are perceived by some as a threat to national or regional cultural distinctiveness.

Traditional political divisions and organizations that have provided the stable framework for political debate, participation and policy-making in so many countries for half a century or more endure, but seem to many to be increasingly out of touch and inappropriate as their traditional constituencies are altered, sometimes dramatically, by successive waves of social and economic change. New political organizations arise with dramatic popular support, often to fade away as quickly as they came. In many places, the difficulties of coping with economic problems and a shifting political landscape have led people to make scapegoats of some of the most powerless in society, rather than to seek reform and development through conventional political channels.

On the other hand, social idealism is far from dead, with a wide range of groups and individuals seeking to mobilize around specific issues such as environmental protection, civil rights for disadvantaged social groups, and the provision of adequate and appropriate health care, sanitation, education and means of making a living to the three-quarters of the world's population who currently live without them. Here too, though, frustration with conventional politics is common, as campaigners experience first-hand the difficulty of producing policy changes that really have an effect in these areas.

The paradox is that in a time of extraordinary political transformation there is apparently such widespread scepticism about, and even downright mistrust of, the formal political system. Perhaps though, this isn't really paradoxical at all. Perhaps it is *because* of the social and economic instability of the contemporary world that familiar political traditions, systems and ways of thinking have come to seem increasingly irrelevant. No leader, party or political movement seems able to find a language (still less a set of policies) which captures the 'spirit of the age'. As the British political thinker and writer Geoff Mulgan says,

> beneath the inertial momentum of elections and offices, the political traditions that became organizing principles for so many societies, dividing them into great tribal camps identified with class, with progress or reaction, with nation or liberty, have lost their potency. They cannot inspire or convince. They do not reflect the issues which passionately divide societies. They are no longer able to act as social glues, means of recognition across distances of geography and culture. What remains is a gap, psychic as much as instrumental. Without great movements, it is much harder to understand your place in society, much harder to picture where it is going. And without coherent political ideas, to organize the fragments of many issues, fears and aspirations, it becomes far harder to act strategically and to think beyond the boundaries of individual lives and relationships. It is not that the great questions have been answered: just that the available solutions have lost their lustre.[2]

Yet politics is not just going to stop. The range of issues and problems facing us seems destined to grow, rather than shrink. Environmental change, health and disease, military conflicts, economic problems, ethnic identity, cultural transformations, global poverty – the list seems endless. However we deal with (or neglect) these concerns, we will be engaging in politics. Directly or indirectly, politics permeates everything we do and influences all our lives. Politics matters.

Politics formal and informal

The common-sense view is that politics is about governments, political parties, elections and public policy, or about war, peace and 'foreign affairs'. These are all important, and they form the focus of much of this book, but they are also limited. They refer to what we shall call 'formal politics'. By 'formal politics' we mean the operation of the constitutional system of government and its publicly-defined institutions and procedures. The implication is that politics is a separate sphere of life involving certain types of people (politicians and civil servants) or organization (state institutions). The rest of us interact with this separate sphere in limited and usually legally defined ways. The political system may accord us formal political rights (such as the right to vote, or to own property) or formal political duties (such as the duty to serve on a jury, or to pay tax). Alternatively, it may from time to time affect the society in which we live, through changes in public policy, for example in the spheres of education or environmental protection. Most of the time, though, many people don't think much about formal politics. Because it seems to be a separate sphere, we can say things like 'I'm not interested in politics' or 'he's not a very political animal'. Formal politics is seen as something that can sometimes *affect* everyday life, but isn't really *part* of everyday life.

One thing we hope this book will show is that the formal political system has much more impact on our lives than is often realized. Of course, the extent to which society is openly controlled or influenced by the government varies considerably. In some countries (such as those still governed by absolute monarchies, for example, or various forms of central planning), the presence of the government in daily life may be clear and explicit. However, even in liberal-democratic countries, the role of the state and the formal political system is wider and deeper than the notion of a separate and limited political realm would suggest. The difference is that in more 'liberal' societies it is easier to *believe* in the separateness of formal politics, because its presence, though significant, is either hidden, or taken for granted and unquestioned.

By contrast, 'informal politics' might be summed up by the phrase 'politics is everywhere'. A good example is the idea of 'office politics'. Office politics obviously doesn't have much to do with the political system of governments and elections, but everyone understands why we refer to it as 'politics'. It is about forming alliances, exercising power, getting other people to do things, developing influence, and protecting and advancing particular goals and interests. Understood like this, politics really does seem to be everywhere. There is an informal politics of the household (parents attempt to influence children, women do more housework than men); of industry (some groups of workers do better out of industrial change than others, the aims of management and workers often conflict); of education (some subjects and points of view are taught while others are not, some children benefit more from education than others); even of television (some people have more chances to have their say on TV than others, certain groups are shown in a more favourable light than others). In fact, if we are talking about *in*formal politics, there is no aspect of life which is *not* political: politics really is everywhere.

It is often said that 'politics is about power'. The ways that power has been understood by social scientists have changed over time. According to the French thinker Michel Foucault, these changes are related to shifts in the ways power is exercised. Foucault argues that in traditional societies power was exercised visibly, in, for example, public spectacles. It often took the form of dramatic acts or displays. In modern societies, by contrast, the exercise of power is much more hidden. To take one of Foucault's own examples, in the punishment of criminals the power of the state in traditional (medieval) societies was displayed through theatrical executions in a public square. These practices gave way during the eighteenth and nineteenth centuries to what Foucault calls the 'disciplinary society'. In the modern disciplinary society, he argues, social control is produced by a complex network of rules, regulations, administrative monitoring, and the management and direction of people's daily lives. This is most strongly developed in institutions and organizations such as prisons, schools and factories. To some extent it applies to all our private lives as well. In the disciplinary society, we all to a greater or lesser extent 'internalize' codes of behaviour and rules of conduct, so that we are unconsciously disciplining ourselves. Instead of being dramatic, public and visible (as in traditional societies), power in modern societies is invisible. It operates behind the scenes, as it were, and in every part of the social order. Instead of something which exists in the centre of society (with the king, say, or the government) and which is consciously used 'against' the powerless, power now flows through all the complex connections of everyday life. Foucault's concept of power in modern societies is sometimes referred to as a 'capillary' notion of power, to imply that power filters down through all our most mundane and ordinary relationships and out into the most routine aspects of human activity.

There is a parallel here with the notions of formal and informal politics. From a 'Foucauldian' perspective, the claim that 'politics is concerned with power' takes on a particular meaning. If power in modern societies saturates the social fabric in the ways Foucault implies, then studying politics should involve at least as much emphasis on 'informal politics' as on 'formal politics'. Moreover, the 'capillary' notion of power implies that power, and hence politics, is part of all social life and all forms of social interaction, however normal, mundane and routine they seem. Thus the way we feel about ourselves and others, how we write and talk, how we work and shop, how we study and play, how we drive and go on holiday — all of these are 'political', as are our religious, recreational, sexual, artistic and academic activities. This is somewhat unnerving, to say the least, and many people may be unhappy to think that their 'private' lives have anything to do with politics.

However, if by 'private' we mean not affecting, or affected by, other people or organizations, it is remarkable how little of modern life can be counted under that heading. Almost all the areas of daily life we have mentioned are likely to involve other people to some extent, even if indirectly. When you shop for food, who grows it, under what conditions and how much are they paid? When you go on holiday, what effects do you have on the places you visit and the people who live there? When you write, what kinds of expressions do you choose to refer to other people, and what kind of representation do you build up of them? We may not feel (or may choose not to feel) *responsible* for the people with whom we have these 'indirect' relationships, but like it or not, we *are* involved with them.

Despite its name, the sub-discipline of Political Geography has not, in the past, dealt with the full range of 'politics' which we have been talking about. It has usually concentrated on *formal* politics, and even then on particular aspects of formal politics: a mixture of those that were commonly studied by the founders of the subject and those which were regarded as being somehow especially 'geographical'. Today it is becoming clearer that virtually all political processes are 'geographical' in some sense. The larger field of *informal* politics is also being widely studied by geographers. In recent years, they have introduced a whole set of new ideas into geography drawn mostly from social and cultural theory, which we believe is particularly useful in thinking about what politics is and how it works. On the whole, however, geographers looking at these broader notions of politics (the politics of everyday life, and so on) choose not to call themselves 'political geographers', and choose not to apply their ideas to the formal politics usually studied under the heading 'Political Geography'. One of our aims in this book is to show *how some of the theoretical perspectives which have helped to illuminate informal politics might assist us in understanding formal politics.*

Understanding politics

Material and discursive practices

Politics involves *material* and *discursive* social practices. The material aspects of social practices are those which involve the organization and use of things. The discursive aspects are those which involve ideas, language, symbols and meanings. Thus eating a meal, for example, involves material practices (the preparation of foodstuffs) and symbolic or discursive ones (an understanding of the role and meaning of meals and mealtimes in society). Writing a book involves material elements (paper, pens, word-processing, the printing process) and discursive elements (the ideas in the book, the significance of literature as a cultural form, and so on).

While material practices and discursive practices can be distinguished for the purposes of analysis, they cannot exist independently of one another. For matter to be used by human beings, they must have a discursive understanding of its role and importance. Equally, discourse is produced materially; whether it involves thought, speech, writing, graphics or takes some other form, the form always exists as matter and (often) has material processes or practices as its subject matter. The material cannot be separated from the discursive, but they are not the same thing. It is common for different writers on politics and geography to emphasize material processes over discursive ones, or vice versa. We want to argue that neither can be understood in the absence of the other. Human life is both material and discursive, and the more we investigate the complex relations between the two, the more difficult it becomes to accord a general primacy to one or the other. This is perhaps particularly true of politics, which, as we outline it below, involves both material interests and discursive argument; both 'modes of production' and 'discursive formations'. Of course, precisely because social processes are both discursive and material, it is difficult to separate the ideas of 'mode of production' and 'discursive formation'. Modes of production are themselves produced in part through discourses (such as those associated with property relations, for example), while discursive formations are produced materially and have material preconditions and consequences (for example, they are dependent on the material means of information circulation). The point of distinguishing them here is to ensure that both aspects are held in mind.

The concept of mode of production refers to the ways in which individuals and social groups are provided with the means of fulfilling their needs and wants, from biological necessities such as food, to the most 'frivolous' luxuries. In complex, modern societies, the mode of production is correspondingly complex. Drawing on ideas from political economy, we may identify a number of key elements. First, the process of production requires the means of production (offices, computers, machines, tools, factories, and so on), raw materials and human labour power. Secondly, the process of production is organized in different ways in different times and places. In craft production, for example, the labourers own the means of production themselves. Under capitalism, the ownership and control of the means of production is separated from the direct producers. Thirdly, there is a division of labour, through which different parts of the production process are allocated to different social groups. Fourthly, there is a system of distribution or circulation through which products can be allocated to consumers. These various elements and the relations between them take different forms in different modes of production. The social outcomes (who gets what, where and how) are usually systematically unequal, although the character and causes of the inequality are different in different social systems.

Like the 'capillary' notion of power, the concept of 'discursive formation' comes from the work of Michel Foucault. According to Foucault, the meaning of language is not transparent and immediately obvious. Words, statements, symbols, metaphors, and so on, mean different things in different contexts. The meaning of a particular statement depends partly on who is saying it and how it is being said, but also on how it 'fits into' an existing wider pattern of statements, symbols and understandings. It is this wider pattern which Foucault calls a 'discursive formation' (which is often shortened simply to 'discourse').

This may be clearer if we consider a simple example. All human beings who live to maturity pass through the ages of 13 to 19. However, it was only in the 1950s that the term and concept of the 'teenager' became widespread. Before then, in some societies, one moved more or less directly from childhood to adulthood. In others, such as in Victorian England, the term 'juvenile' was often used, but crucially it did not mean the same, and did not have the same connotations, as 'teenager'. In most societies, specific ages or ceremonies were important in marking the transition from childhood, often at a customary age, such as 21 (the age of majority in nineteenth-century England), or a religious rite of passage, such as the Jewish *bar mitzvah*. In America during the 1950s, however, the stage between childhood and adulthood emerged as separate and was labelled 'teenage'. Human beings were still biologically the same, and yet Western society was transformed by the emergence of 'the teenager'. In Foucault's terms, this was the result of a 'discourse of the teenager'. The 'statements' which made up the discourse were indeed dispersed throughout society. They appeared in many different media: in political speeches, in films, in popular music, in advertising, in newspaper columns, in parental discussions, and so on. However, they all had enough in common, in their object of analysis, in their mode of language, in the terms used and in their tone, to be considered part of a unified 'discourse'. The 'teenager', therefore, was a 'discursive construction' which was 'made real' by the discourse. While it referred to the same span of years as the Victorian concept of 'juvenile', the effects of the two discourses were very different.[3]

Throughout this book we will be stressing the importance for politics of the relationship between discursive and material practices. We will consider both how discourse makes things real, and how material practices enable or constrain discourse. To pursue the teenager example, material processes were important in enabling the discursive construction of the teenager. These include the growth of the American economy, which provided the wealth and resources for clothes, records and cars; the availability of leisure time and of extended education; changing demographic and family patterns; and the construction of a material geography in American cities of coffee bars, movie theatres, shops, sports facilities and high schools. This link between discursive changes and material conditions is significant in most areas of politics and something we will explore in the rest of the book.

Our approach

Our approach views politics as a process that is made up of geographically and historically situated social and institutional practices. As we have seen, those practices are both material and discursive in character. They are also, at least in part, purposeful and strategic, and they depend on the availability of unequally distributed resources. Let's unpack this in a little more detail, by outlining six key elements of the interpretative framework that will inform the rest of the book.

(1) People and their competing needs

It is people and the relationships between them which make politics: political processes are produced by human activities and *human agency*. As human beings, we all, individually and in social groups, have *needs, desires, wants* and *interests*, which, with the possible exception of basic biological necessities, are constructed (made meaningful) through discourse. *Politics* arises from the impossibility of reconciling the wants, needs, desires and interests of all individuals and groups instantly and automatically.

(2) The role of strategic action

We develop and pursue *strategies* (purposeful practices) in support of (our understanding of) our interests. Strategies need not be grand or comprehensive: they may be mundane or small scale. Our strategies are never wholly rational, since our knowledge of the circumstances in which we act is always partial and imperfect, and many of the factors which influence outcomes are beyond our control. This means in turn that while our strategies have effects, their effects are often *unintended*. Strategic action potentially brings actors into *conflict* or *alliance* with others pursuing similar or opposed strategies, and can consequently generate both *struggle* and *co-operation*.

(3) Resources and power

The ability of different groups and individuals to pursue strategic action varies, as does its effectiveness, depending on the differential availability of *resources* within society. Resources may be of many kinds. These include: our bodies; other material resources of all sorts; 'discursive' resources (such as knowledge, information, language, symbols, and ways of understanding); the compliance of other people; means of violence; and organizational resources (the ability to co-ordinate, deploy and monitor other resources). Unequal access to such resources accounts for differences in *political power*. Where conflicting strategies are being pursued, the exercise of political power generates *resistance* (counter-power).

(4) Institutions

Strategic action often leads to the development of *institutions* of various sorts. Once established, though, institutions 'escape' from the intentions of the initial strategy and develop independently. Institutions are then political actors themselves, pursuing strategies which may be unrelated to those which established them. Institutions also have their own internal politics, which also consist of individuals and groups pursuing strategic action. The strategies of institutions are the (often unintended) products of internal politics. As such they may be (and often are) contradictory. Institutions exist on a different temporal (and often spatial) scale from individual action. The fact that they endure over time and are stretched over space is one source of their political power, and helps to explain why and how they can become harnessed to very different strategies from those intended by their creators.

(5) Authority and sovereignty

Individuals, groups and institutions typically advance *claims to authority*, through which they aim to secure the compliance of other individuals, groups and institutions with their own strategic action. However, there are no absolute grounds on which authority can be justified. All claims to authority are assertions, rather than statements of fact. Claimants to authority usually pursue (often again through strategic action) attempts to legitimate their assertion: that is to secure consent to their claim from both other claimants and those whose compliance to authority is sought. The process of *legitimation* is a discursive one involving attempts to construct frameworks of meaning through which authority is made to seem legitimate. Legitimation is rarely completed or absolute, but is a continual struggle against those who contest it. In the absence of (or additional to) consent, compliance with claims to authority may be pursued through *coercion*, where the necessary resources (means of violence) are available. A claim to *sovereignty* on the part of an institution is a special type of claim to authority: a claim to being the *highest* authority for some defined group or area. Like all claims to authority, it is rarely established and uncontested.

(6) Political identities

Our pursuit of different strategies and our positions in relation to the strategies and claims to authority of others, constitute us in a variety of ways as *political subjects* with particular *political identities*. These are thus partly the products of our conscious intentions, but partly the outcome of the discursive and material practices of others. To say that we are political subjects means that we each, as human beings, have relationships to politics. Part of 'who we are' is produced through our political positions. For instance, we all relate to the state in different ways, perhaps as voters, as users of public services, as asylum seekers, as pupils in state schools or universities, or as the focus of various forms of legal regulation. In different times and places, we take on different political identities, sometimes deliberately, as part of a 'strategy' and sometimes unwillingly or even unconsciously.

This may seem a little abstract, but in the chapters that follow we will show how this kind of perspective can help us to understand political change in different contexts, which should help to flesh out the framework in more detail. It is important to note, however, that this perspective is not a rigid theory which can be applied like a template to all political situations. Rather, we want to use it as a *way of thinking* about politics. This means that there will be times when we use other, more detailed theories to talk about particular aspects of political change. There are, for example, substantive theories of international relations, imperialism, state formation and social movements. In the chapters dealing with those topics, we will want to discuss some of those more specific theories and their strengths and weaknesses, using the above framework as a kind of guide for assessment.

Politics and geography

So much for politics: what about geography? Of course, the term 'geography' can refer to quite a wide range of ideas. Traditionally, 'geography' has been defined broadly as the study of the earth's surface. As far as human activity is concerned, this is often thought to involve four (overlapping) aspects:

(1) *Space.* Geographers study the spatial distribution of human activities and institutions of all kinds and their causes and effects. They are also interested in the influence of spatial organization on social, political, economic and cultural processes.

(2) *Place.* Geography involves the study of place: the character of places, the relationship between people and their places, and the role of places and the difference between them in human activities.

(3) *Landscape.* Geography focuses on the development of landscapes and the meaning and significance of landscapes for people.

(4) *Environment.* Geographers are interested in the relationship between people and their environments, including their understandings of environments and their use of environmental resources of all kinds.

All of these traditional concerns remain central to human geography today. All of them, however, have been subject to considerable rethinking and reformulation over the years. To take one example, the relationship between society and space has been the focus of much debate within human geography. In the past it was often assumed that space and society were separate things which may have *influenced* each other in various ways, but which could, in principle, be examined and analyzed independently. More recently, geographers have insisted that spatial relations are inseparable from society. All social relations are constituted spatially, and there can be no possibility of a 'non-spatial' social science.[4]

To understand what this entails for Political Geography consider some of the components of politics outlined above. Human agency and strategic action are always *situated* in particular geographical contexts, which condition strategies and make some options available and others impossible. The resources on which agents draw in developing strategies are made available to them partly by virtue of their spatial organization. Our access to money, materials and organization is partly a function of where we (and they) are, while knowledge, information and symbolic understandings are the product of geographical contexts and on many occasions have places and geography as their subject matter. Moreover, space and spatial organization is itself a resource. Studying the control of key sites and territories has a long history in Political Geography, but the principle may be extended much further. For example, the spatial organization of institutions such as schools, factories and prisons is a central element in their control and monitoring. Finally, social and cultural geographers have studied how the production of political subjectivities and identities is bound into space and place. All of this suggests that in studying politics, geography is not an optional extra, or a particular perspective. Instead, politics is intrinsically geographical, and can be studied in that light.

Political geography

Human geography has traditionally been divided into a number of 'sub-disciplines': urban geography, social geography, historical geography, and so on. Each sub-discipline represents a more limited and specialized field of study supposedly corresponding to a coherent part of 'geographical reality'. However, universities, where, for the most part, academic human geography is practised and developed, are not the rational, ordered places they some-times like to claim to outsiders. While some writers have tried to argue for the development of a more rational sub-disciplinary structure,[5] the activities of human geographers seem unlikely to fall neatly into ordered categories. This is because the discipline of human geography has evolved over time and has been created in particular social and political conditions. As a result, some sub-disciplines are stronger than others, with more research, more academics working in the field, more conferences, books and papers, and so on. In addi-tion, academic research and writing is continually developing and changing. Understandings of the world and the subject form and reform; schools of thought and theoretical traditions arise and then fade; and the substantive issues studied change over time. In some cases, a sub-discipline can be dom-inated for some time by a single person; others may be more diffuse.

All this means that while human geography and its sub-disciplines are *about* social phenomena, they also *are* social phenomena in their own right. They are the products of historical accidents, debates, disputes, personal and institutional success and failure, and their social, political, cultural and eco-nomic surroundings. In fact, they are what we have referred to as discourses or discursive formations.

Foucault's concept of 'discourse' has implications for how we think about academic subjects like human geography. If disciplines and sub-disciplines are discourses, then they do not provide immediate and transparent windows on to the world. The world is not divided neatly and rationally into economic aspects, cultural aspects, geographical aspects, and so on, with each part the subject of a corresponding academic discipline, and each discipline looking down on 'its' object of analysis from a detached viewpoint. Instead, as dis-courses, academic subjects are *part* of the world. Not only that, they are influ-ential in making the world the way it is. As we shall see, just as the discourse of the teenager helped to bring the phenomenon of the teenager into exis-tence, so the discourse of geography helped to shape the modern world (some-times in violent and destructive ways).

One of the standard sub-disciplines of human geography is 'Political Geography'. It has all the trappings of a formal sub-discipline. It has a journal, also called *Political Geography*. It has representation in learned societies: for example, the Association of American Geographers has a 'Political Geography

Specialty Group' while the Royal Geographical Society/Institute of British Geographers has a 'Political Geography Research Group'. It has its 'Great Thinkers of the Past': Friedrich Ratzel, Halford Mackinder, Ellen Semple, Isaiah Bowman and Richard Hartshorne. It also has university courses and textbooks devoted to it. As well as an institutionalized sub-discipline, 'Political Geography' is also a discourse, in the sense we have outlined above.

This has a number of implications. First, the sub-discipline does not refer transparently, straightforwardly and comprehensively to some easily definable 'politico-geographic' aspect of the world. Despite its journals, textbooks and courses, there is no universally accepted definition of the field of inquiry called 'Political Geography'. Moreover, any attempt at definition will almost certainly throw up anomalies, when compared with what actually appears in the courses and textbooks. Many 'textbook' definitions cite, in some form, the relationship between space and place (geography) and politics (or power, or government) as the core focus of political geography. In one sense, this seems to be stating the obvious, but it really only begs the further questions of how one defines 'politics' (and 'geography'!).

However, even if we could answer these additional questions, the problem with attempts to define the 'essence' of 'Political Geography' is that they give an inaccurate picture of the actual *discourse* of Political Geography. That discourse overlaps only rather haphazardly with these 'essentialist' definitions. A discourse operates by setting the agenda, establishing the boundaries of legitimate debate and marking some statements and arguments as meaningful and as making sense (i.e., within the discourse) and others as not meaningful, (i.e., outside the discourse). To some extent these consequences of a discourse may be part of a deliberate strategy. Often, they are unintentional, though that does not make them any less significant. An important point about discourses is that they are not (or only very rarely) controlled by a single person or organization. Indeed, part of their power comes from their being widely accepted. When a discourse is produced and reproduced through the speech and actions of a large number of people and institutions, it can come to seem like common sense – like part of the taken-for-granted background to everyday life. In fact, a discourse is always the product of a specific set of historical circumstances, and always operates in favour of certain interests and social groups. Many people who participate in the propagation of discourses may not have given much thought to the social and political circumstances which produced them, and might not even approve of the interests which they sustain.

The discourse of the sub-discipline of Political Geography has in the past been marked by the inclusion of certain characteristic topics and points of view and the general exclusion of others. Think of some of the main political shifts over the last quarter-century. In many countries, the women's movement has, by any reckoning, been one of the most influential and important political forces of recent years. It has involved political campaigns and struggles, new legislation, reams of comment in the political media, the founding of political and academic journals, the development of feminism as a political philosophy and practice, not to mention counter-attacks and a so-called male backlash since the late 1980s. In all respects it has been one of the biggest political controversies of its day. Moreover, it is hugely geographical. Women's lives vary from country to country and place to place, as does the form and content of their political campaigning. Control of space and of places goes to the heart of the issue, as may be seen in, for example, attempts to reduce the threat of male violence both in the home and on city streets.

Yet, until quite recently, both feminism as a perspective, and the women's movement as a political phenomenon were marginal to the discourse of Political Geography. Geographers have been working on these topics for many years. Indeed, they represent some of the liveliest and most innovative areas for contemporary geographical research. For the most part, however, the resulting papers and reports have not 'counted' as Political Geography according to the (unwritten) rules established by its discourse. This highly political work has tended to appear in journals and books devoted to cultural or social geography, or those dedicated to studies of gender. This is now changing and a strong field of feminist Political Geography is emerging. And of course, in one sense it may not matter. If the work is done, and it is published, then perhaps it isn't important whether we call it 'Political Geography' or 'Cultural Geography'.

Fair enough. There are, though, two reasons why such 'turf disputes' may be significant. First, the example illustrates how conventional academic divisions do not reflect a rational ordering of reality (or even their own definitions of their fields), but a particular path of intellectual, social and institutional development. Secondly, as we mentioned above, discourses are the products of, and in turn sustain and promote, particular social and political interests. Discourses involve mobilizing meanings in association with relations of power. If the discourse of Political Geography constitutes the sub-discipline around (among other things) the geopolitical world order, while simultaneously marginalizing issues of gender and the politics of the women's movement, then the inference that students, policy-makers and other academics are likely to draw is that geopolitical transformations are not connected to (or even that they are more politically significant than) gender politics. Arguably, such a discourse implies that geopolitical change is not even of concern to women: that it is men's work.

Like other discourses, Political Geography is marked by its origins. Early Political Geography was concerned mainly with the relationship between physical territory, state power and global military and political rivalries. Throughout the twentieth century Political Geography took those concerns as its starting point, and they are, of course, important issues. Nevertheless, the result was a rather 'top-down' view of the subject. *People* appeared rather infrequently in the textbooks of Political Geography. Political geographers now take social and political struggles and social movements much more seriously than in the past. Movements of labour, women, lesbians and gay men, minority ethnic groups, disabled people and environmental campaigners, are now taking centre-stage in research on political geography. Political geographers draw more on ideas from social and cultural theory as well as political economy. A new wave in the development of Political Geography is underway. This book tries to map some of its directions.

Notes

1. Painter, Joe (1995) *Politics, Geography and 'Political Geography': A Critical Perspective.* London: Arnold.
2. Mulgan, Geoff (1994) *Politics in an Antipolitical Age.* Cambridge: Polity Press. pp. 7–8.
3. Thanks to Miles Ogborn for this point.
4. See, for example, Soja, Edward W. (1989) *Postmodern Geographies: The Reassertion of Space in Critical Social Theory.* London: Verso; Doreen Massey (2005) *For Space.* London: Sage.
5. Dear, Michael J. (1988) 'The postmodern challenge: reconstructing human geography', *Transactions of the Institute of British Geographers*, 13: 262–74.

Further reading

Political geography is a lively and rapidly developing field. Two comprehensive collections of essays convey this breadth and dynamism particularly well. They are:

Agnew, John, Mitchell, Katharyne and Toal, Gerard (eds) (2003) *A Companion to Political Geography*. Oxford: Blackwell.

Cox, Kevin, Low, Murray and Robinson, Jennifer (eds) (2008) *The SAGE Handbook of Political Geography*. London: Sage.

The journals ***Political Geography*** (Elsevier), ***Space and Polity*** (Taylor and Francis) and ***Geopolitics*** (Taylor and Francis) are all essential for keeping up with current developments in the field, while ***Progress in Human Geography*** (Sage) publishes reviews of recent research in regular progress reports on political geography.

Those interested in the history of political geography can explore it with:

Agnew, John (2002) *Making Political Geography*. London: Arnold.

TWO

State Formation

On 10 June 2004 elections took place in Britain for the European Parliament and local government. Both of these exercises in representative democracy had a history of low turnouts and voter apathy. During the run-up to the 2004 votes, a series of advertisements were placed in British newspapers by the Electoral Commission, the body that oversees the conduct of elections in the UK. Each advertisement drew attention to the effect of political decisions on a different aspect of daily life, including commuting, sport, food and having a night out. The last of these read:

> How politics affects your night out. It decides where and when you can buy an alcoholic drink. Says at what age you can buy an alcoholic drink. Sets the amount of tax that you have to pay every time you buy one. Decides where and when you can listen to music and whether it can be played live. Controls how loud that music can be and whether or not you're allowed to dance to it. Decides what is acceptable behaviour when you're under the influence and what is liable to get you arrested. Affects the number of police officers patrolling town centres at night. Says what substances are illegal and what will happen to you if you're caught with them. Decides what time trains and buses stop running and whether or not there will be a night service. Says how much you can legally drink and still drive home. Controls the licensing of taxis. Controls the licensing of doormen and bouncers. Decides how long you've got to finish that pint.

The aim was to persuade people (particularly young people) that political decisions matter to their lives and that it is worthwhile seeking to influence them through the ballot box. At the same time, the adverts illustrated to great effect how daily life is permeated by the institutionalized practices of the state, often in unrecognized ways. It is difficult, particularly in the most economically privileged parts of the world, to think of any aspect of life that is not touched in some way by the workings of the state. In this chapter, we explore how this has come about and what its implications are.

OVERVIEW

In this chapter, we consider the historical geographies which gave rise to the global system of modern states that we know today. We begin by looking at the relationships between space, place and the 'global jigsaw' of modern states. We then consider how to define the state before examining some of the main conceptual issues surrounding the state: the process of state formation, the relationship between 'high' and 'low' politics and the notion of sovereignty. We then discuss in more detail the processes that gave rise to the typical form of the territorial state. Two processes are emphasized: the preparation for and the waging of wars on the one hand, and the building of the administrative systems of the state apparatus on the other. We conclude by looking beyond Europe to consider some of the reasons why a political form which developed in one small part of the world has become the dominant system of territorial organization throughout the world.

States in space

A recurring theme

The state has been a central concept in political geography since German geographer Friedrich Ratzel wrote about the state as an organic, living entity in the nineteenth century. As a territorial form the state is the basic building block of the world political map. Traditionally, political geographers have emphasized the geographical form of states in absolute spatial terms — their borders, land areas, and even shapes.[1] They have also been interested in the forces which promote or disturb territorial integration within states ('centripetal' and 'centrifugal' forces, respectively) and territorial differentiation of states from their neighbours. This led to a focus on issues such as the role of transport and communications networks.[2]

Since the 1970s geographers' understandings of the state have taken new paths. Initially, ideas drawn from political economy (notably Marxism) provided conceptual tools to strengthen the rather descriptive approach of traditional political geography and to show how state policies, state elites and state finance were bound into the social relations of capitalism and processes of capital accumulation. More recently, political geographers have increasingly turned to social, political and cultural theory, and to concrete accounts produced by historical sociologists. A range of questions and issues have been newly highlighted (or revisited). These include questions of war, militarism and violence; of bureaucracy, organization and surveillance; of culture, discourse and meaning; and of authority, citizenship, rights and resistance. Our discussion of the state is divided into three chapters. In this chapter we look at the geographies of state formation. In Chapter 3 we focus on the changing character of the welfare state, and in Chapter 4 we look at the geographies of democracy, citizenship and elections.

The global jigsaw

Despite challenges from transnational corporations, social and religious movements, global terrorism and non-governmental organizations, states remain the pre-eminent forms of political authority in the modern world. No agencies assert their power over us quite so insistently as the states in which we live. We will come back to the issues of power and authority later, but we need to begin with questions of definition.

We are all used to the political map of the world in which the land surface (with the exception of Antarctica) is completely divided up into the territorial areas called states. To be sure, there are a few blurred edges, especially where wars have left territorial disputes unresolved. In the vast majority of cases, though, we reside in places which are each clearly within the territory of one particular state, with clear boundaries separating it from its neighbours.

This situation seems so normal to us that it is difficult to imagine how things could be otherwise. The difficulty of thinking outside the framework of states is demonstrated in part by the problems in finding solutions to many territorial political conflicts. In Israel/Palestine, for example, two groups both claim the same territory, and both insist on their right to a state. Since, in our 'normal' way of thinking, no two states can occupy the same territory, it seems impossible to reconcile both demands simultaneously. In the modern world, achieving state-hood has been made to seem the ultimate goal for any group defining itself as a nation. Yet there is nothing inevitable or natural about states. Like all human institutions they are products not of nature, but of social and political processes.

They are, moreover, extremely recent products. Human beings emerged some 400,000 years ago, but it was not until 8,000 years ago that anything that might be called a state appeared. And for most of the time since then, states of whatever form have only occupied a small part of the earth's surface. It is only in the last 300 years that distinctively modern states have developed and only in the last 50 years that the modern form of the state has become more or less universal.

Even today, the variety of state forms is quite large, and for most of the modern period the characteristics of different states have been highly diverse. So it is difficult, and in many ways downright misleading, to try to construct a theory of 'the' state. Such a theory depends on identifying the 'essence' of stateness, as it were. Because states are political and social institutions, they are in a continuous (albeit slow) process of change and mutation: if we define the 'essence' of the state in one place or era, we are liable to find that in another time or space something which is also understood to be a state has different 'essential' characteristics.

In order to avoid such 'essentialist' interpretations, we need to give due weight to historical and geographical differences in the nature of states. Rather than trying to find a central unifying principle that is shared by all states, we prefer to understand states as (1) complex networks of relations among a (shifting) mixture of institutions and social groups, and (2) the product of their own processes of institutional development and historical change (as well as important 'external' influences).

States and geography

The geographical character of the modern state is evident in five of its distinctive features. First, we take it for granted that the territories of modern states are ordered by relatively precise boundaries. Their positions may be contested, but such disputes strengthen, rather than undermine, the principle that modern states are defined by clearly demarcated linear boundaries. The boundary dispute between India and Pakistan in Kashmir has made the India–Pakistan border elsewhere the focus for nationalist sentiment. The Wagah border crossing in Punjab (Figure 2.1) sees a daily evening display of ceremonial confrontation between the Indian and Pakistani border guards that attracts large crowds of spectators on both sides.

Figure 2.1   Spectators at the India–Pakistan border, Wagah © Joe Painter

But such boundaries are a fairly recent invention. The precise borders that emerge with modern states are associated with the capacity of states to spread their power relatively evenly throughout a territory. In earlier times, because of technical, resource and organizational limitations, state power tended to be much stronger in the centre of the territory than towards its edges. States had frontier zones, rather than borders, where the weak influence of one or more states overlapped, or state power petered out into areas not occupied by any state.[3] The neat boundaries of modern states, therefore, are symptoms of states' ability to 'project' their administrative capacity across the whole of their territories.

Secondly, most modern states occupy large territories, and seek to administer them through various systems of territorially organized institutions. These range from loose confederations at one end of the scale, through federal systems (such as those in Germany or the USA) and systems of regional and local government (city councils, for example), to local offices of the central state at the other end (such as a local tax office).

Thirdly, we need to consider the institutional geography of the state – offices, courts, parliaments, military bases, and so on must be located somewhere (and where they are located can make a difference to how they work and what effects they have). They also have social and symbolic geographies too. Parliament buildings, for example, embody certain meanings. They form part of various discourses, about state power, for instance, or 'democracy'. The Australian Federal Parliament in Canberra has a sloping grass roof so that members of the public can walk on top of the building (see Figure 2.2). The design is intended to symbolize the pre-eminence of 'the people' in the political system.

Fourthly, the apparatus of the state, spread throughout the territory, allows state organizations to monitor, govern and attempt to control the population.

Figure 2.2   Australian Federal Parliament, Canberra © Joe Painter

This capacity to keep an eye on what is going on depends both on the territorial reach of the state, and on what we might call the spatial density of the mechanisms and practices through which monitoring occurs. These include the *physical* surveillance of space by police and other state employees and, increasingly, electronic surveillance using cameras. Less obviously they also include technologies of record-keeping and data-gathering, through which the activities of the population are monitored either at the aggregate level or the individual level, through personal records relating to birth, marriage, death and a whole range of other aspects of our lives. It is no coincidence that the words 'state' and 'statistics' share the same linguistic root.

Fifthly, this monitoring activity has tended to increase over time.[4] However, it is never absolute (even in so-called 'totalitarian' societies). There are always gaps in the state apparatus in which resistance of various forms may develop — spaces of resistance, if you like. In the former Soviet Union there were networks of dissidents in which ideas and literature officially banned by the state were able to circulate (albeit in a highly restricted way), and in many countries state authorities either tolerate popular protest over a whole range of issues or do not have the resources to prevent it.

Finally, geography as *place* is significant in the formation of states. At particular times, dominant groups may pursue deliberate 'state-building' strategies (perhaps after independence from a colonizing state). In these circumstances, a discourse of the state as 'homeland' is developed as a means of legitimating the state.

States and state formation

Defining the state

It is famously difficult to define 'the state'. On the face of it, the term seems to refer to an institution or an organization, but no state consists of a single unified organization and once we start to look at organizations in detail, it is often difficult to work out which are part of the state and which are not. Another common approach is to define the state in terms of what it does – its functions. But here too there are problems. Almost all the activities undertaken by the state today could be performed by other agencies. Indeed, at one time or another most of them have been. In the past, providing education and health care, building roads, and even fighting wars have been private activities, and in many countries today there is a shift back towards private provision in these areas. It seems we can't draw a neat line between 'state' and 'society', because their organization and functions overlap.

It is also difficult to come up with a comprehensive theory of the state in all its forms. Political theorist Bob Jessop distinguishes between 'strong' and 'weak' theories:

> A strong theory would provide an integrated account of the state in terms of a single set of causal mechanisms. It would explain all the institutional and

operational features of a state in a given conjuncture. Even with the best will in the world, however, a strong theory could not be constructed. For it is simply impossible methodologically to develop a single, all-encompassing theory of so complex an entity as the nation-state in all its historical specificity.[5]

Instead, Jessop suggests, attention should be focused on developing a 'weak' theory — a useful set of guidelines and principles which will assist analysis of particular states, but which do not assume that everything can be explained by a single set of mechanisms.

Some have argued that we should see the state as an idea, a myth, or a symbolic construct, rather than a thing or an object. One difficulty with this proposition is that it might be taken to mean that the state is an illusion and does not really exist. Yet we can see the very real effects of the state all around us, particularly when we move from the territory of our own state to that of another. Suddenly we find ourselves subject to different laws, using a different currency, and without the rights and obligations accorded to us in our own state by our citizenship. Our passport may be stamped in the name of the state, if we infringe the law we may be arrested in the name of the state, if we travel we may use public transport provided in the name of the state, if we buy goods or services we use money issued in the name of the state, and so on. If the state is mere illusion how can it have such far-reaching effects?

Part of the answer is that 'myths', 'ideas' and 'symbols' are far from illusory. In fact, they are powerful and durable social phenomena. Through constant repetition and by being embedded in daily life, they organize thought and action in profound ways. Much of what we think of as the state's power 'over' us actually works *through* us because our habits and everyday behaviour have been gradually shaped through our upbringing, education and social interactions so that most of the time we act in accordance with the state's norms without much conscious effort. When we get in our car to drive to work in Britain, we don't need to deliberately remember to drive on the left of the road; we do so apparently without thinking about it. In most states the law requires drivers to keep to the right and when British residents drive in other countries they definitely do need to think carefully about which side of the road to use! Not all such social conventions are the effects of the state, of course. No law requires us to hold doors open for each other or to wait in line at a ticket booth. But many of our most routine and mundane activities do unintentionally reinforce the apparent existence of the state as an overarching provider of order in society.

The political theorist Timothy Mitchell has pursued this line of thinking about the state for a number of years. He suggests that the state is not only present in our thoughts and actions, but in a variety of material forms too:

> The importance of the state as a common ideological and cultural construct, I argue, should be grounds not for dismissing the phenomenon ... but for taking it seriously. ... A construct like the state occurs not merely as a subjective belief, incorporated in the thinking and action of individuals. It is represented and reproduced in visible, everyday forms, such as

the language of legal practice, the architecture of public buildings, the wearing of military uniforms, or the marking out and policing of frontiers.[6]

In previous work one of us has suggested that the state should not be seen as an actual entity separate from the rest of society, but is better understood as an 'imagined collective actor', in whose name individuals are identified 'as citizens or subjects, aliens or foreigners', and which is 'imagined as the source of central political authority for a national territory'.[7] In the rest of this chapter (and the rest of the book) we will often have cause to refer to 'states' and 'the state'. This is partly a matter of convenience and partly because the writers we draw on use those words. As you read, however, bear in mind that, for us, 'the state' is not an object, an entity or a unified political actor. Rather, it is the name we give to the effect of the social process that make such an object, entity or actor appear to exist.[8] That may sound somewhat strange and elusive, but so, we think, is the state.

State formation as a social process

One of the benefits of defining the state as the effect of social processes is that it emphasizes the continual formation of the state over time. The state is constantly becoming. To begin with, the process of state formation was a by-product of other activities, which were not themselves intended to give rise to the state. However, once state institutions and practices start to emerge, once they gain their 'institutional materiality', they become the focus of attention. People start to pursue strategies in relation to the state. Such strategies never arise on a blank surface, however; there is always an historical legacy — a set of institutions and conventions inherited from the immediate past. These provide the resources with which actors pursue strategies for the future, but they also limit the range of options. On a day-to-day basis, change is often piecemeal rather than dramatic, although piecemeal changes can add up to complete transformations over a long period. Occasionally, in the cases of revolutions, previous structures may be almost wholly dispensed with, although even here it is likely that the revolutionary strategy itself will have been heavily conditioned by the previous forms which were the context for its development. For example, historians studying Russia have often remarked on the extent to which the Tsarist state influenced that established by the Bolsheviks, following the Russian revolution in 1917.

Bob Jessop draws out the basis for his weak theory of the state from the work of Michel Foucault and Nicos Poulantzas. From Poulantzas he takes the idea that the state is an 'institutional ensemble' — the mix of institutional forms and practices which Poulantzas calls the institutional materiality of the state. For Jessop, the state may be defined as 'a specific institutional ensemble with multiple boundaries, no institutional fixity and no pre-given formal or substantive unity'.[9] It implies that there is no inherent division of functions between state and non-state institutions, that states are multifarious in their activities and that there are gaps, both geographical and organizational, in the extent to which society is 'penetrated' by the state, even in those functions for which the state is responsible.

Jessop has developed what he calls a 'strategic-relational approach' to the state along three axes. First, the state system is seen as a site of strategy; as the place, if you like, where political strategies 'happen'. However, access to this site is easier for some than for others, and the form of the state apparatus is more suited to some strategies than others. Secondly, the state 'is also the site where strategies are elaborated'. In other words, state officials and thus elements of the state apparatus act strategically in their own right. Jessop points out that this may mean that different parts of the state are operating according to different (and maybe even opposed) strategies, and that therefore the 'formal unity' of the state is not matched by a 'substantive unity'. Thirdly, the state apparatus and the conventional ways of acting of state officials and institutions are themselves the products of past strategies. 'Past strategies' may mean the strategies of previous state institutions and officials, or those of other political actors, in the economy, the wider society or the international arena.

Political strategies are important to state formation but they rarely turn out as expected. They are also multifarious. The development paths of modern states have not been unilinear. State formation should certainly not be seen as a process of steady development towards the modern form of the state. Along the road many other forms emerged, grew and declined: city states, absolutist monarchies, empires, satellites, religious governments and others rose and then, for the most part, fell. State formation is not a process in which a 'more effective', 'more democratic' or 'more enlightened' system of political administration arose inevitably from 'inefficient', 'despotic' or 'ignorant' predecessors. While medieval states were no doubt all of these things from time to time, modern states have hardly done away with all forms of domination, inefficiency and irrationality.

High and low politics

State security and social security

Before outlining some actual examples of state formation it will be helpful to add to the concepts of formal and informal politics, which we considered in Chapter 1. *High politics* refers to the politics of war, peace, diplomacy, the state's claim to sovereignty and constitutional change. It touches on the very existence of the state, and the ways in which it deals with threats to that existence. Its strategies commonly (though not exclusively) involve the people who occupy elite positions in the state apparatus. Since it is involved with the 'big' questions of the state's existence and broad organization, we might think of it as dealing with state security.

By contrast, *low politics* refers to more 'mundane issues' such as economic policy, public health, education, routine administration, welfare benefits and environmental protection, the kinds of issues over which states rarely, if ever, go to war, but which today occupy a large part of their attention and resources. The strategies and practices concerned do involve state elites, especially in producing legislation, but are carried out overwhelmingly by the 'ordinary' personnel of the state — the junior civil servants, employees of municipal councils, teachers and social workers.

As in the case of formal and informal politics there is a degree of overlap between the two — they are not mutually exclusive. Thus the provision of social welfare may be used to assert the legitimacy of a state's claim to authority, while the 'protection' of state security commonly involves the routine monitoring of many more 'ordinary' people than is often realized. However, the high/low distinction is different from the formal/informal one. High politics involves informal politics (such as personal relations between heads of state) as well as formal politics (in the shape of diplomatic missions, constitutional commissions, and the like). Similarly, low politics involves the formal arenas of parliament and civil service, as well as informal politics within a council department or an educational institution.

From high to low

The balance between high and low politics has moved back and forth over time. During war, for example, high politics comes to the fore. Over a relatively long period, however, there has been a tendency for high politics to decline in importance relative to low politics, at least in the West. In pre-modern states, government was dominated by high politics. Rulers were concerned first and foremost with issues such as territorial conquest and expansion, securing the constitutional succession for monarchic dynasties and gaining wealth and prestige relative to other states. The daily lives of their subjects were of very little concern to them, at least by contrast with the situation today. Provided 'the masses' did not pose a threat to the state, they were, for the most part, ignored. With the emergence of the modern form of the state, in which the state becomes distinct from the person of the monarch, the balance began to shift. More and more states became concerned with the everyday affairs of their resident populations. To begin with, this was a by-product of the state's increased demand for resources with which to finance its own activities. Raising more taxes required more knowledge and information on the population and its activities, and this led to a growing tendency to keep tabs on what was going on 'at home'. At the same time, doing more to and for ordinary people required its own kinds of resources. These were not just a question of money, but also required new forms of technology, such as the means to collect and record data.

According to Michel Foucault, the idea of government was not originally associated with what we now consider to be 'politics'. Initially, 'government' referred to government of oneself — the exercise of self-control. The term then came to refer to government of the family or the household (by, for example, the father). Until the sixteenth century, Foucault suggests, the ruler of a state was concerned with the preservation of the state, rather than with governing: 'to be able to retain one's principality is not at all the same as possessing the art of government'.[10]

The notion of government in its modern, political sense only arises when the management of the state comes to be understood in the same way as a father's management of a family. That is, that the governor (father) comes to be concerned with the ordering of the people, activities and things of the state (household) and with their interrelations. This is a different concern from simply ensuring the survival of the state or protection of the monarchy from overthrow. With the shift to what Foucault calls governmentality, the ruler of a state begins to take an interest in, and to pursue strategies towards, the people who live in the territory of the state, and their affairs, including economic activities, social norms, and so on. Previously, what the people did was of little concern to the prince unless they threatened the state. Central to this change was the identification of the people of the state *as a population*, which was understood as the proper focus of the art of government. For Foucault, the discourses and practices of 'governmentality' emerge during the sixteenth century together with the objects of government: the population of a particular territory.

The shift towards low politics involved increasing the 'density' of relations between state and society. In order to provide public health measures, mass education, environmental improvements and welfare benefits, the state has to penetrate society much more intensively, which requires additional resources of all kinds: staff, institutions, buildings, knowledge, systems of organization and frameworks of understanding. While states are in general more highly militarized than ever, there has been a relative shift away from high politics, with the decline of war-making as a routine activity, at least in the West. Wars continue to be fought from time to time, and the twenty-first century has seen a definite resurgence with the conflicts in Iraq and Afghanistan. But in most Western countries the day-to-day role of states, and the expenditure of state revenues, has become dominated by low politics.

This shift is less marked in the Global South, where a much higher proportion of state resources and activities are commonly devoted to 'high' politics. This is in part a consequence of the smaller overall resources available to Southern states. Since state security (both material and symbolic) is widely regarded (by state elites) as the first priority, it is common for the first call on resources to be allocated to military and diplomatic activities. Where resources are limited, this may leave little for anything else. The absence of successful economic policies and the lack of social welfare provision, may, of course, exacerbate the threat to the survival of the government, or even of the state, from 'below'.

A growing concern with low politics is partly the product of strategies 'from above'. Tax-gathering, for example, both serves the immediate purposes of the state and involves 'low politics'. More often, however, it is the result of pressures, or responses to perceived threats, 'from below'. The long-term trend towards low politics developed especially strongly in the context of the dramatic industrialization and urbanization of the nineteenth century. These changes produced large, impoverished urban populations (see Table 2.1), removed from many of the traditional ties of rural life and less able to rely on local sources of support. Living and working conditions were often dangerous and unhealthy. Such dramatic transformations gave rise to popular social movements which pressed for reforms and the provision of social welfare, health services and education. At the same time, regardless of the actual conditions in large cities, the urban poor were regarded by the wealthy and by the state as a source of disease, moral laxity and social unrest. The strategies of the poor and the fears of the rich constituted a pressure on the state for social reform which had not previously arisen. In addition, industrialization gave rise to a new set of social interests, of industrialists, capitalists and entrepreneurs, who were concerned that the state should turn its attention to economic matters and to trade policy. In the twin processes of industrialization and urbanization, therefore, lay the seeds of the two major concerns of twentieth-century 'low politics' in industrial economies: economic progress and social welfare.

Table 2.1   Urbanization in Europe west of Russia (after Tilly, 1990)

Year	People living in cities of 10,000 or more (millions)	Percentage of population living in cities of 10,000 or more
1590	5.9	7.6
1790	12.2	10.0
1890	66.9	29.0
1980	c.250	c.55

Claiming sovereignty

No higher authority?

In the modern world, states are the foremost claimers of authority, an authority which is simultaneously claimed to be legitimate. In other words, states claim to have the right to require residents of their territories to behave in certain ways and to refrain from certain activities, that is, to receive compliance. The fact that these 'rights' of the state are (within limits) more or less universally accepted in most states should not mislead us into thinking that they are absolute or can be legitimated in any permanent way. They remain claims and assertions, albeit ones which are conventionally accepted, both by residents and by other states. The discourse of 'sovereignty' raises the stakes still further. As Joseph Camilleri and Jim Falk argue:

> Sovereignty is a notion which, perhaps more than any other, has come to dominate our understanding of national and international life. Its history parallels the evolution of the modern state. More particularly, it reflects the evolving relationship between state and civil society, between political

authority and community. ... [D]espite loose talk about the way it is acquired, lost or eroded, sovereignty is not a fact. Rather it is a concept or a claim about the way political power is or should be exercised.[11]

A claim to sovereignty is a claim to being the highest authority within an area, or over a particular group. When Paul Bremer, the Head of the US-led 'Coalition Provisional Authority' in occupied Iraq handed nominal control of the country to the Iraqi government on 28 June 2004, the US Secretary of State Condoleezza Rice passed a note to President George W. Bush that read 'Iraq is sovereign'. Bush scrawled 'Let freedom reign' across the note before returning it (Figure 2.3). Many critics have argued that the assertion of formal sovereignty contained in this now famous note is belied by the practical control over Iraqi affairs subsequently exercised by the occupiers.

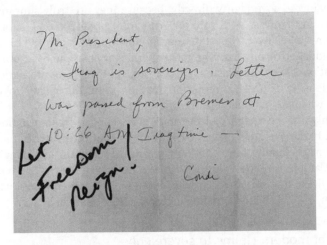

Figure 2.3   Note from Condoleezza Rice to President Bush

Source: http://frwebgate.access.gpo.gov/cgi-bin/getdoc.cgi?dbname=browse_usc&
docid=Cite:+17USC105

Modern states' claims to sovereignty are conventionally recognized by other states, although some states are not regarded as sovereign or legitimate by all others. For example, the state of Northern Cyprus is not recognized as *legitimate* by any European countries apart from Turkey, although it operates in most other regards as any other state. An institution would be entirely sovereign if there were no organization or institution which could require its compliance in any field of activity and if it were free to pursue its own policies unhindered, at least within its own territory. It is doubtful whether states have ever been sovereign in this sense. Today there are numerous challenges to the sovereignty of states.

First, the globalization of economic processes undermines the ability of the state to plan, steer and govern the 'national' economy. Increasingly, multinational corporations, international financial services companies and multilateral financial institutions such as the World Bank have been able to take decisions with little or no regard to the wishes of individual governments. The room for economic manoeuvre of governments and the scope for macro-economic intervention has been significantly diminished.

Secondly, we have seen the growth of new forms of political authority and governmentality which operate alongside state governments. Many international political institutions are wholly intergovernmental, that is, they operate, at least in theory, on the basis of mutual agreement between participating states. The United Nations and its various agencies are perhaps the most developed example. In practice, however, power within intergovernmental organizations is often not distributed evenly between participants (as a result of the differential distribution of resources). In the case of the United Nations, for example, the role of the USA has been central to many of the policies it has adopted, particularly where military intervention in an individual state is concerned.

Thirdly, there are new forms of political authority which challenge the state's claims to sovereignty directly, because they are truly supranational in character. In contrast with intergovernmental organizations, supranational bodies have taken over from states certain functions which used to be fulfilled by individual governments. The most significant example of a supranational organization is the Commission of the European Union. In international trade negotiations it is the Commission, rather than European governments directly, which act on behalf of Europe.

Fourthly, the sovereignty of the state is challenged by international belief systems. In the past, this included communism, but the principal focus now is on the world religions. Many of the major world religions, including Judaism, Roman Catholicism and Islam, are able to exercise a degree of what is effectively political authority over at least some of their adherents which is separate from, and implicitly a challenge to, the sovereignty of states.

Origins of modern claims to sovereignty

The doctrine and discourse of sovereignty developed in Europe in tandem with the modern state itself. In Feudal Europe, power was in many ways highly decentralized. The broad normative and legal framework was regarded as fixed, and divinely ordained, rather than the product or possession of the 'government'. The monarch may have ruled by divine right, and been regarded as the ultimate temporal authority, but was almost wholly detached from the daily lives of ordinary people. Power was exercised through a highly hierarchical, but simultaneously decentralized, system. The local lord was a far more important (and powerful) figure in the everyday lives of villagers than their king or queen.

As the feudal system began to disintegrate, the power of monarchs was strengthened. The system of absolutist monarchies which came to dominate Europe in the sixteenth and seventeenth centuries, saw the concentration of power (in principle, 'absolute' power) in the hands of the monarch. According to Anthony Giddens, however, unlike medieval monarchs, whose power was embodied in their very person, the sovereignty of absolute monarchs was, *in principle* at least, separable from the individual known as the sovereign. This allowed a shift, with the growth of a centralized state apparatus that extended beyond the court, from the sovereign-as-monarch to the more impersonal 'sovereign state'.[12] This is neatly illustrated by the frontispiece to the book *Leviathan* (1651), written by the English political thinker Thomas Hobbes (see Figure 2.4). The image shows a monarch overseeing his kingdom wearing what looks like chainmail. On closer inspection the 'chainmail' turns out to be composed of tiny human figures: the subjects of the ruler.

Figure 2.4   Frontispiece from *Leviathan* by Thomas Hobbes (1651)

Of crucial importance to this process was the emergence of a number of absolutist states *together* and the resulting development of the *interstate system*. Since sovereignty can't be grounded in any absolute foundations, it is constructed in practice through a system of mutual recognition. A state's claim to sovereignty is 'made to stick' as it were by showing that other states regard it as a legitimate claim. In one sense, this is a circular exercise, since those acknowledging the claim have an interest in getting their own claims recognized. Nonetheless, it has provided the preconditions for the hugely powerful system of territorial administration of modern states, by providing a bounded space in which the massive apparatus and complex practices of the modern state could develop relatively free, under 'normal' circumstances, from external intervention.

One of the key moments in this mutual recognition process came at the end of the Thirty Years' War in 1648. The Treaty of Westphalia secured the foundations of the modern state system by agreeing that individual territorial states, rather than the empires of which they were a part, should have the right to conduct their own diplomatic relations with other states, and that, in principle, states should be regarded by other states as sovereign within their own borders. Thus it can be seen that far from being a natural and universal 'norm', the modern territorial 'sovereign' state is the product of quite particular historical circumstances.

Rulers, resources and wars

State formation as the product of war

The Treaty of Westphalia was the outcome of warfare. The historical sociologist Charles Tilly has argued that preparations for war and the waging of wars were crucial to the process through which the modern European state system developed, and that this has often been underestimated. Tilly suggests that the ability of states to prepare for and wage war depended on the kinds of resources (or capital) available to rulers. Rulers' strategies in relation to war generated state institutions and practices largely unintentionally. Moreover, the strategies that were pursued, and thus the processes of state formation, were strongly affected by the strategies and institutions of other rulers and states.[13]

Preparing for, and waging, war are influential in state formation for a number of reasons. Making war is expensive and complicated. It requires large resources of people and equipment and significant levels of organization. It therefore requires taxation, recruitment into the armed forces and the development of new institutions. According to Tilly, these form the core of the process of state formation. In addition, 'successful' wars may increase the territorial possessions of rulers, and start to demarcate the more precise boundaries associated with modern states. Of course this process relies heavily on *coercion* rather than *consent*:

> Why did wars occur at all? The central, tragic fact is simple: coercion *works*; those who apply substantial force to their fellows get compliance,

and from that compliance draw the multiple advantages of money, goods, deference, access to pleasures denied to less powerful people.[14]

The extent of war during the period of the emergence of modern states was dramatic (Table 2.2).

Table 2.2 Temporal extent of war between great powers (after Tilly, 1990)

Period	Number of wars	Proportion of period war underway (%)
16th century	34	95
17th century	29	94
18th century	17	78
19th century	20	40
1901–75	15	53

Wars are expensive, requiring the maintenance of large armies which are not engaged in production, and the acquisition of equipment, much of which has to be continuously replenished. Paying for all this involves taxation (in a broad sense), or borrowing against future taxation. Certain forms of taxation, such as direct and arbitrary collection of money or goods (which Tilly calls 'tribute'[15]), can be garnered by *ad hoc* and coercive means. More systematic and dependable taxation regimes require organization and monitoring of the population, and a monetary economy.

In addition, the armed forces had to be organized and managed, and as warfare itself became increasingly large-scale and complex, so too did military organizations. According to Christopher Dandeker, the sixteenth and early seventeenth centuries saw a revolution in military organization:

> The state transformed military organization from a system comprising autonomous, largely self-equipped mercenary formations, employed by contracting captains, to one based on professional servants of the state, disciplined in a bureaucratic hierarchy and owing allegiance to the state alone.[16]

Despite the importance of coercion, the dependence of the war-mongering states of early modern Europe on the wider economy and society for the *resources* for war, forced their ruling elites into relations of strategic alliance and compromise with other social groups. These other groups were often pursuing very different interests and strategies, but they were sometimes able to secure their aims in a process of negotiation with the dominant elite:

> In fact, rulers attempted to avoid the establishment of institutions representing groups outside their own class, and sometimes succeeded for considerable periods. In the long term, however, those institutions were the price and outcome of bargaining with different members of the subject population for the wherewithal of state activity, especially the means of war. Kings of England did not *want* a Parliament to form and assume ever-greater

power; they conceded to barons, and then to clergy, gentry, and bourgeois, in the course of persuading them to raise the money for warfare.[17]

These processes and strategies resulted in the emergence of state institutions from which developed modern states. Among the key institutions involved were treasuries, state banks, taxation departments, diplomatic corps, military administration, military academies, armies and navies, and, as a product of bargaining with other social groups, (partially) representative institutions, such as parliaments. These organizations formed the cores of the apparatuses of modern states. On the whole, none of them was established *in order delib-erately to construct* modern states — for one thing the idea would have made little sense to those involved at the time. Rather, they were the by-products, the unintended consequences of strategies pursued for other reasons, most notably the preparation for, and waging of, wars.

The character of states: variations, then convergence

During the middle ages the political map of Europe was both fragmented and complex. Hundreds of rulers governed a multifarious patchwork of statelets, cities, dukedoms, principalities, caliphates and larger empires. Within the largest units (such as the dynastic empires) dozens of local potentates pursued their own interests and strategies largely independently from those of their ultimate overlords.[18] As state formation proceeded through the pursuit of war, different states developed in very different ways. By the middle of the twenti-eth century, however, states had become much more alike. While significant differences remain, modern states have much more in common with each other in terms of their activities and forms of organization, than did their early modern ancestors. This process of differentiation and then convergence is central to Charles Tilly's account of state formation.

The resourcing of armies and wars through various forms of taxation over a sustained period depended upon the ability of the economy to generate suffi-cient production to maintain not only the general population, but also the mil-itary activities of the state. According to Tilly, this means that the capacity of states and their rulers to pursue militarist strategies was heavily influenced by the reciprocal relationship between *coercion* and *capital*. We have already seen the importance of coercion, but it was the various different ways in which coercion combined with the availability of capital that led to variation in the character of states.

Geography, in the form of the spatial structure of the relations between cap-ital and coercion, was of crucial importance. According to Tilly, the means of coercion were characteristically mobilized by states and their rulers. Capital, by contrast, was concentrated in cities: the home of banks, merchants, traders, markets and craft workers. Cities were in many respects rivals to the emerging states. Cities had their own institutions and resources, and were concerned above all with production and trade, rather than war and the acquisition of territory. In some cases, they formed states in their own right – city-states. In others, they existed more or less uncomfortably *within* the territories or spheres of influence of emerging states.

States and their rulers relied to a greater or lesser extent on the resources which cities could provide. The precise balance varied, and Tilly identifies three contrasting trends in state development: capital-intensive, coercion-intensive and an intermediate 'capitalized coercion' path. These alternatives were not deliberate strategies, but represented the response of states to the different environments in which they found themselves.

In the capital-intensive mode, 'rulers relied on compacts with capitalists — whose interests they served with care — to rent or purchase military force, and thereby warred without building vast permanent state structures'.[19] By contrast, where coercion dominated, 'rulers squeezed the means of war from their own populations and others they conquered, building massive structures of extraction in the process'.[20] The intermediate path involved aspects of each, and included 'incorporating capitalists and sources of capital directly into the structures' of the state.[21] According to Tilly, examples of the first approach include Genoa and the Dutch Republic, of the second Brandenburg and Russia, and of the third, France and England.

In due course, however, the loose federations of city-states at one end of the scale and the massive tribute-taking empires at the other both lost out to the 'intermediate form' – the modern state:

> Which sort of state prevailed in a given era and part of Europe varied greatly. Only late in the millennium did national states exercise clear superiority over city-states, empires, and other common European forms of state. Nevertheless, the increasing scale of war and the knitting together of the European state system through commercial, military, and diplomatic interaction eventually gave the war-making advantage to those states that could field standing armies; states having access to a combination of large rural populations, capitalists, and relatively commercialized economies won out. They set the terms of war, and their form of state became the predominant one in Europe. Eventually European states converged on that form: the national state.[22]

Tilly's work shows how different relationships between capital and coercion shaped different state forms. However, the cultural aspects of state formation were also important, as Philip Corrigan and Derek Sayer argue in their book, *The Great Arch* (1985).[23] What does it mean to say that state formation is cultural? First, it implies that it is a symbolic as well as organizational or material process. State institutions and practices embody a wide range of meanings, in their buildings, spatial arrangements, discourses, flags, costumes, ceremonies and routine activities. A be-robed and be-wigged judge symbolizes something different from one wearing a business suit. The elaborate ceremonials of the British monarchy carry a different set of coded meanings from the more austere rituals of a federal republic such as the USA. A conscript army *means* something different from one made up of volunteers. A parliament which meets in an ancient and grand palace is governing (symbolically) in a different way from one which meets in a purpose-built, modern office building.

Secondly, it implies that the production of meaning is central to the progress of state development. The state is not only a set of institutions, but also a set of understandings — stories and narratives that the state tells about itself and which make it make sense (in particular ways) both to its personnel and to the general population. These might include myths and legends, the 'official history' of the state, or fictions and dramas which represent the state, its people and its government in particular (usually heroic!) ways. In a related vein, Mark Neocleous has analyzed how the state has at various times been imagined as a body, a mind and a personality.[24]

Thirdly, state activities are 'performed' by the actors involved. State bureaucrats behave in bureaucratic ways because they have an understanding of what it is that bureaucrats do, with which they try to 'fit in'. Armies, police forces, tax inspectors, administrators, teachers and politicians all work with a set of cultural codes about what it is to be a soldier, police officer, tax inspector, and so on.

Crucially, these aspects can vary markedly between different states as their formation progresses. Even modern state institutions, such as parliaments or bureaucratic departments, which may seem organizationally similar, may have very different effects and roles as a result, in part, of the different discourses, symbols and performances embedded within them. According to Corrigan and Sayer, it is these cultural differences which account for much of the distinctiveness of the English state as it developed from the middle ages onwards. Among other things, they emphasize the discourses of the state and its role in moral regulation as key aspects of its cultural formation. The discourses of the state are multiple (and sometimes contradictory). They include legislation, court judgments, inquiries, regulations, official reports, histories, educational material, public pronouncements and political arguments. The work of Corrigan and Sayer suggests that, over time, these discourses, through their rhetorics, characteristic language and symbolic content, serve to mould the state as a series of cultural forms.[25]

'Moral regulation' refers to the processes by which the state tries to represent itself as the neutral guardian and protector of a unified 'whole' people, which is actually a heterogeneous mixture of different and often conflicting social groups and interests. The state tries to 'pull together' and integrate society, in part by representing itself as the embodiment of society. How often, for example, do we hear journalists speak of 'the British' or 'the Americans' or 'the Chinese' when what they actually mean is 'the British government' or 'the US administration' or 'the Chinese authorities'? The widespread confusion of states with their populations is evidence of the success of state strategies in trying to represent themselves as normal and natural expressions of a 'homogeneous' and 'united' people.

Administrative power and state apparatus

Power and information

Administrative power is central to modern states. It began with the development of writing, and the use of recorded information in traditional states. In pre-modern societies, technological and resource limitations prevented the large-scale storage of detailed information. Nonetheless, the fact that some kind of recording was undertaken was a key breakthrough. Writing and information storage and retrieval allowed a gradual shift away from power as the immediate expression of the will of the monarch and towards power as the capacity of institutions to co-ordinate large-scale resources for strategic objectives. As Antony Giddens writes:

> As good a single index as any of the movement from the absolutist state to the nation-state is the initiation of the systematic collection of 'official statistics'. In the period of absolutism, such data-gathering was particularly concentrated in two areas, at least as regards the internal affairs of states. One was that of finance and taxation, the other the keeping of population statistics – which tended, however, until the eighteenth century to be localized, rather than centralized. ... The official statistics that all states began to keep from about the middle of the eighteenth century onwards maintain and extend these concerns. But they also range over many sectors of social life and, for the first time, are detailed, systematic and nearly complete. They include the centralized collation of materials registering births, marriages and deaths; statistics pertaining to residence, ethnic background and occupation; and ... 'moral statistics', relating to suicide, delinquency, divorce and so on.[26]

The sociologist Michael Mann has drawn a useful distinction between *despotic power* and *infrastructural power*.[27] Despotic power refers to the power of state elites to do things without reference to the rest of society. As Mann graphically puts it:

> Great despotic power can be 'measured' most vividly in the ability of all those Red Queens to shout 'off with his head' and have their whim gratified without further ado – provided the person is at hand.[28]

By contrast, infrastructural power is the ability of the state to 'penetrate' society and reach out across geographical space to influence events throughout its territory. States which were despotically strong, but infrastructurally weak, had great powers over life and death in theory, but did not possess the logistical means to carry them out. Where states have great infrastructural power, but limited despotic power, they typically have huge bureaucracies reaching into every part of the land, but are unable to use them to produce rapid or effective results. Mann identifies a range of types of state depending on the combination of infrastructural and despotic power (Table 2.3).

Surveillance

Those of us who live in modern states with a high degree of infrastructural power would find it very difficult, probably impossible, to pursue our everyday lives entirely independently from the state. The state monitors our births,

Table 2.3   Despotic and infrastructural power (after Mann, 1988)

	Infrastructurally weak	Infrastructurally strong
Despotically weak	Feudal	Bureaucratic
Despotically strong	Imperial	Authoritarian

marriages and deaths, our work and income, our child-rearing, our health, our housing, transport and travel, our education, our entitlement to public assistance, our political activities, our law-breaking and much else besides. Some of this information is held anonymously, but much of it is in named records. Electronic information storage has greatly expanded the ability of states to keep tabs on its population. Most information-gathering is not undertaken by specialized 'security services'. Instead, it is the by-product of a huge range of routine daily interactions between people and state institutions.

Geography is crucial to the state's capacity to undertake such routine surveillance. Surveillance requires a high level of infrastructural power, and it thus depends on a spatially dense and comprehensive set of institutional practices through which whole populations, from Miami to Seattle and from Lands End to the Orkneys, can be drawn into the knowledge circuits of the state. The 'institutional materiality' stretches the state's practices throughout its territory, usually through a spatially dispersed network of offices, courts, registries and agents. Although the coverage is never complete, this allows the expansion of state power away from the centre and right up to the boundary, giving us the sharply-drawn borders of modern states.

Administrative power is also expressed through 'internal pacification'. In traditional states, the centre had very little capacity to suppress internal dissent or unusual behaviour. Giddens mentions two developments which led to an increased emphasis on the state suppression of what gradually came to be defined as 'deviance'.[29] First, the growth of a large class of landless and dispossessed people led to rural unrest, poverty and rapid urban growth. Secondly, the state became increasingly concerned with the separation and treatment of specific social groups constructed as 'deviant' or 'abnormal'. These included those suffering from mental distress (the 'insane'), those with certain diseases, those committing criminal offences and those regarded as immoral or morally degraded, such as prostitutes and unmarried mothers. These twin shifts produced further parts of the state apparatus: the police, the internal security forces and 'carceral' institutions, such as prisons, workhouses and mental institutions, each with its own distinctive geography.

The spread of modern states: statehood as aspiration

State formation is not a neat process. Modern states are the products of centuries of sporadic, *ad hoc* developments and unintended consequences. War and the resourcing of war has been a key influence. So too has the growth of administrative power, both through surveillance and population monitoring on the one hand and through the emergence of strategies for internal pacification and social control on the other. These processes have all involved particular uses of space and the production of spaces, and all of them involve cultural as well as political, economic and military transformations. During the twentieth century they spread across the world as the idea of the nation-state took on global significance.

The worldwide spread of modern states was intimately tied to European imperialism and colonialism. For one thing, during the rise of Europe's overseas empires, the imperatives and cultures of imperialism were of great importance in conditioning the formation of states in Europe. Then, during the period of decolonization, the territories and administrative apparatuses bequeathed to the newly independent areas by the departing imperial powers were central to the formation of states in the Global South.

Colonialism influenced the development of states throughout Asia, Africa and Latin America. Imperial administrations operated in territories that had been mapped out through the processes of colonization. Territorial boundaries were partly the product of conflict between imperialist powers over territory, partly the results of conflicts between colonizers and the colonized, and partly a consequence of the imperialists' desire to organize space to facilitate the exploitation of resources.

With eventual decolonization, the newly independent states stepped into the administrative map of the colonizers, even though it rarely bore much relationship to the social or political geography of the pre-colonial societies. They also inherited state institutions that were culturally alien and had been designed for the twin purposes of subduing the local population and facilitating the transfer of resources to the metropolitan core. While this legacy hardly provided a propitious start for many newly independent states, there was in practice little that they could do other than adopt the model of the modern state.[30] As we have seen, though, the elaborate edifice of the modern state is expensive. Supporting it has sometimes added to, rather than solved, the economic difficulties of poorer countries. The failure of many states in the South to secure 'development' has often produced cycles of political instability with more liberal regimes being succeeded by more authoritarian ones and vice versa. Political geographer Ron Johnston suggests that this is because the difficulties of generating economic 'development' lead to a loss of legitimacy of the existing form of government and political instability, which allows a 'dictator' to take power on the basis of promises to restore order and encourage investment. The repression involved leads to a loss of legitimacy for the new regime and, eventually, a return to democracy.[31]

The political scientist Jean-François Bayart takes a rather different view of states in the Global South. Focusing on sub-Saharan Africa, he counsels against seeing states in the Third World as inherently unstable, weak, ineffective and corrupt.[32] Such images, he suggests, are both offensive and inaccurate. African states are not 'failed' versions of European states, fatally undermined by a combination of indigenous inadequacy and the global economic order. Rather, African politics and state formation must be understood in their own terms and be seen as ordinary and human, not as pathological deviations from some Western norm or ideal.

At the same time, it is unlikely that any society could avoid the general model of the modern state — bureaucratic, territorial, complex and militarized — since the pressures which generated it in Europe have to some extent become global in their scope.[33] The importance of Bayart's work is to point out that within this general model, states in different societies can take very different forms, and that those forms have to be understood as the products of their own histories and trajectories.

The *idea* of the modern state has also taken strength from another great movement of the twentieth century: nationalism. The anti-imperialist struggles which led to the creation of independent states were one form of nationalism and led in some cases to what has been called 'flag nationalism' or 'state nationalism': the attempt to develop a sense of nationhood and national belonging on the basis of nothing more than residence in the same state's territory. Other nationalisms, grounded in various constructions of ethnic identity, pursue the ideal of the modern state understood as a nation-state. In such campaigns, a discourse of statehood is developed in which the 'destiny' of the 'nation' is presented as dependent upon achieving statehood — a territorial space in which the 'community' of the nation can govern itself. Such arrangements are mythical of course — as we have seen, the actual processes of state formation are not quite like that. But they are also extremely powerful, as the nationalist war in the former Yugoslavia, which began in 1991, attests. These issues are pursued in more detail in Chapter 7. Next, though, we turn to the changing geographies of a particular form of the modern state: the welfare state.

Notes

1. Glassner, Martin and Fahrer, Chuck (2004) *Political Geography*. New York: John Wiley. pp. 65–8.
2. Soja, Edward W. (1968) 'Communications and territorial integration in East Africa: an introduction to transaction flow analysis', *East Lakes Geographer*, 4: 39–57.
3. Giddens, Anthony (1985) *The Nation-state and Violence*. Cambridge: Polity press. pp. 49–51.
4. Giddens, *The Nation-state and Violence*.
5. Jessop, Bob (1990) *State Theory: Putting Capitalist States in Their Place*. Cambridge: Polity press. p. 249.
6. Mitchell, Timothy (1991) 'The limits of the state: beyond statist approaches and their critics', *American Political Science Review*, 85(1): 77–96. p. 81.
7. Painter, Joe (2006) 'Prosaic geographies of stateness', *Political Geography*, 25(7): 752–74. p. 758.
8. Mitchell, 'The limits of the state'. p. 94.
9. Jessop, Bob, *State Theory*. p. 267.
10. Foucault, Michel (1979) 'On governmentality', *Ideology & Consciousness*, 6: 5–21. p. 8.
11. Camilleri, Joseph and Falk, Jim (1992) *The End of Sovereignty?* Aldershot: Edward Elgar. p. 11.
12. Giddens, *The Nation-state and Violence*. pp. 94–5.
13. Tilly, Charles (1990) *Coercion, Capital and European States: AD 990–1990*. Oxford: Blackwell. pp. 14–16.
14. Tilly, *Coercion*. pp. 70–1.
15. Tilly, *Coercion*. p. 87.
16. Dandeker, Christopher (1990) *Surveillance, Power and Modernity: Bureaucracy and Discipline from 1700 to the Present Day*. Cambridge: Polity press. p. 57.
17. Tilly, *Coercion*. p. 64.

18. Tilly, *Coercion*. pp. 39–40.
19. Tilly, *Coercion*. p. 30.
20. Tilly, *Coercion*. p. 30.
21. Tilly, *Coercion*. p. 30.
22. Tilly, *Coercion*. p. 15.
23. Corrigan, Philip and Sayer, Derek (1985) *The Great Arch: English State Formation as Cultural Revolution*. Oxford: Blackwell.
24. Neocleous, Mark (2003) *Imagining the State*. Maidenhead: Open University Press.
25. Corrigan and Sayer, *Great Arch*.
26. Giddens, *The Nation-State and Violence*. pp. 179–80.
27. Mann, Michael (1988) *States, War and Capitalism*. Oxford: Blackwell. p. 5.
28. Mann, *States, War and Capitalism*. p. 5.
29. Giddens, *The Nation-State and Violence*. p. 182.
30. Tilly, *Coercion*. p. 192.
31. Johnston, Ron J. (1993) 'The rise and decline of the corporate welfare state: a comparative analysis in global context', in P. Taylor (ed.), *Political Geography of the Twentieth Century*. London: Belhaven, pp. 115–70.
32. Bayart, J.-F. (1993) *The State in Africa: The Politics of the Belly*. London and New York: Longman.
33. Tilly, *Coercion*. pp. 192–225.

Further reading

A good account of the modern state is provided by:

Pierson, Christopher (2004) *The Modern State* (2nd edition). London: Routledge.

Geography's changing understanding of the relationship between state and society is surveyed in:

Painter, Joe (2005) 'State: society', in Paul Cloke and Ron Johnston (eds), *Spaces of Geographical Thought: Deconstructing Human Geography's Binaries*. London: Sage. pp. 42–60.

Charles Tilly's arguments about capital and coercion are set out in:

Tilly, Charles (1990) *Coercion, Capital and European States: AD 990–1990*. Oxford: Blackwell.

Bob Jessop's influential strategic-relational approach to the state is set out in a series of books and papers, including:

Jessop, Bob (2008) *State Power: A Strategic-Relational Approach*. Cambridge: Polity Press.

Finally, if you want to follow up our own approaches to the geography of the state in more detail you might be interested in:

Painter, Joe (2006) 'Prosaic geographies of stateness', *Political Geography*, 25: 752–74.

and

Jeffrey, Alex (2006) 'Building state capacity in post-conflict Bosnia and Hercegovina: the case of Brčko district', *Political Geography*, 25: 203–27.

THREE

From Welfare State to Workfare State

In the early 1980s, when one of us (Joe) left school with plans to take a year out of education before going to university, unemployment in the UK was at record levels. For a short period, regular visits to the job centre and the unemployment benefit office became part of my life. With hindsight, two features of the experience stand out. Each fortnight I was asked 'Have you done any work since you last signed on?' This was the only check of my eligibility to claim benefit. And when I went to the job centre to look for work I was left alone to peruse the advertisements at my leisure. I was offered no help or encouragement in my search for work, and was placed under no particular pressure to find a job within a specified time. This reflected the ethos of the welfare state that had grown up in Britain after the Second World War. The system of unemployment benefits was understood as a kind of safety net. It was assumed that periods of unemployment would be relatively short and that it was largely up to the would-be worker to find work. If, in periods of economic downturn, jobs were scarce, unemployed people could not be blamed for their inability to find work. The benefits system would provide the means of survival until the economy picked up, when jobs would be available and the unemployed could return to the labour market.

Things are rather different today. Job centres (now called 'Jobcentre Plus') have been transformed into proactive agencies assisting job-seekers in all aspects of their search for work. A glossy magazine called *Inspire* is packed with advice on everything from childcare to CV preparation, information about training, financial planning, and case studies of successful job-seekers to inspire others. Unemployment benefit has been renamed 'job-seekers allowance' and for some social groups it has been made conditional on participation in an active programme of intensive job searching and preparation for work. Instead of the simple inquiry 'Have you done any work?', people receiving benefits are increasingly being asked to prove that they have been diligent in their search for employment. And unemployed people are no longer understood by the state to be victims of economic circumstances, but instead as individuals responsible for their own employability. In today's Britain, the implication seems to be, if you are able to work but don't have a job, it's nobody's fault by your own.

OVERVIEW

The chapter begins by setting the welfare state in its global context, noting the limited spread of state welfare provision worldwide. We then consider two overarching definitions of the welfare state: that part of the state that provides welfare services (a narrow definition) or as a particular type of state in which the welfare of the population is a core policy concern (a broad definition). We then look at two geographies of the welfare state: international differences in welfare regimes and internal spatial variation in the quantity and quality of public service provision. The next sections of the chapter focus on the contradictions and crises of the welfare state and on the restructuring of the welfare state since the 1980s. In many countries, eligibility for welfare benefits has been steadily restricted and made conditional on claimants making themselves ready and able to participate in the labour market. This has led some geographers to argue that the welfare state is giving way to the workfare state.

The Welfare State in a Global Context

As we saw in Chapter 2, the modern state was forged in Europe through warfare. While military expenditure still accounts for a significant part of the budget of most states, their warlike origins have been partly obscured by the growth of social expenditure and a concern with economic policy – activities we called 'low politics' in Chapter 2. This chapter focuses on 'low politics' and specifically on the development and transformation of the welfare state.

If, like us, you grew up in Western Europe in the second half of the twentieth century you will have grown up with the welfare state all around you. The state may have provided your education. It may have supplemented your family's income. It may have supplied your housing and health care. And it may have paid your grandparents' pensions and arranged care for them when they were no longer able to care for themselves. For a few generations, citizens of the world's richest countries have been entitled to a range of such social benefits either free of charge or subsidized by the state. As we shall see, in many places that universal entitlement is now being eroded and the welfare state is being transformed, but for half a century or so after the end of the Second World War those fortunate enough to live in the wealthier parts of the planet could take for granted the idea that the state would look after their basic needs 'from cradle to grave'.

Elsewhere the picture was very different. In large parts of Asia, Africa and Latin America state welfare provision was limited or non-existent. In poor countries, often dependent on primary production to service manufacturing industries in the Global North, there was little or no economic surplus available to fund universal education or health care, to pay old-age pensions or unemployment benefits, or to subsidize good quality housing. For hundreds of millions of people all over the world this remains true today. For example, Table 3.1 shows the number of countries providing different levels of public

Table 3.1   International variations in health expenditure

Annual public expenditure on health per person 2004 (purchasing power parity)	Number of countries
>US$4,000	5
US$3,001–4,000	10
US$2,001–3,000	10
US$1,001–2,000	14
US$501–1,000	34
US$101–500	70
US$51–100	24
US$21–50	18
<US$21	3

Source: United Nations, Human Development Report 2007–8

expenditure on health. To make the comparison more meaningful, the data have been adjusted to account for variations in prices between different countries (purchasing power parity).

Thus when we talk about 'the' welfare *state*, we are in fact referring to a rather small number of particular *states* that historically have had both the resources and the political commitment that have allowed them to provide high levels of social welfare for their citizens. A global commitment to providing a basic level of well-being for everyone was expressed in the United Nations' Millennium Development Goals. The goals include the eradication of extreme poverty and hunger, the provision of universal primary education, and specific improvements in health.[1] However, the achievement of the goals (which in any case remains a distant prospect) need not, and in most cases would not, involve the establishment of welfare states in the form we know them today.

Traditionally, the term 'welfare state' referred only to countries with liberal-democratic political systems and capitalist market economies. Countries with authoritarian political systems and centrally planned economies were usually ignored in most discussions of the welfare state in Western social science. Searching Google in 2008 for 'Danish welfare state' gives 13,700 results, whereas 'Chinese welfare state' brings up just 30. Although one of the defining features of state socialist systems was the extensive state provision of social benefits, the label 'welfare state' was usually reserved for countries with market economies with more limited state provision. Why? Because the welfare state came to be understood as a form of political compromise. At a time when most Western governments viewed communism as an alien threat to their favoured political and economic system, the welfare state was seen in part as a way of reducing the appeal of more radical solutions to poverty, inequality and inadequate access to education, health care and housing. If a basic standard of living could be guaranteed for all through public provision, then the risk of widespread social unrest and the possible overthrow of the capitalist economic system would be reduced. So it proved. In the 1990s, it was state socialism that collapsed in most of the countries where it had been established. And in most cases today it is the welfare state, rather than capitalism, that faces serious political pressure for reform and restructuring.

'From cradle to grave': the geography of 'welfare' states

What is the welfare state?

In this section we will examine the development of the welfare state and its geographies, while in the next we consider some of the processes which are undermining its dominance as the principal form of the state in wealthy industrialized countries.

The term 'welfare state' has two meanings. It is used to refer to the collection of state institutions that provide health, education and other 'welfare' services. But it can also be used to mean a *type* of state. In the first case, we might say that France (for example) *has* a welfare state; in the second, that France *is* a welfare state. In line with the perspective on state formation we are adopting in this book, our view is that the uneven, patchy and contested emergence of particular institutional innovations came first. The tentative diagnosis that those innovations add up to an integrated, functional whole called *the* welfare state follows only later.

State welfare services started to develop in the last quarter of the nineteenth century. The last decade of the nineteenth century and the first quarter of the twentieth saw the beginnings of social insurance schemes. In a social insurance system workers make a small regular financial contribution to a public insurance fund and can then claim compensation for industrial injuries, receive financial support if illness prevents them from working, and other benefits such as a retirement pension. By the time of the First World War, at least some of the population in most European countries was covered by some form of public social insurance for industrial injuries, health and old-age pensions. In the USA, similar schemes were introduced in the 1930s under the 'New Deal' promised by President Franklin Roosevelt (1882–1945). The 'New Deal' was a response to the severe economic crisis of 1929–33 (the Great Depression). Roosevelt (Figure 3.1) introduced numerous programmes to revitalize the American economy, to provide financial relief to poverty-stricken families, and to improve economic regulation and stability. Although many of the original New Deal programmes were wound up or substantially reformed, one of the most important programmes, Social Security, has continued to the present. US Social Security is an insurance-based system that provides financial assistance in old age, unemployment benefits, and assistance with health costs for children, low-income households, disabled people and people over the age of 65.

In Britain, the welfare state was strengthened and enlarged after the Second World War. During the war the British government asked William Beveridge (1879–1963), a senior academic, former civil servant and subsequently a

Figure 3.1   US President Franklin D Roosevelt

Liberal politician, to write a report on the reform of the social security system. The *Beveridge Report*, as it became known, stated that:

> social insurance should be treated as one part only of a comprehensive policy of social progress. Social insurance fully developed may provide income security; it is an attack upon Want. But Want is one only of five giants on the road of reconstruction and in some ways the easiest to attack. The others are Disease, Ignorance, Squalor and Idleness.[2]

Each of Beveridge's giants was attacked by a different pillar of Britain's post-war welfare state. Ignorance was the target of the Education Act of 1944, which introduced free secondary education. Disease was to be tackled by establishment of the National Health Service in 1948 (Figure 3.2). The New Towns Act of 1946 and the Town and Country Planning Act of 1947 sought to reduce Squalor by providing for urban redevelopment after the destruction of large amounts of housing in wartime bombing. Finally, Idleness (unemployment) was to be reduced through a policy of full employment based on a further report by Beveridge, published in 1944 under the title *Full Employment in a Free Society*.[3]

The idea that governments could and should influence the level of employment in a capitalist economy was developed by Beveridge's contemporary, the British economist John Maynard Keynes (1883–1946). The principles of

Figure 3.2   An NHS hospital: icon of the British welfare state © Joe Painter

Keynesian economics were set out in his great work *The General Theory of Employment, Interest and Money*, published in 1936.[4] Keynes argued that governments' could influence the level of demand for goods and services in the economy which would, in turn, affect employment levels. In a recession, the government should boost demand to stimulate production and encourage employers to take on more workers. Demand could be boosted either by cutting taxes, or by increasing public expenditure. Governments' might need to borrow money in the short term to do this. The debts would be repaid when the economy recovered, tax revenues rose and public expenditure could be reduced. In an economic boom, governments could act in the opposite manner to reduce overall demand. This would ensure that the supply of labour was not outstripped by the demand from employers, which might lead to excessive wage inflation or a rise in imports and a crisis in the balance of payments. The social security system helped to regulate demand too. Without social security payments, a recession could lead to a collapse in demand (as in the Great Depression). By providing a minimum living standard for those out of work, social security helps to set a floor to the overall level of economic consumption. In theory, such measures should help to prevent a recession turning into another depression.

There is thus an intimate link between economic policy, labour market regulation and the welfare state. Some writers use the term 'Keynesian welfare state' to highlight these connections. Keynesian economics seems to work best when national economies are relatively independent of each other. As economic activities become more internationalized over time, and as capital in particular can move more freely between countries, it becomes more difficult to use Keynesian techniques to regulate demand and influence the level of employment. This adds another element to our picture of the geography of the welfare state. We have already seen that in global terms welfare states are geographically limited to the richest parts of the world. Now we can see that they are also characteristically 'national' in scale. We will consider how this may be changing later in the chapter. First, though, we want to look at two other aspects of the geographies of welfare states: differences in the nature of the welfare state in different countries and spatial variations in the activities and impact of the welfare state within countries.

Spaces of welfare I: contrasting welfare 'regimes'

In 1990, the Swedish political scientist Gøsta Esping-Andersen published *The Three Worlds of Welfare Capitalism*, which has become a landmark text in research on the welfare state. The book is of particular interest to geographers because, as its title suggests, it focuses on the geographically uneven development of welfare provision. In the book, Esping-Andersen identifies three broad types of welfare state, which he calls 'welfare regimes'. He labels these the 'conservative', the 'liberal' and the 'social democratic'. These labels correspond to the dominant politics associated with the development of the welfare state in each case.

The liberal state was founded on the basis of the freedom of the individual, with minimal state interference. Conservatives tend to stress tradition, the importance of religion, the family, social status and social order. Socialists argue that the 'liberties' of liberalism are illusory, because they are based on private property and the capitalist economic system which tend to generate systematic inequalities and a social structure in which wealth is accumulated by the few at the expense of the many. Socialists seek to overthrow capitalism or bring about its radical reform. Social democrats argue that the social problems generated by capitalism can be reduced or eliminated by using democratic parliamentary means while retaining the basic capitalist system.

Esping-Andersen's account of the welfare state stresses three key components. The first is the degree to which welfare provision occurs outside the market, that is, in 'de-commodified' form. The second is the relative mix of market provision, state provision and family or community provision of welfare services. Following from these, the third component is that welfare states cannot be understood simply in terms of the 'rights' of citizens to particular benefits, but must be analyzed according to the ways in which the benefits are provided, and from what source. States do not divide rigidly into three groups but form clusters according to their mixture of liberal, social democratic and conservative features. Esping-Andersen outlines the 'liberal' welfare state as follows:

> In one cluster we find the 'liberal' welfare state, in which means-tested assistance, modest universal transfers, or modest social-insurance plans predominate. Benefits cater mainly to a clientele of low-income, usually working class, state dependants. In this model, the progress of social

reform has been severely circumscribed by traditional, liberal work-ethic norms. ... Entitlement rules are therefore strict and often associated with stigma; benefits are typically modest. In turn the state encourages the market, either passively – by guaranteeing only a minimum – or actively – by subsidizing private welfare schemes. ... The archetypal examples of this model are the United States and Canada.[5]

The second group is the 'conservative-corporatist' group which includes Austria, France, Germany and Italy:

In these conservative and strongly 'corporatist' welfare states, the liberal obsession with market efficiency and commodification was never preeminent and, as such, the granting of social rights was hardly ever a seriously contested issue. What predominated was the preservation of status differentials; rights, therefore, were attached to class and status. ... The corporatist regimes are also typically shaped by the Church, and hence strongly committed to the preservation of traditional familyhood. Social insurance typically excludes non-working wives, and family benefits encourage motherhood. Day care, and similar family services, are conspicuously underdeveloped; the principle of 'subsidiarity' serves to emphasize that the state will only interfere when the family's capacity to service its members is exhausted.[6]

Finally, the smallest group has the widest extension of the principles of universalism and decommodification. In the 'social democratic' welfare states,

[r]ather than tolerate a dualism between state and market, between working class and middle class, the social democrats pursued a welfare state that would promote an equality of the highest standards, not an equality of minimal needs as was pursued elsewhere. ... In contrast to the corporatist-subsidiarity model, the principle is not to wait until the family's capacity to aid is exhausted, but to preemptively socialize the costs of familyhood. The ideal is not to maximize dependence on the family, but capacities for individual independence. In this sense, the model is a peculiar fusion of liberalism and socialism. ... Perhaps the most salient characteristic of the social democratic regime is its fusion of welfare and work. It is at once genuinely committed to a full-employment guarantee, and entirely dependent on its attainment. On the one side, the right to work has equal status to the right of income protection. On the other side, the enormous costs of maintaining a solidaristic, universalistic, and de-commodifying welfare system means that it must minimalize social problems and maximize revenue income. This is obviously best done with most people working, and the fewest possible living off social transfers.[7]

This case most closely approximates to the Scandinavian countries.

Esping-Andersen's arguments fit well with the approach to understanding state formation which we have outlined. For example, we have already stressed the importance of giving full weight to the contrasting processes of state formation in different places. The relative balance of liberal, conservative and social democratic elements in different welfare states reflects the contrasting balance of social forces and the pattern of social struggles and political strategies adopted. Moreover, the development of welfare states is never 'completed', but is an ongoing and shifting field of conflicts and alliances. Although Esping-Andersen does not deal with the impact of the cultural and discursive aspects of state formation in any detail, the significance of cultural processes in differentiating between the three regime types is implicit in his account. Thus the importance of the church and the family in the conservative cluster is perpetuated through a set of cultural understandings about the role of religious institutions, family life and the gender division of labour. In more liberal regimes, the role of the free market is not guaranteed, but must be continually reinforced against opposition through discursive strategies, while in social democratic systems, universalism, full employment and high levels of public expenditure are legitimated in part in terms of their material benefits, but also through discourses which construct them *as* benefits (rather than as costs, for example).

Spaces of welfare II: the geography of public services

We have already seen how the modern state is distinguished by its ability to reach across its territory in exercising its administrative power. One of the features of most welfare states is a political commitment by the state to use that capacity to promote a geographical universalism in the provision of public services. The declared intention is that, while particular welfare benefits and services may be available only to certain social groups (through eligibility criteria, such as means testing), access should not be influenced by place of residence. In other words, all those who are eligible for a specific welfare service according to 'national' standards should be able to receive it, regardless of geography. In practice, however, things are rarely so straightforward. Although state provision is often more geographically even than market provision (which has inherent tendencies to uneven development[8]), the geography of public services is by no means wholly uniform.[9] In a simple sense, of course, the unevenness of public service provision reflects the unevenness of population distribution. What is of more significance, however, is the way in which the location of public services can produce more or less equitable outcomes in terms of social justice.[10]

A concern with 'territorial justice' in the *material outcome* of public service provision is clearly of considerable importance, not least to the users of public services. In addition, of particular interest within the framework of this book are the ways in which a doctrine or discourse of 'territorial justice' may be mobilized by different political actors inside and outside the state. Although it was not always couched in explicitly spatial terms, most welfare states have in the past stressed universal accessibility to public goods such as social services, health care and education. In many countries, the planning of public services formalized political demands that public hospitals, schools, housing finance and so on, should be distributed geographically in order to achieve wide population coverage. Recently, however, this discourse of geographical equity has been contested by the neo-liberal critique of the welfare state (see below). According to this perspective, the free market is capable, if unhindered by the state, of producing the greatest overall social benefit, while the welfare state has grown to the extent that it has 'crowded out' the private sector, which is regarded by neo-liberals as the only genuinely 'productive' part of the economy.[11] During the 1980s, many governments used parts of the neo-liberal argument in developing political strategies to 'roll-back' the welfare state, and in some cases this involved challenges to the concept of spatial evenness in public service provision.

In the USA, for example, the Reagan administration of the 1980s introduced sharp reductions in welfare finance provided by the Federal Government. Because of the characteristics of the federal system, in which considerable power and institutional capacity resides at the (lower) state level, federal programmes in a range of fields play an important role in underwriting a degree of geographical evenness, and thus spatial equity. If federal taxes and spending are cut back, then there is a net transfer of resources from poorer groups to richer groups in the population, and, by extension, from poorer areas, to richer areas. At the same time, the remaining provision, at the state level, tends to generate further unevenness because the political strategies of state governments and their resulting policies can vary quite widely.

The discursive elements of such changes are crucial, but they are not straightforward. It is an unusual government that explicitly proclaims that its intention is to increase social inequality. Rather, tax- and welfare-cutting programmes are organized through other discourses, such as 'the encouragement of investment', 'enhancing individual responsibility' or 'increasing flexibility'. In many cases, such discourses contain an explicit geographical component. 'Flexibility', for example, may be couched in terms of 'giving increased flexibility' to elected local governments and local administrators, which implicitly sanctions greater geographical variation in provision.

Neo-liberal thinking is often linked with rational choice theory, which is applied to the provision of public goods and services as 'public choice theory'.[12] According to this perspective, individuals act rationally and in their own self-interest to maximize their welfare in terms of the mixture of public services they receive and taxation costs they bear. One geographical application of this was proposed by C.M. Tiebout. Tiebout argued that there should be a large number of small local government units each providing a different mixture of taxes and services.[13] If the assumptions of rational choice theory hold, then individuals would move to the local government area which provided the particular mix of taxes and services which maximized their welfare. Such a scenario clearly depends on the decentralization of political decision-making about taxation and public expenditure to the local level and actively promotes unevenness in the provision of public services. In Britain in the 1980s, the Conservative government of Margaret Thatcher introduced a new form of local taxation (the community charge, which became widely known as the 'poll tax'). Initially, this was promoted through a discourse of local accountability and consumer choice which owed much to the thinking behind the Tiebout model.[14]

The Contradictions of the Welfare State

It is difficult in a large and complex society to guarantee completely uniform coverage of public services. However, the post-war welfare state, particularly in its social democratic form, did aim to be universal and equitable. In many countries this commitment to universality waned during the 1990s. Increasingly, government budgets were stretched and some governments sought to target spending on particular groups, rather than offer the same to all. The rise of consumer culture has also fuelled a political discourse of 'choice' in public service provision. In this discourse, citizens are transformed into consumers who are to be given the right to choose between different services. For example, parents might be invited to choose between different schools for their children, or patients might be given the right to choose the hospital at which to be treated. Whether these choices are real or illusory, ideas about targeting and choice are certainly helping to reshape individual public services and the wider basis of welfare state. We will come to the politics of these changes later, but let us look first at some of their underlying causes.

A number of writers have argued that the problems of the welfare state arise from logical contradictions within its apparatus and functioning, and in the relationship between state and society. A second group of critics have pointed out how some social groups have been excluded from the full rights of 'social citizenship' on which the welfare state is based (see Chapter 4). Challenges to the state come from a whole variety of different sources and from all points on the political spectrum. The sheer size and power of the state apparatus, and the multifarious character of state functions and roles, makes it almost inconceivable that it could act always in ways which please everyone. When we add to that 'logistical' constraint, the surveillance and monitoring functions of the state, the fact that state resources are distributed in systematically unequal ways, and the cultural formation of the state in ways which exclude certain groups, the potential for opposition to the state is large. This does not mean that welfare states have not achieved increases in welfare for large numbers of their citizens. On the other hand, it does mean that we need to take seriously Poulantzas' injunction that the state is the site and product of social and political struggles, and not some kind of neutral observer, 'above the fray' (see Chapter 2).

Our perspective in this book has emphasized the administrative, social and cultural aspects of state formation, and we have not so far paid much attention to those approaches which focus on the *political economy* of the welfare state. The political economy of the welfare state is important because it details the relationship between the state and the capitalist system of production. Although a huge range of state activities contribute either directly or indirectly to the reproduction of capitalist social relations and to the process of accumulation of capital, the state itself rarely engages directly in production for profit. Indeed, the liberal heritage of the modern state means that its claims to legitimacy depend on state intervention being used only in supposed cases of 'market failure', and not becoming a general principle across the broad range of economic production. This means that modern welfare states are almost wholly dependent for resources on production in the private sector. Even where finance is borrowed by the state, for example by issuing government bonds, the commitment to repayment implies an expectation that future resources can be obtained from the private sector.

States in capitalist countries can raise money in three main ways: by borrowing, by taxing profits, income or consumption, or by selling or leasing state-owned assets (for example, by charging television companies a fee for the right to broadcast, or oil and mining companies a royalty for the right to extract minerals). In a capitalist economy, all these forms of revenue depend directly or indirectly on private production. Capitalist production thus pays for the state, but also gains from it, as the state provides infrastructure, a legal system, an educated and healthy workforce, and so on. However, the size and complexity of the state apparatus, and the political strategies of dominant political and bureaucratic groups within it, means that there is no direct and straightforward functional relationship between the state and capital accumulation.

We argued in the previous chapter that the modern state did not develop *for the purpose* of supporting capitalism. Rather, the development of capitalism in particular places allowed certain states to acquire the resources with which to undertake other activities (such as waging war). The process of political bargaining for access to resources certainly involved the state increasingly in policies which furthered the interests of at least some sections of capitalism, but the state does not exist because capitalism 'needs it'. Since the state is an arena of social struggle between a wide variety of social interests, other groups besides those of capital can and do make demands of, and gains from, the state. The establishment of the British National Health Service, for example, was strongly opposed by the private medical establishment and other sections of capital. While some of its activities feed into the capitalist system by providing healthier workers, it is difficult to see how others, such as the care of elderly people, or of those suffering mental distress, has any significant benefit for the process of capital accumulation. The fact that the state does engage in such 'non-functional' (for capitalism) activities shows the extent to which it is able to pursue its own agendas and political strategies.

Nevertheless, if state policies did have a consistently negative impact on the overall capacity of the capitalist sector, in the medium to long term there would be considerable negative consequences for the state itself. First, it will be faced with increased levels of social problems as a product of economic decline and the resultant increased costs. Secondly, it will find its own resource base stagnating, or even shrinking. The simple solution to this might appear to be for the state to attend extremely carefully to the requirements of capitalist production. However, such a strategy has its own difficulties. First, it will encounter opposing strategies within and outside the state apparatus. Secondly, there is no one singular 'capitalist interest' which might be prioritized. In Britain, for example, many commentators have written on the conflicting interests of the finance sector based in the City of London and the manufacturing sector.[15] If the state is to prioritize the needs of capital, which section of capital should it target? Thirdly, one of the functions that the welfare state has characteristically fulfilled has been the mitigation of some of the inherent conflicts in the capitalist mode of production. However, since such conflicts are endemic in modern societies, they cannot be permanently resolved by the state, but only postponed.

The state is thus the focus of *contradictory* pressures. If it undertakes strategies to try to resolve difficulties in one sphere, it tends to exacerbate them in others. Some commentators have argued that this means that the state in capitalism is dogged by inherent crisis tendencies. Three of the most important writers here are James O'Connor, Jürgen Habermas and Claus Offe.[16] Although there are differences of emphasis between their accounts, their approaches are broadly compatible, and we will use Claus Offe's account of the 'crisis of crisis management'. According to Offe, the modern state in capitalist societies is marked by tendencies to *fiscal crises*, *rationality crises*, and *legitimation crises*.

Fiscal crises

A tendency to *fiscal crises* arises because the budget of the state has a tendency to grow more quickly than its resource base. For Offe, the political crises of the welfare state are displaced economic crises. As capitalist economies expand, he argues, they tend to become organized more and more by the state. This does not mean necessarily that the state takes over the actual management of firms, although this can happen. Rather, the continued reproduction of the capitalist relations of production increasingly depend on state activities in other areas, such as the regulation of the banking and credit systems, the organization of markets, the stimulating of demand, the provision of physical infrastructure and investment in human capital such as education and training. The paradox at work here is that as this process continues, the state has a tendency to absorb a greater and greater proportion of the gross national product, leaving a declining proportion for profit-making investment by the private sector and the process of capital accumulation:

> Budgetary decisions concerning revenues and expenditures have the double function of creating the conditions for maintaining the accumulation process as well as partially hampering this accumulation process by diverting value from the sphere of production and utilizing it 'unproductively' in the capitalist sense. ... This contradictory process can be seen as analogous to that of physiological addiction: the addict requires ever larger drug doses at the same time as the potential withdrawal phenomena that would follow a reduction of these doses become more and more crucial.[17]

Rationality crises

According to Offe, 'administrative rationality ... is the ability or inability of the political-administrative system to achieve a stabilization of its internal "disjunctions"'.[18] In order for the state to act 'rationally', it must fulfil five criteria. First, it must maintain an operational distance from the immediate political demands. Secondly, it must be able to separate internally those functions which are concerned with economic management 'steering' from those involved with securing legitimation 'mass loyalty'. Thirdly, it must be able to co-ordinate its various agencies to prevent them acting in contradictory ways. Fourthly, it must have, or be able to acquire, sufficient information on which to take decisions. Fifthly, it must be able to forecast adequately over the same timescale on which it aims to plan its activities.

The tendency to rationality crisis arises when the state is chronically unable to meet these criteria. Given our previous discussion about the porous and differentiated character of the state apparatus, it should come as no surprise to discover that in general, welfare states are rarely able to meet these criteria, and thus exhibit tendencies to rationality crisis.

Legitimation crises

Finally, the *legitimation crisis* of the state develops because the state has a chronic inability to secure, in any stable way, mass loyalty for its activities. Offe identifies five problems here too. First, the welfare state is based on a commitment to provide high (and often rising) levels of social welfare for its population. Because this is an avowed aim of state policy, any failure to maintain welfare outputs has a greater impact on public support than failures in policy areas which are not a central and defining feature of the state. Secondly, the symbolic resources which might promote social integration increasingly decline as pre-industrial ways of life are eroded. Thirdly, there are contradictions between social and cultural norms and understandings which destabilize the political culture. For example, the Protestant work ethic is in conflict with a growing hedonism. Fourthly, as symbols promoting social cohesion and integration increasingly become drawn into the marketplace, they lose their validity as focuses of popular solidarity. Finally, as the state draws more and more aspects of social life out of the market ('decommodification'), people's working lives are less and less subject to the 'discipline' of the labour market (for example) and their expectations consequently rise.

Summary

To summarize, Offe argues that there are inherent tendencies to crisis in the welfare state because (1) its activities undermine inputs which are essential to its survival (namely fiscal revenue and mass loyalty) and (2) its internal decision-making processes are inadequate to the growing range of tasks which it attempts to undertake. Although Offe does not emphasize the role of practice and strategy explicitly, the tendencies towards crisis he identifies may be understood in our perspective as the unintended outcome of strategies pursued for other purposes. For example, institutional strategies intended to generate legitimacy, such as the provision of welfare benefits in line with popular expectations, may have the unintended consequence of contributing to the development of a fiscal crisis, through the resulting increased demand for taxation revenue.

It is important to stress that the processes identified by Offe are only crisis *tendencies*. An actual crisis (leading, for example, to the complete breakdown of the welfare state and its replacement by something new) will probably only develop if it becomes a political crisis. It is to these directly political challenges to the liberal-democratic welfare state which we now turn.

The Politics of Welfare State Restructuring

Offe's arguments are compelling, but they are constructed at the level of inherent, logical tendencies in the structural relationships and typical dynamics of the state. They cannot explain why particular states at particular times come to be the focus of certain kinds of political strategy, or exhibit a particular concrete form of crisis. These issues can only be addressed by returning to a focus on the discursive constitution of the political and strategic political behaviour on the part of situated social groups.

Bob Jessop's 'strategic-relational' approach to the state is useful here. Jessop argues that the state was itself the site of conflicting strategies between and within social groups, political parties and state employees. All of these are themselves more or less institutionalized, and the success of different strategies has varied markedly. In Chapter 6, we will show how different social movements are able to achieve differing levels of political success according to the package of resources that they can command. The same applies here. Different strategies within and towards the state have different effects depending, in part, on the range of organizational, material and discursive resources that actors command. Here, though, we will focus on the discursive side and look at the critiques which have been developed from different perspectives in relation to the liberal-democratic welfare state. Such critiques are numerous and highly varied. They have been developed from a range of political perspectives. Here are the main elements of some of the more important arguments.[19]

The conservative critique: the permissive state

The social-democratic welfare state which places such store on the provision of welfare benefits and social rights, has been under political attack from the right of the political spectrum since the 1980s. In many countries after the Second World War, there developed a broad political consensus between right and left. Although the level of agreement should not be overstated, in many places there was a general acceptance of the existence of the welfare state. During the 1980s, this consensus broke down and welfare states became the focus of significant critiques and restructuring, which originated among right-wing thinkers, but became more general, as even nominally socialist or labour governments (for example, in France, New Zealand and more recently the UK) began to move towards more market-oriented provision.

However, the right-wing critique was itself contradictory, combining both conservative and liberal arguments. The neo-conservatives attacked the welfare state for its supposed role in undermining the traditional structures of the family, religious life and voluntary self-help. In Britain and the USA, for example, neo-conservative thinkers suggested that state welfare benefits systematically encouraged young, single women to have children without getting married, or establishing a secure home environment. According to this point of view, the state provision removed the need for a male breadwinner, and thus for the conventional nuclear family.

Such arguments have proved enormously controversial. Many opposing views have been put forward, suggesting, among other things, that the state is responding to wider social changes (in family structures, for example) rather than producing such changes, and that the conventional nuclear family need not be regarded as the only legitimate, or even the best, household form.

The neo-liberal critique: the nanny state

Neo-liberal views are in many ways at odds with conservative ones (although they are often combined in the thinking of right-wing political parties). For example, a liberal perspective, with its emphasis on individual freedom, might stress the right of people to live in any form of household that they choose, free from state interference. While neo-liberals might shares conservatives' misgivings about welfare payments to single mothers, that is because they have doubts about the state welfare in principle. In its purist form, neo-liberalism argues that the state provision of welfare should be cut to the bare minimum and that the state should not engage in *any* kind of 'social engineering', whether in favour of or against the traditional nuclear family.

In general, neo-liberalism prioritizes market provision over all other forms and is critical of what it sees as the 'nanny state', protecting and cushioning households and companies from the rigours of market relations. The assumption of neo-liberalism is that the free market, left to its own devices, will secure the 'greatest happiness for the greatest number'. It assumes that state intervention is bound to fail in the long run, and that the state is less efficient in promoting well-being than the market. In contrast to these arguments, critics on the left argue that, left to themselves, market forces do not produce social justice, but operate in systematically unequal ways, leading to greater inequality and, for those at the bottom, increasing hardship.

Feminist critiques: the gendered state

A very different perspective comes from feminist writers, who have criticized a wide range of state activities on the basis of their gendered characteristics. Feminism is very diverse, but in general feminism focuses on the unequal position of women and the feminine relative to men and the masculine. Liberal feminism emphasizes the struggle for equal rights for women within the existing social system, while socialist and radical feminists argue that the existing social system is the source of gender inequalities and needs to be radically transformed. Socialist feminists suggest that capitalism plays an important (or even an overriding) role in producing gender inequality, while radical feminists stress the role of patriarchal social relations. This has led socialist feminists to focus more on issues such as the position of women in the labour market and the role of women's domestic labour in supporting capitalist production, and to radical feminists to stress the role of men and masculine ideology in exploiting and oppressing women through, among other things, control over their bodies and through violence. Three examples will illustrate how these concerns connect with our discussion of the welfare state.

The role of male violence is important in the state in a number of ways. We saw how the formation of the modern state was intimately connected to war. Modern states are also highly militarized. The majority of the armed forces of modern states are men and that throughout history wars have been almost always fought between men. From a feminist perspective, preparing for and waging war are gendered masculine, a gendering which is reinforced in modern, Western culture through popular media – war films. At the same time, it is often women who are left to pick up the pieces of war (through support on the home front, for example) and who are directly affected as civilian casualties. Press coverage of the 1991–1995 war in the former Yugoslavia, for example, stressed the extent to which territorial conquest is often followed by the sexual domination of women (through rape) by the victorious forces.

Feminists have also argued that the welfare activities of the state are gendered to the advantage of men. This varies from state to state, and Esping-Andersen's work emphasizes the ways in which welfare benefits that help women have been introduced to a greater extent in the social-democratic regime cluster than in the conservative regime cluster (see above). In many cases, however, state welfare provision is supplementary to, and assumes the continuation of, women's domestic caring activities. In Britain, for example, the architect of the welfare state, William Beveridge, was clear about the gendered assumptions on which the British system was based:

> In any measure of social policy ... the great majority of married women must be regarded as occupied on work which is vital though unpaid, without which their husbands could not do their paid work and without which the nation could not continue. In accord with the facts, the plan for Social Security treats married women as a special insurance class of occupied persons and treats man and wife as a team. ... That attitude of the housewife to gainful employment outside the home is not, and should not be, the same as that of the single woman. She has other duties. ... Taken as a whole, the plan ... puts a premium on marriage in place of penalising it.[20]

Furthermore, some commentators have stressed the ways in which bureaucratic forms of organization, such as those typical of welfare states, are gendered.[21]

Thirdly, liberal feminism, which stresses legal rights and equality of opportunity, has emphasized the state's role in providing (or failing to provide) the legislative and legal frameworks to ensure that women have the same formal access to jobs, political participation and the 'public sphere' as men. Thus, in many countries, governments have enacted equal rights legislation, making it illegal for prospective employers to discriminate between employees on the grounds of sex. A key focus here is the notion that citizenship, in its various forms, has not been universal in the past, in as much as it tended to exclude women, either deliberately or by default.

Finally, it is important to stress that the gendered character of the state in all its forms has been the focus of resistance from women. The growth of feminism was been one of the most important political, as well as intellectual, developments of the twentieth century. In Chapter 6 we will consider the geography of social movements in more detail.

Socialist challenges: the bourgeois state

Feminists have emphasized one axis of domination in which the state is implicated, that of gender. Socialist arguments also focus on domination, but tend to stress its class character. The socialist critique of the welfare state holds that the state operates in favour of the middle class and in the interests of capital to the detriment of the working class. Some socialist writers have stressed the ways in which the key decision-making roles in the state apparatus tend to be filled disproportionately by the bourgeoisie. Others have argued that the state is simultaneously the site, medium and outcome of class struggles.

Charles Tilly argues that the process of state formation is the outcome in part of the development of class alliances.[22] The same can also be said of the modern welfare state. While it is able to provide welfare services, such as health and education, to a broader cross-section of the working class than ever before, it also acts in the interests of capital, as we showed in the discussion of Offe's work, above. One of the ways in which the state acts 'for capital' is through a discourse which seeks to identify state policies with 'the national interest'. According to the socialist critique, the 'national interest' is in fact the interests of capital in disguise.

States also base much of their claim to authority and legitimacy on economic policy. Given that the economic system is dominated by capitalist relations of production, which, according to socialist analysis, depends on the perpetual accumulation of capital and class exploitation, the promotion of economic growth is inevitably the promotion of the interests of capitalism. The picture is complicated, however, because in advanced capitalist economies, the class structure is much more complex than a simple division between the capitalist class and the working class. Much of the means of production is owned by large institutional investors, whose funds come ultimately from savings accumulated by ordinary employees (for example, in pension funds). Control of the means of production, however, is largely vested elsewhere among senior management and corporate executives. Many workers occupy intermediate positions in the spectrum of possible class relations, particularly those who work in service functions, such as banking, insurance and advertising. Such employees are not straightforwardly members of a capitalist class, but they service the needs of capital. At the other end of the social scale, most advanced capitalist countries now have a large proportion of their populations in a state of permanent or semi-permanent un- or underemployment. Again, such people are not straightforwardly members of a unified 'proletariat', but at various times may be more or less excluded from the social relations of capitalist production altogether.

The links between the state and these various relationships are complicated. On the one hand, the state's resources stem ultimately from the production undertaken by the capitalist sector. On the other hand, at any particular point in time, the state can pursue a variety of strategies in relation to different social groups. This 'relative autonomy' of the state provides scope for class-based (or indeed other) strategies of resistance.

Traditionally, class-based resistance to the state came through the formation of labour movements. With the growth of welfare provision came the growth of the state's own workforce. This meant that the state was increasingly involved directly in the constitution of class relations through its own role as an employer. Challenges to the state by the labour movement could (and in many cases did) now come not just through the political system (for example, through the growth of labour and socialist parties), but also through industrial actions on the part of state workers.

State formation and social struggle

All of these perspectives, as well as critiques based on anti-racist and environmentalist thinking,[23] might suggest that the welfare state has few friends left. However, while the state is the object of critiques from a variety of political positions, the social and political movements based on those critiques seek, for the most part, changes in the state, rather than its abolition.[24] In other words, the construction of alternative discourses and political strategies usually represents an engagement with the state, rather than a complete rejection of it. As we have suggested, states are not static, finished products. Rather, they are subject to continuing processes of formation and development. Moreover, states are the products of social struggles and alliances which will shape their development and future formation. This suggests that while the state is changing, it is not necessarily disappearing. The future characters of particular states depend on the political success of different strategies and social movements, of which these critiques are the basis. Politics is a fluid, unpredictable and contingent process, and it is impossible to foretell exactly where the welfare state is going. Some tendencies are clear, however, and in the final sections we will consider one of the main trends – the rise of the workfare state.

The rise of the workfare state

Although the work of Offe and others points to the inherent crisis *tendencies* of the state, the evidence of actual crisis is ambiguous.[25] Although a fiscal crisis in New York in the mid-1970s brought the city to the verge of bankruptcy, national welfare states have not been subject to complete collapse. While they have certainly been significantly restructured, governments continue to spend large proportions of their budgets on welfare and related activities. In most countries, there is still a lot of support for the provision of key public services by the state. Even when governments committed to rolling back the welfare state have come to power, the proportions of state finance spent on welfare have proved remarkably resilient. What *has* changed are the ways those budgets are divided up and the ways services are delivered.

The previous section outlined a series of political challenges to the traditional Keynesian welfare state. The challenge of neo-liberalism is the one that has made most headway since the 1990s. This has produced a much more interventionist welfare policy, often targeted at particular groups. Welfare provision has become more conditional. In many places it is no longer seen as a universal entitlement, but something that has to be earned. For example, unemployed people may have to agree to undertake job training or to participate in directed job-search programmes. Those in receipt of sickness or disability benefits may be more rigorously assessed while some health treatments may be made conditional on behaviour and lifestyle modifications.

This growing emphasis on *conditionality* has led some commentators to refer to a shift from the welfare state to the 'workfare' state. The notion of workfare has a complex history.[26] The idea of workfare originated in the USA in the late 1960s and early 1970s. Initially, it referred to programmes that required people living on welfare to work to 'earn' their benefits. Workfare, in this narrow sense, is relatively rare. What we might call workfar*ism*, on the other hand, is becoming increasingly widespread. Workfarism is an approach to labour market policy in which benefit recipients have to earn their money through behavioural changes and active participation in official programmes that are supposed to make them ready for work and more employable.

Workfarism reinforces the idea that work, or rather paid employment, should be the social norm for adults. It aims to move people off welfare and into work (so-called 'welfare to work' programmes). In line with neo-liberal thinking, workfarism is based on the idea that unemployment does not occur because there are too few jobs available, but because unemployed people are ill-suited to the jobs that exist, unwilling to take them up, or unattractive to potential employers. In addition, neo-liberals believe that in areas where jobs really are scarce, a workforce that has been prepared for employment in line with the workfarist approach, will either be more willing and able to move to find work elsewhere, or will appear a more attractive proposition to potential investors in the local economy. In each case, the aim is to shape individuals more closely to meet the needs of potential employers. The concern with social discipline that played such an important role in the early development of the welfare state has returned with a vengeance, with the onus placed firmly on potential workers to turn themselves into diligent and productive employees prior to taking up employment.

The economic geographer Jamie Peck has charted the changing geography of workfarism from its beginnings.[27] Peck notes that although the term was coined in the USA in the 1960s, it came into much wider use during the 1980s during the Presidency of Ronald Reagan. Reagan restricted eligibility for welfare and encouraged state governments to establish welfare to work programmes. In the 1990s, a bipartisan consensus around workfare meant that by 1996 President Bill Clinton boasted that '73 percent of welfare recipients nationwide are receiving their benefits under some sort of "workfare" reform program'.[28] Throughout this book, we stress the central role of discourse in the shaping of political geographies. Nowhere is this more true than in the development of workfarism, and Jamie Peck emphasizes that 'the shift toward workfare (and the associated crisis of welfare) must in part be understood as a discursive project.'[29] Moreover, geography is central to this. As Peck puts it:

> policy knowledges about workfare have been *spatially* as well as socially constructed. There is a renewed ideological faith in 'local solutions,' [...] while] models and stories of workfare – from California to Wisconsin – have been disembedded from the local contexts on which they are dependent, translated into the kind of universal technocratic language suitable for 'fast policy transfer,' and then taken up in a transformative way into national (and international) policy discourses.[30]

The emphasis on local solutions – often initiated as 'experiments' – has been particularly important in the US context. The leading states included California, Wisconsin and Massachusetts, and the development of workfarism has been markedly uneven across America, in terms of both implementation and discourse.

The welfare reform introduced in Massachusetts in 1995 is a good example of workfarism in practice. It involves a wide range of measures, including the following:

- Able-bodied parents receiving benefits under the Aid to Families with Dependent Children programme must work 20 hours per week once their children are of school-age.
- Welfare benefits are limited to 24 months in any 60-month period.
- Reduction in the value of cash benefits to make employment more attractive, but recipients will be able to keep more of their earnings from employment before benefits are reduced.
- Parents under the age of 20 must have a high-school diploma or equivalent or be enrolled in education.[31]

In Europe, with its tradition of social-democratic forms of welfare provision, there has been much more wariness among politicians about adopting the discourse of workfare. On the other hand, during the 1990s the *ethos* of

Figure 3.3   Jobcentre Plus: gateway to the world of work? © Joe Painter

workfare has been developing in a number of European countries. In fact, there has been a long history of active intervention in the labour market, notably in Scandinavia, and the term 'active labour market policy' or ALMP is often used in place of the more controversial-sounding 'workfare'. In Britain after 1997, the New Labour government of Tony Blair introduced a series of welfare reforms, centred around the 'New Deal' programme for unemployed people. In their study of the geography of workfarism in Britain, Peter Sunley, Ron Martin and Corinne Nativel identify workfare as a particular form of ALMP.[32] Sunley et al. focus on the largest element of the New Deal programme – the New Deal for Young People (NDYP). Under the programme, 18–24 year-olds who have been claiming Job Seekers' Allowance for six months are required to participate in NDYP, organized by Jobcentre Plus (Figure 3.3). There are three stages. Stage one ('Gateway') lasts for 16 weeks and involves weekly meetings with a personal adviser. Stage two ('Options') lasts for 13 weeks and involves the provision of education, training or work experience. Stage three ('Follow through') can last for up to 26 weeks, with further advice and guidance. The emphasis throughout the

NDYP is that young people should be involved in either paid employment, education, work experience, or voluntary service. The government insists there should be no 'fifth option' of merely continuing on benefit. Other 'New Deal' programmes have been developed – for lone parents, disabled people and older workers, for example – but to date the NDYP is the most 'workfarist' in approach.

Like many of the workfare initiatives in the USA, and in line with neo-liberal approaches to social policy, the NDYP was designed with a degree of decentralization in mind. According to Peter Sunley and his colleagues, however, in practice decentralization has been limited in the New Deal programme. In addition, relatively little attention has been paid to the local economic context faced by New Deal participants, or to the uneven outcomes of the programme. As Sunley et al. note, the British government has tended to treat the labour market in national terms and has downplayed the significance of areas of persistent high unemployment. This is consistent with the neo-liberal workfarist leanings of the New Deal programme, which tend to treat unemployment as an individual problem (stemming from a lack of skills, training or experience) rather than a wider social or structural problem (stemming from a lack of jobs).[33]

The conditions in local labour markets are important though, especially when employment and unemployment are geographically very uneven. Sunley et al. show that there is great variation in the success of the New Deal programme in finding jobs for young people. Table 3.2 shows the proportion of NDYP participants in different cohorts of the programme who found employment in different types of labour market area.

The data show that NYPD participants in rural and rural/urban areas were considerably more likely to find jobs than participants in urban areas. The areas with the worst problems of youth unemployment, the inner cities, had the lowest success rates, suggesting that local labour market conditions have affected the performance of the New Deal programme. When we look at the proportion of participants remaining in jobs after 26 weeks, another highly uneven pattern is revealed. On this measure, the scheme was least successful at finding secure employment for young people in older industrial areas in northern England and central Scotland, where unemployment is highest. The government claims that high unemployment levels in particular places are not due to a lack of available jobs, but to educational, cultural and practical barriers that make it difficult for unemployed people to access the jobs that are available. On the basis of their research, Sunley et al. conclude that this claim is wrong and that the geography of labour market demand does affect the ability of individuals to find work.

Interpreting the Workfare Regime

The work of Peck and of Sunley et al. shows that the recent restructuring of the state welfare provision has clear workfarist characteristics, of which its localized geographies are a key part. But how should we interpret the transition from the welfare state to the workfare state? One of the most developed

Table 3.2 Percentages of NYDP participants finding employment in different types of area (April 2000)

Type of area	Cohort 1	Cohort 2	Cohort 3	Cohort 4	Cohort 5	Cohort 6	Cohort 7
Rural tight labour market	65.2	61.7	59.2	59.6	59.7	53.9	39.7
Rural high unemployment	65.0	58.1	55.8	59.9	51.2	50.2	40.5
Rural/urban tight labour market	61.1	55.0	53.3	56.3	53.1	48.5	39.4
Rural/urban high unemployment	60.4	57.0	54.7	58.9	55.4	49.6	38.6
Urban tight labour market	57.5	53.9	53.2	53.7	53.3	48.8	38.4
Urban high unemployment	58.2	53.8	51.3	54.5	52.8	49.1	36.7
Inner-city high unemployment	47.0	44.9	41.6	43.1	41.7	36.9	28.1

A 'tight' labour market is one where there is a high demand for labour relative to supply.
Source: Based on Sunley, Martin and Nativel (2006), p. 72.

accounts of the changing nature of the state is to be found in the work of Bob Jessop. Jessop argues that the Keynesian national welfare state (KNWS) is being replaced by the 'Schumpeterian post-national workfare regime' (SPWR).

The KNWS was *Keynesian* and *national* because it used Keynes' economic theory to promote full employment through demand management of the national economy. It was a *welfare state* because the state offered a universal minimum level of provision on the grounds of social welfare as much as for economic reasons. By contrast, according to Jessop, in the internationalized economy of the twenty-first century, the first priority for governments is typically economic competitiveness rather than social welfare. To promote competitiveness the state intervenes on the supply side of the economy to boost innovation. Jessop calls this approach *Schumpeterian* after the economist Joseph Schumpeter (1883–1950), who was particularly concerned with the economics of innovation. The system is *post-national* because policy-makers no longer treat the national economy as a self-contained unit, but see it as shaped by international economic forces. The SPWS involves *workfare* because it uses reform of the benefits system to make it more conditional, to shape a more compliant and flexible workforce and to place responsibility on individuals for readying themselves for employment. Those who cannot or will not adapt will be left with, at best, a residual level of income protection, or in some cases no income at all. Finally, the SPWS is a *regime* rather than a form of the state, because instead of central direction through mainstream state institutions it involves a more diffuse pattern of international policy transfer, partnership working, local solutions and governance networks.

Increasingly, private companies and voluntary sector organizations are the mechanisms through which workfarist policies are delivered. This reflects wider moves towards the privatization of the welfare state. While it has never been possible to draw a completely rigid line between public and private welfare provision, there was a widespread acceptance until the 1980s that the public sector, if not inherently superior to the private sector, was essential to ensure that social benefits were distributed evenly and universally. Typically, the state continues to be involved in the financing of service provision, at least for the most disadvantaged social groups, but the provision of the services themselves is often undertaken by private or voluntary organizations under contract. This process of privatization has proceeded in a geographically uneven way both between and within different countries. The growing importance of the informal and not-for-profit (or voluntary sectors) has led some commentators to talk about the emergence of a 'shadow state' – a set of institutions which are gradually taking over state functions, partly as a result of political strategy on the part of the state, and partly through default.[34]

While governments often insist that there is little alternative to neo-liberal policies, some commentators believe that the SPWR is not the only game in town. For example, the journalist and commentator Will Hutton[35] argues that, far from being dead, Keynesian economics provides part of the answer to Britain's social and economic ills. Hutton identifies a resurgence of interest in Keynesian ideas. The neo-liberal, free-market approach which has dominated the thinking of many governments (including Britain's) in recent years, is based on an inaccurate picture of the economy. The free-market approach is based, Hutton points out, on the assumption of a 'level playing field' between all participants, in terms of information, market power and capacity to influence prices. Without such a level starting-point, the operation of free markets can only produce markedly (and increasingly) uneven levels of economic and social welfare. Left to their own devices, markets do not tend towards equilibrium. Hutton argues that attention needs to be paid to reforming the institutions of the economy in tandem with constitutional reform of the state itself. Only then, he suggests, will the state have the capacity to manage and regulate the economy adequately and thereby to prevent the kinds of social dislocation that workfarist solutions may generate. Whether Hutton is right about the details or not, his intervention highlights an important truth. The future of the state is not predetermined. It is a political matter – and will be shaped by political struggles and political choices.

Notes

1. www.un.org/millenniumgoals/(accessed 18/07/08).
2. Beveridge,Willam (1942) *Social Insurance and Allied Services*. London: HMSO. p. 6.
3. Beveridge, Willam (1944) *Full Employment in a Free Society*. London: Allen and Unwin.
4. Keynes, John Maynard (1936) *The General Theory of Employment, Interest and Money*. London: Macmillan. pp. 20–1.
5. Esping-Andersen, Gøsta (1990) *The Three Worlds of Welfare Capitalism*. Cambridge: Polity press. pp. 26–7.

6. Esping-Andersen, *The Three Worlds of Welfare Capitalism*. p. 27.
7. Esping-Andersen, *The Three Worlds of Welfare Capitalism*. pp. 27–8.
8. Smith, Neil (1984) *Uneven Development*. Oxford: Blackwell; Harvey, David (1982) *The Limits to Capital*. Oxford: Blackwell.
9. Pinch, Steven (1980) *Cities and Services*. London: Routledge and Kegan Paul; Bennett, Robert (1980) *The Geography of Public Finance*. London: Methuen; Curtis, Sarah (1989) *The Geography of Public Welfare Provision*. London: Routledge.
10. Smith, David M. (1994) *Geography and Social Justice*. Oxford: Blackwell.
11. The 'crowding out' argument is particularly associated in Britain with the work of Roger Bacon and Walter Eltis. See Bacon, Roger and Eltis, Walter (1978) *Britain's Economic Problem: Too Few Producers*. London: Macmillan.
12. Archer, J. Clark (1981) 'Public choice paradigms in political geography', in Alan D. Burnett and Peter J. Taylor (eds), *Political Studies from Spatial Perspectives*. New York: John Wiley. pp. 73–90.
13. Charles M. Tiebout (1956) 'A pure theory of local expenditures', *The Journal of Political Economy*, 64(5): 416–24.
14. Hepple, Leslie (1989) 'Destroying local Leviathans and designing landscapes of liberty? Public choice theory and the Poll Tax', *Transactions of the Institute of British Geographers*, 14: 387–99. The decentralizing force of the measure was quickly undermined when it became clear that far from resulting in general downward pressure on local taxation and spending, local governments and their electors were in many cases opting for a tax-service mixture which did not fit in with the central government's strategy of constraining public expenditure and curbing the expansion of local government.
15. Ingham, Geoffrey (1984) *Capitalism Divided: The City and Industry in British Social Development*. London: Macmillan; Hutton, Will (1995) *The State We're In*. London: Jonathan Cape.
16. O'Connor, James (1987) *The Meaning of Crisis*. Oxford: Blackwell; Offe, Claus (1984) *Contradictions of the Welfare State*. London: Hutchinson; O'Connor, James (1973) *The Fiscal Crisis of the State*. New York: St Martin's Press; Habermas, Jürgen (1976) *Legitimation Crisis*. London: Heinemann.
17. Offe, *Contradictions of the Welfare State*. p. 58.
18. Offe, *Contradictions of the Welfare State*. p. 58.
19. Christopher Pierson provides further details in relation to each of these critiques. See Pierson, Christopher (2006) *Beyond the Welfare State: The New Political Economy of Welfare* (3rd edition). Cambridge: Polity press. Other useful material is in: Drover, Glenn and Kerans, Patrick (eds) (1993) *New Approaches to Welfare*. Aldershot: Edward Elgar; Burrows, Roger and Loader, Brian (eds) (1994) *Towards a Post-Fordist Welfare State?* London: Routledge; Lewis, Jane (ed.) (1993) *Women and Social Policies in Europe: Work, Family and the State*. Aldershot: Edward Elgar; Williams, Fiona (1989) *Social Policy: A Critical Introduction*. Cambridge: Polity press.
20. William Beveridge, quoted in Clarke, John, Cochrane, Allan and Smart, Carol (1987) *Ideologies of Welfare: From Dreams to Disillusionment*. London: Hutchinson. p. 101.
21. See, for example, Savage, Mike and Witz, Anne (eds) (1992) *Gender and Bureaucracy*. Oxford: Blackwell.
22. Tilly, Charles (1990) *Coercion, Capital and European States: AD 990–1990*. Oxford: Blackwell. pp. 62–6.
23. For details, see Pierson, *Beyond the Welfare State*. pp. 77–96.
24. The main exception is anarchism, which seeks to develop a society without a state.
25. For a review, see Pierson, *Beyond the Welfare State*. pp. 143–70.
26. Peck, Jamie (2001) *Workfare States*. New York: Guilford press.
27. Peck, *Workfare States*.
28. Cited in Peck, *Workfare States*. p. 88.
29. Peck, *Workfare States*. p. 89.
30. Peck, *Workfare States*. p. 89. Original emphasis.
31. Peck, *Workfare States*. pp. 150–1.
32. Sunley, Peter, Martin, Ron and Nativel, Corinne (2006) *Putting Workfare in Place: Local Labour Markets and the New Deal*. Oxford: Blackwell.

33. Sunley, Martin and Nativel, *Putting Workfare in Place*.
34. Wolch, Jennifer (1989) 'The shadow state: transformations in the voluntary sector', in Jennifer R. Wolch and Michael Dear (eds), *The Power of Geography: How Territory Shapes Social Life*. Boston, MA: Unwin Hyman. pp. 197–221.
35. Hutton, *The State We're In*.

Further reading

A good overview of the development of the welfare state and contemporary challenges to it is provided by:

Pierson, Christopher (2006) *Beyond the Welfare State? The New Political Economy of Welfare* (3rd edition). Cambridge: Polity Press.

For more on the geographies of the welfare state, see:

Pinch, Steven (1997) *Worlds of Welfare: Understanding the Changing Geographies of Social Welfare Provision*. London: Routledge.

For the full details of Esping-Anderson's influential study and the concept of welfare state regimes, see:

Esping-Andersen, Gøsta (1990) *The Three Worlds of Welfare Capitalism*. Cambridge: Polity Press.

The shift from the Keynesian welfare state to the Schumpeterian workfare regime is elaborated in:

Jessop, Bob (2002) *The Future of the Capitalist State*. Cambridge: Polity Press.

Two important studies by geographers provide a wealth of information about the emergence of workfarism in the USA and the UK:

Peck, Jamie (2001) *Workfare States*. New York: Guilford Press.

Sunley, Peter, Martin, Ron and Nativel, Corinne (2006) *Putting Workfare in Place: Local Labour Markets and the New Deal*. Oxford: Blackwell.

FOUR

Democracy, Citizenship and Elections

Queues formed outside the polling station in Bishkek, the capital of the Central Asian Republic of Kyrgyzstan, as citizens sought to vote in the 2007 elections. Kyrgyzstan had experienced two volatile years since the government of President Askar Akayev was overthrown in a popular revolution in March 2005. As the voters made their way through the polling station doors, their thumbs were sprayed with a clear liquid before they proceeded to the voting booths to cast their vote. This 'inking' technique was used to attempt to reduce voter fraud, in particular the practice of double voting. The liquid used to mark voters' thumbs was a permanent ultraviolet marking. As voters make their way into the polling station they passed their hands under a neon light. If the individual had already voted the ultraviolet marking would emit a florescent glow. Since all the polling stations in the election were directed to utilize this technology, the idea was that voters could not travel between stations and continue to cast votes by assuming the identity of other citizens. But despite these lengths, the Organization for Security and Co-operation in Europe (OSCE), the primary election monitoring body, declared that the election was a 'missed opportunity' and 'fell short of public expectations'.[1] In particular, they cited irregularities in the voting process, indicating that the inking of voters was 'neither checked nor properly applied in some 15 per cent of polling stations visited'.[2]

The act of marking citizens during elections is not unique to Kyrgyzstan. States such as Serbia, Indonesia and Turkey have also recently utilized the technology. Nor is Kyrgyzstan unique in attempting to combat voter fraud. Every state that holds open elections has to confront attempts to manipulate the outcome of the vote (both by individual citizens and those in power). We highlight the practice of inking to demonstrate the multiple geographies of democracy, citizenship and elections. The practice of voting serves as one of the most tangible aspects of democratic participation, but we should be mindful that this serves both to include and to exclude. Only those with a right to vote would have been queuing outside the Bishkek polling station. Those excluded (for example, certain immigrants and convicted criminals) would not have had the right to participate. The use of ink to inscribe the body is a tangible way in which the state marks its citizens as included in the electoral process and then subsequently monitors their circulation through the use of florescent lighting. Perhaps it is instructive that this technology has had its widest application in upland sheep farming, to provide the farmer with a rapid counting mechanism to monitor her or his sheep. But as the OSCE report notes, this is not a system of perfect surveillance since it requires human diligence and consistency in its application. The site of the polling station and the constituency it serves is also important: as we will see, the spatial organization of elections can have a profound impact on the subsequent results. Finally, the example of the Kyrgyz election illustrates the importance of international agencies such as the OSCE in monitoring elections and declaring their outcome 'free and fair'. The democratic performance enacted at elections is not simply undertaken for domestic purposes, but also to demonstrate the democratic competence and trustworthiness of an individual state on the world stage.

OVERVIEW

This chapter has two objectives that reflect the broader interpretative framework of the book. The first is to illustrate the spaces produced and inhabited within concepts of democracy, citizenship and elections. The focus on space is important, since it serves to highlight the highly unequal nature of political rights, responsibilities and legal duties. In addition, focusing on political practice draws attention to the incomplete nature of democracy, citizenship and legal rights as they are enacted in the world today. The second, and related, objective is to highlight the significance of socio-cultural theory to our understanding of these political concepts and practices. Drawing on the wealth of recent scholarship examining the spaces of democracy, citizenship and elections, this chapter will argue that these concepts are embedded in social and cultural networks. In many ways, these concepts serve as tangible illustrations of the entangled nature of political and cultural phenomena.

The chapter is organized into three parts. In the first, we outline the historical roots of concepts of individualism and liberty, focusing in particular on how these have been institutionalized and codified in democratic government. Drawing on the work of geographers James Bell and Lynn Staeheli, we suggest that the emergence of democracy can be best understood as a series of *diffusions*, both across the globe (and not necessarily from a single point) and within individual states. These diffusions have been incomplete and imperfect, leading to the differentiated levels of democratic participation on both global and national scales.

These arguments are developed in the second section of the chapter, where we explore in detail the spaces of citizenship. This topic has received sustained scholarly attention over the past two decades, reflecting the importance of this term within the discourses of national and regional state institutions. We critically engage with this work and argue that citizenship is more than simply a useful concept for narrating disparities in participation in political and social life. It is also a normative concept that identifies how political entitlements should be distributed. These arguments are productively explored through recent scholarship exploring insurgent and cosmopolitan forms of citizenship whose rights and responsibilities conflict with conventional understandings of state-based citizenship.

The final section builds on this analysis by considering what is often perceived to be the most explicit element of democratic participation, voting in elections. Electoral geography is a vibrant aspect of political geography that explores the distribution of voting patterns and the territorial arrangements of electoral competition, often in relation to social, cultural and economic disparities.

Introduction

In the previous chapter we outlined the spatial and political consequences of the shift from 'welfare' to 'workfare' resource provision within contemporary liberal-democratic states. In this chapter we will further consider this transition through an exploration of the relationship between individuals and political communities. In particular, we will examine three concepts that structure this relationship: democracy, citizenship and elections. As we introduced in Chapters 2 and 3, the nature and capacities of state sovereignty has changed in recent years. Scholars such as Bob Jessop argue that the state has been 'hollowed out', suggesting that the emergence of global circuits of capital, labour and technology has changed the role of states in governing the lives of their population. In addition, the rise to prominence of concerns such as climate change and human rights abuse has led others to suggest we now live in a 'postterritorial' age, where rights and responsibilities beyond the borders of the state motivate individual political actions. While this chapter will explore these claims, it uses the liberal-democratic state as its starting-point. This is not to reify this unit as a universal form of political community, but rather to recognize its historical importance as a model of political arrangements which claims to provide social justice and political freedom.

The Enlightenment and liberal democracy

The discourse of the freedom of the individual is deeply ingrained in our dominant ideas about politics and societies in the West. Yet the individual view of human liberty is no more 'natural' than any other, nor is it a universally accepted ideal. In fact, it was the product of a unique set of social, political and intellectual circumstances that came about in the eighteenth century and that we refer to as the Enlightenment.

The Enlightenment project

Along with urbanization, industrialization and the development of capitalism, the formation of the modern state has been a key element of 'modernity'.[3] As well as these shifts in social, political and economic geography, however, modernity has also involved a new set of human experiences and new ways of understanding the world and our place in it. Central to these is what is sometimes referred to nowadays rather grandly as 'the project of the what is European Enlightenment'. In a narrow sense, the term 'Enlightenment' refers to the ideas of a group of eighteenth-century thinkers. More broadly, however, it has come to signify a wider intellectual movement which developed strongly after the Protestant Reformation. This wider movement valued rationality and human reason above superstition and unthinking religious observance, and established a philosophical case for social change and social progress.

Understood narrowly, the Enlightenment refers to the work of the French *philosophes*, among them Diderot (1713–84) and Voltaire (1694–1778). Foremost of the works of the *philosophes* was the great *Encyclopédie* (*Encyclopaedia*), published in 35 volumes between 1751 and 1776. The writings of the *philosophes* challenged many of the traditional ideas of feudal society in Europe. Most importantly, they were highly critical of superstition and conventional beliefs. They sought to establish human reason and rationality, and the possibility of scientific and social progress as the dominant world view (the Enlightenment is also known as the 'Age of Reason').

Understood more broadly, the Enlightenment refers to the wider development of scientific learning and rational thinking in the natural sciences, political economy and philosophy during the seventeenth and, especially, eighteenth centuries. The 'Enlightenment project', therefore, represents the various attempts to continue and to develop scientific reason and social progress in the period since, as well as the 'world view' associated with them. Many writers now argue that in the late twentieth century this 'project' has begun to falter. The experience of two world wars, the growth of environmental problems, the obvious lack of social progress in many parts of the world and the feeling that the world is becoming dominated by technology, rather than served by it, have all contributed to a questioning of the Enlightenment ideals. In addition, a number of writers have argued that the Enlightenment faith in rationality gave special priority to one particular way of seeing the world: detached, all-encompassing and masculine. This, they argue, has led to a downgrading of other forms of understanding, including those prevalent in non-Western cultures and those seen as feminine.

The Enlightenment and the individual

The source of human reason is the human mind, and the Enlightenment project thus accorded human beings a central place in the world. Nowadays, we rather take this for granted, but at the beginning of the modern age it was much more common to place God at the centre of things, and to see human beings as just one part of divine creation (and a flawed part at that). Moreover, people were not treated as individuals, but as components of a social order, with the church, the monarchy and the nobility at the top; traders, merchants, teachers and doctors in the middle; and peasants and labourers at the bottom. The *philosophes* were hardly democrats themselves. However, their challenge to traditional ideas and forms of social organization led to their principles being adopted within the wider 'Enlightenment project' by those who wanted to build human political freedoms on to the intellectual freedom that they had propagated.

The political thinking that grew out of the Enlightenment was quite new. In contrast with the ordered social world of medieval Europe, political philosophy began to emphasize individual liberty. The ancient powers of the absolute monarchs were decisively challenged, in some cases violently. In their place, the beginnings of various forms of representative rule were established. These changes did not happen all at once, or to the same degree everywhere, but where they did occur they put into practice politically some of the philosophical ideas of the Enlightenment. These shifts are often labelled the 'bourgeois revolutions'. They challenged the old power structures based on inherited authority and the nobility or aristocracy. In their place, the 'new class' of traders, industrialists and capitalists (the 'bourgeoisie') rose to power across much of Europe. Only the most radical of the political thinkers argued that *all* people should have a say in government. Most writers gave women no role in formal politics, and in many cases working people without independent wealth were also excluded. However, although not *all* individuals were to be included, by the end of the eighteenth century individualism *as an idea* or a political principle had come to dominate thinking about government and economics, at least in northern Europe.

Liberalism

Individualism was the basis of *liberalism*. Today 'liberalism' is often used to refer either very narrowly to the ideas of a particular political party or very widely and rather vaguely to a tolerant or even permissive outlook. In the eighteenth and nineteenth centuries, however, its meaning was much more precise. In those days, 'politics' and 'economics' were not treated separately in the way they often are today. Instead, writers referred to themselves as 'political economists'. What we might call 'classical' liberalism stressed the importance of individuals and individual freedom in both politics and economics, seeing the two as completely interlinked.

According to John Gray, a liberal political theorist writing today, liberalism is the political philosophy of modernity. He writes:

> Liberalism – and most especially liberalism in its classical form – is the political theory of modernity. Its postulates are the most distinctive features of modern life – the autonomous individual with his [*sic.*] concern for

liberty and privacy, the growth of wealth and the steady stream of invention and innovation, the machinery of government which is at once indispensable to civil life and a standing threat to it – and its intellectual outlook is one that could have originated in its fullness only in the post-traditional society of Europe after the dissolution of medieval Christendom.[4]

This does not mean, of course, that liberalism has not been challenged. From different points of view, both conservatives and socialists have criticized the assumptions and practices of liberalism. However, conservatism and socialism are really *responses* to modernity (albeit ones which have fed back into it and conditioned its development). Liberalism, on the other hand, was central to the emergence of modernity in the first place.

Liberal writers included many of those involved in the French Enlightenment, as well as a group of Scottish writers who are often referred to as members of a Scottish Enlightenment. Among the latter were David Hume (1711–76) and Adam Smith (1723–90). They argued that the individual should be free from any interference from the government, unless it was necessary to protect others. This freedom included, most importantly, freedom to own property, to trade and to establish commercial enterprises. The assumption (and it is only an assumption) was that the best thing overall for society was to allow individuals to pursue their own selfish interests unhindered. This could best be achieved, the liberals argued, if the government was limited to the bare minimum of activities: just enough to allow individuals to carry out their own wishes unhindered by others (hence the close link between economic and political liberalism). This meant that classical liberalism did not guarantee, or imply, representative government. Liberal writers were concerned that rule by majority vote could result in restrictions on the individual freedoms which they valued above everything else.

Liberal democracy: the extension of formal politics

While there is no inevitable link between parliamentary democracy and the philosophy of liberalism, the pressures towards more representative forms of government came out of the same social and intellectual circumstances as liberalism. Many eighteenth-century political radicals, such as Thomas Paine (1737–1809) and the other American revolutionaries of 1776, and the French revolutionaries of 1789, based their calls for political freedoms on the same notion of individualism. In nineteenth-century Britain, liberals and political radicals called for the reform of Parliament to extend the franchise to a larger number of voters. This process began with the 'Great Reform Act' of 1832, which extended the right of men to vote to a large part of the growing middle class. In 1848, popular protests demanding more representative government erupted across Europe, following further revolutionary upheavals in France which established the short-lived Second Republic and universal male suffrage. In Britain, the Chartists teetered on the brink of revolution before their demands for a radical extension of political participation finally failed.

In the following decades there were piecemeal expansions of the extent of formal political rights, although it was not until well into the twentieth century that the universal adult franchise was established throughout today's 'liberal democracies'.[5] Nonetheless, it was the movement towards more representative forms of government that marked the shift from 'liberal states' to 'liberal-democratic' ones.

Charles Tilly argues that in the process of state formation rulers cede power selectively to other social groups (in the nineteenth century this mainly meant the bourgeoisie, and then the skilled working class) while 'bargaining' for resources. The sentiment behind the American revolutionaries' slogan of 'no taxation without representation' was a powerful weapon in the struggle to secure full political citizenship for the widest number of people. The impact of pressures from outside the state apparatus for increased participation in the formal political process can thus be understood in relation to Bob Jessop's 'strategic-relational' theory of the state. Social struggles for civil rights and state attempts to resist them bring different groups of state officials, ruling elites and popular protesters into strategic alliance and strategic conflict with one another. The outcome reflects both the differential resources available to the different parties, and the strategic trade-offs which groups are prepared to make in attempts to secure their own ends.

Diffusion of democracy

The history of the emergence of democratic states highlights the centrality of struggles by individuals and groups to achieve representation. This contestation should be remembered, since the current ubiquity of discourses of 'democracy' and 'democratization' among hegemonic state actors (such as the USA and the UK) could lead to the assumption that the struggle over democratic rights is somehow consigned to history. For example, 'democratization' has become an unquestioned virtue within the foreign policy strategies of the USA, as evidenced by the opening words of the 2002 US National Security Strategy:

> The great struggles of the twentieth century between liberty and totalitarianism ended with a decisive victory for the forces of freedom – and a single sustainable model for national success: freedom, democracy, and free enterprise.[6]

Underpinning this comment is the idea that democracy is inherently a universal human value that will inevitably spread across the globe. A number of high-profile contributions to debates around democracy have helped to communicate a sense that we are currently experiencing a triumphant conclusion to struggles over democracy. Samuel Huntington's thesis of the 'Third Wave' of democratization reflects this paradigm.[7] Huntington isolated three distinct 'waves' of democratization taking place in 1828–1926, 1943–64 and from the 1970s up to 1991, where formerly authoritarian or colonial states transformed into democracies. Huntington's thesis suggests that a counter-movement against democracy followed each wave, though this does not affect the broad outline of his argument. The culmination of Huntington's model is the fall of the Berlin Wall in 1989 and the subsequent democratic transformations in the previously Communist states of Central and Eastern Europe. This moment of democratization also forms a key element of the argument of political philosopher Francis Fukuyama in *The End of History and the Last Man* (1992).[8] In this book, Fukuyama deploys Darwinian terminology to celebrate the 'ideological evolution' of humanity in its choice of liberal democracy as the 'final' form of government. Fukuyama's thesis has received sustained criticism. For example, scholars have argued that his celebration of political freedom underplays the increasing political exclusions and material inequalities of populations within purportedly democratic states.

Such critiques of Fukuyama draw attention to a key concern of political geographers, namely the extent to which the existence of democratic states actually leads to increased political freedom for the population. In particular, geographers have suggested that democratic rights do not travel unhindered across the territory of the state, but rather diffuse across space in an unequal fashion. In a paper in the journal *Political Geography*, James Bell and Lynn Staeheli explored this point through the distinction between procedural and substantive approaches to democratization. Procedural approaches focused on the institutions, rules and practices of democratic government (for example, electoral competition and a free press (see Figure 4.1)), while substantive approaches to democratization focused on the *outcomes* of democratic government. 'Democracy from this perspective', they suggest 'is evaluated in terms of equality, fairness, and justice; normative concerns about outcomes are explicit, rather than latent or irrelevant'.[9]

Developing Bell and Staeheli's distinction, it could be argued that the democratic transitions outlined by Huntington have clearly increased the number of procedural democracies across the world, but the question remains whether these transitions have resulted in substantive democratization in terms of reducing the exclusion of individuals from participating in political and civic life. Certainly, popular measures of democratization rely more on the tangible elements of civic engagement (procedural factors) than soliciting the more empirically challenging details of the feeling and perceptions of individual members of the population (substantive outcomes). This primacy of the tangible can also be noted in external attempts to foster democratization following conflict, such as the cases in Bosnia-Herzegovina in 1995 or Iraq in 2004, where commentators have suggested that elections were held promptly following the cessation of hostilities in order that intervening states could demonstrate the successful adoption of democratic norms.

The relationship between procedural and substantive approaches to democracy requires further examination. As we have discussed, political geographers, with their interest in the multiple scales and spaces of political action, are well placed to engage with such a distinction. Rather than crudely dividing the following sections into 'procedural' and 'substantive' aspects of

Figure 4.1   Procedural democracy in action: a voter in the Bosnian election, 2003 © Matthew Bolton, 2003

democratization, we consider both these approaches in relation to two key aspects of democracies: first through the changing geographies of citizenship, and then later through the spatial arrangement of elections.

Citizenship

In this section we will explore the other rights and responsibilities connected to citizenship and examine how these attributes are unevenly distributed, both internationally and within the nation-state. In doing so, we will consider recent work exploring 'insurgent citizenship', or forms of participation that seek to create new spaces of political action outside the nation-state. We will also consider the need for, and possibilities of, cosmopolitan forms of citizenship operating at a scale 'above' that of the nation state. These discussions will highlight that there is no fixed definition of citizenship; it is a term that is interpreted in a number of different ways. This is a consequence of fact that citizenship is a concept rather than a distinct theory, and thus it is deployed in a range of different arenas to support divergent political projects.

Although the roots of the term and the concept lie in the city-states of ancient Greece and the empire and republic of classical Rome, the modern concept of citizenship developed in tandem with the creation of the modern state. Its emergence was charted in a classic essay by T.H. Marshall in 1950.[10]

Marshall argued that there are three aspects to the modern concept of citizenship, each of which involves a different form of rights: civil rights, political rights and social rights. He suggested that, historically, the development of these different forms of rights matched the development of the English state from the liberal state of the eighteenth century, through the liberal-democratic state of the nineteenth century to the social democratic welfare state of the twentieth century. Many contemporary writers would be more cautious than Marshall in assuming that there is a neat linear progression at work here, and would hesitate to apply the same evolutionary scheme to other states. Moreover, as we shall see, it would be a mistake to assume that the modern state involves the incorporation of its residents into full citizenship in any uniform way. However, while Marshall's thesis cannot be taken as a complete account of the relationship of actual states to their citizens, it is useful in clarifying the different dimensions that citizenship *can* involve.

The first dimension, *civil rights*, is closely linked to the liberal doctrine of the protection of the freedom of the individual. As we saw, liberalism argues that the state should be sufficiently limited in its powers so as not to unreasonably restrict individual liberty, but sufficiently effective to underwrite and protect that liberty from other threats. Thus the liberal state maintains military defences, institutions of law, order and justice, and protects the rights of its citizens to ownership of private property, to freedom of speech and to freedom from duress. The second dimension, *political rights*, involves the right to participate in the government of society, whether directly, through some form of 'participative democracy', or indirectly through the elections of representatives. The third dimension, *social rights*, involves the recognition by states that citizens have a right to a certain standard of economic and social well-being, which has involved the establishment of welfare and educational services of various kinds within a 'welfare state'.

In accordance with the interpretative framework outlined in Chapter 1, it is important to see these aspects of citizenship as both the objects of social and political struggles and strategies, and the means by which those strategies are pursued. The extension of citizenship at each stage was not granted by the state without a fight, and involved demands from different social groups for the extension of rights. On the other hand, once the institutions of one form of citizenship were adopted, they could then be used as resources with which to campaign for other forms. Thus Parliament (one of the 'sites' of political citizenship) became part of the battleground in the struggle for social citizenship – welfare provision being introduced by Act of Parliament, for example. In addition, there is a 'discourse' of citizenship, which is used in and produced by participants in political struggles. Hence the state seeks to define discursively who is and who is not a citizen, and to insist that, for those who are included, citizenship is equal and universal. By contrast, those campaigning for civil, political and welfare rights use the same discourse of citizenship in arguing that certain groups are excluded from the benefits which citizenship brings. Both the meaning and the practices of citizenship are therefore changing and contested.

Spaces of citizenship

Reading Marshall's account of the emergence of citizenship could give the impression that we are near the completion of a protracted struggle to emancipation and liberty, but there is a wealth of scholarly literature that would encourage more caution. Geographers have been at the forefront of attempts to stratify understandings of citizenship in order to pay attention to mechanisms through which certain individuals are excluded from achieving or exercising their citizenship. This work has highlighted that conceptions of citizenship involve a continual process of demarcating 'insiders' and 'outsiders'. How these mechanisms of exclusion are formulated and communicated is the subject of intense social and political conflict. In order to capture this conceptually we can speak of *formal* and *informal* limits to citizenship. *Formal* limits apply to the legal extension of citizenship as set out in a constitution or codified in statutes and treaties. But simultaneously, there are *informal* practices and mechanisms that serve to discriminate against certain individuals or groups exercising their citizenship rights. Corresponding to this distinction, we can subsequently speak of *de jure* citizenship (citizenship in law) and *de facto* citizenship (citizenship in practice). This distinction highlights that though an individual is recognized as a citizen by legal indicators, there may be social barriers preventing the person taking an active part in civic life. In this instance, we could say the person has *de jure* but not *de facto* citizenship. Similarly, there may be cases where an individual is taking an active part in civic life but is not recognized by constitutional or legal criteria, thereby exhibiting *de facto* but not *de jure* citizenship. It is important to keep in mind that these labels are not fixed in time or space, but rather represent means through which the citizenship claims of individual actors can be interpreted in specific examples.

The assignment of *de jure* or *de facto* citizenship is neither politically neutral nor does it occur by chance. As successive studies have demonstrated, the exclusion of individuals from participation in their rights and responsibilities as citizens is shaped by their gender, social class, ethnic origin, religious affiliation, age, disability, sexuality and place of birth. Exploring the political significance of such entangled and dynamic identity traits has required patient intellectual labour. At the forefront of such work, feminist scholars have critiqued the exclusion of women from both *de jure* and *de facto* citizenship. In almost all European democracies, women were enfranchised later than men. For example, in the UK, a select cohort of women were finally granted the right to vote in the 1918 Representation of the People Act, 37 years after men. But scholars have argued that such procedural understandings of equality, structured around the expansion of *de jure* citizenship, miss the continued social exclusion of women, a denial of their *de facto* citizenship. This perspective has reshaped citizenship studies, since feminist scholars have argued that the universalism and rationality at the heart of conventional understandings of citizenship (such as Marshall's, discussed above) embodies masculinist assumptions. These studies have consequently suggested that the normal citizen is encoded as male. In place of such a unitary understanding, feminist scholars have voiced more embodied and situated theorizations of the dynamics between citizenship and gender. This has led to research highlighting the patriarchal nature of Western capitalist society, a structure that discriminates against women through their absence in positions of power, the inequality of income between men and women and the poor incorporation of women's issues into mainstream policy-making.

While feminist scholars agree that men and women have different experiences of citizenship, there is less consensus as to how such a situation can be resisted or transgressed. The early feminist movement of the 1970s argued that there were three main elements to the oppression of women: the bureaucratic state, capitalism and the patriarchal family. Within this model the public and the domestic are conflated as arenas of oppression, thereby suggesting that there are no spatial exclusions from masculine dominance. Over the early 1980s, a number of feminist scholars rejected this image of the domestic sphere, arguing that women should reclaim mothering as a distinct aspect of a feminist political consciousness, highlighting the potential of 'maternal thinking' as an alternative mode of being in the world. This viewpoint unsettles the formerly unitary understanding of the spatiality of women's citizenship, arguing that the domestic sphere becomes a distinct site of political expression. This shift towards the celebration of the domestic sphere as a space of empowerment for women has not itself been without critics, with political theorist Mary Dietz suggesting it 'distorts the meaning of politics and political action largely by reinforcing the one-dimensional view of women as creatures of the family'.[11] This criticism is supported by emerging work examining sexuality and citizenship, scholarship that critiques the inequalities faced by gay and lesbian groups and individuals as a consequence of the dominance of heterosexuality in theories and practices of citizenship.

While these debates do not settle on a neat conclusion regarding the emancipatory potential of the domestic sphere, they do highlight the multiple spaces through which citizenship is enacted. Since the 1980s, a number of feminist geographers have moved away from a specific focus on gender relations to consider the wider social exclusions of individuals that deviate from an imagined ideal citizenship. This focus is reflected in a recent study by Gill Valentine and Tracey Skelton, where the authors explore the complexity of *de jure* and *de facto* citizenship through a consideration of the social exclusion of Deaf[12] people in the UK in the early twenty-first century.[13] They argue that though Deaf people hold *de jure* citizenship, they are not always able to exercise their rights because they lack the linguistic ability to participate in the dominant oral-based hearing society. They suggest that Deaf people are discriminated against in terms of democratic participation since 'democracy not only involves the formal process of voting but also informal activities such as debating and exchanging political views'.[14] Valentine and Skelton chart alternative spaces of political engagement, such as 'Deaf clubs', where Deaf people articulate their citizen rights of debate and discussion independently of the hearing-dominated conventional public spheres.

At first blush Valentine and Skelton's account could be interpreted as a fragmented and localized citizenship, but the authors go on to suggest that Deaf clubs are increasingly deploying the rhetoric of universal human rights and attempting to make connections with other Deaf groups outside the UK. In particular, they suggest that the use of British Sign Language (BSL) has emerged as 'a powerful affective bond of belonging and collective social and political identity'.[15] This example of the exclusion of Deaf people highlights the complexity of geographies of citizenship. On the one hand, Valentine and Skelton's argument highlights the disenfranchisement of Deaf people from *de facto* UK citizenship on the grounds that their hearing loss prevents engagement with the debates of public life. On the other, their shared linguistic culture (BSL) serves to create new spaces of citizenship operating at both local and global scales.

The case of Deaf citizenship seems to support Anthony Giddens' assertion that individuals can be both subordinate within hierarchical power relations and simultaneously active agents in their own lives, 'capable of exercising power in the "generative" sense of self-actualization'.[16] This also reflects Egin Isin's observation that the act of exclusion is not simply negative, but rather constitutive of new forms of citizenship that inhabit alternative public spaces.[17] But we need to exercise caution when interpreting the normative aspects of such an argument. Though the paper celebrates the emergence (and political potential) of a post-national solidarity among the Deaf community, the authors also stress that this does not replace the need for new strategies through which Deaf people can participate in wider civic and political life.

The examples considered so far have emphasized the point that individuals can be granted *de jure* citizenship and simultaneously remain excluded from exercising their *de facto* citizenship. But this can also be true in reverse, where individuals or groups may play an active part in civic or political life but are denied the legal benefits and protections of citizenship. Migrant workers are often cited as a key example of such patterns of exclusion, where their labour is a valuable asset to the efficient running of a state and yet they are not extended full citizenship rights. This is a particularly important field of study in an era of increased transnational flows of capital and labour. In cases of migration, state borders act as the defining instruments of exclusion, where those born within the territory of a state are granted *de jure* citizenship while those travelling in from outside are often subject to exclusion or only partial citizenship. Studies of migrant workers have outlined the mechanisms at the disposal of hegemonic states to allow temporary residence without citizenship, from the use of three different 'levels' of UK passport introduced by the government of Margaret Thatcher in the 1980s through to the *gastarbeiter* ('guest worker') label for migrant workers in Germany following the Second World War. There are two key points to make regarding such examples. The first is that these exclusions are often discussed in media and policy circuits in economic terms, that the migrant restrictions are a necessary part of defending the economic interests of a state. But studies by political and cultural geographers have stressed that such exclusions are more crucially connected to defending the mythical cultural homogeneity of a given state. The migrants are viewed as outsiders and, consequently, they are perceived to pose a threat to the cultural constitution of a given state since they do not 'fit' the mainstream citizenship ideal. Secondly, the example of migrant citizenship creates tensions in our understanding of citizenship as inclusion or exclusion from a single state. In the case of migrant labour, immigrants will often retain social and political linkages with their country of origin, establishing political institutions that transcend the boundaries of states.[18] Again, we must be careful with the political consequences of such an argument. We are not suggesting that transnational links are an adequate alternative to increased rights for migrant workers in a host country, but rather that migration creates new spatial networks of responsibility and belonging that do not cohere with a simple state–citizen binary.

Insurgent citizenship

> Oh, I can hear more gunshots (rubber bullets) outside the Paramount, police chasing protestors. Bottles being thrown. Looks like the Anarchist from Eugene group are trashing things again. (They are the ones doing most of the violence, the other groups are trying to pick up after them.) These guys are dressed in black, smashing into the buildings, slingshot rocks to break windows ... other protestors trying to stop them from doing the violence. No police in that area right now. They are several blocks away ... spray painting everything including the newsman's camera ... vandalizing Bank of America ... still no cops there...[19]

This first-hand account provides a snapshot of the violence that surrounded protests against the World Trade Organization (WTO) meeting in Seattle on 30 November 1999. In scenes that would be repeated at subsequent meetings in Genoa and Cancun, protesters sought to disrupt the meeting, damage the urban landscape of Seattle and consequently draw media attention to their protests at the economic and social consequences of WTO policies. These acts mark one aspect of a recent rise in direct political action, operating purposefully outside the formal spaces and institutions of the state. Examples of protests are all around us, and Figures 4.2 and 4.3 illustrate a recent demonstration against the Danish cartoons depicting the Prophet Mohammed and a protest held by Jewish elders and rabbis against Iran on the streets of New York City. Though such acts can involve legal transgression, we want to discuss a potentially more radical form of citizenship action, termed 'insurgent citizenship'. This is a concept of citizenship that functions in forcible opposition to lawful authority and seeks to disrupt the operation of the state. This should not be taken to mean that objectives of such forms of political action are necessarily opposed to those set down in the constitution of any individual state (for example, equality, observation of human rights, access to basic services), but rather that they emerge from what could be termed a radical scepticism

Figure 4.2   Protest against the Danish cartoons of the Prophet Mohammed ©
Matthew Bolton, 2006

Figure 4.3   Protest by Jewish elders and rabbis against Iran in New York City ©
Matthew Bolton, 2007

that the state will fulfil such duties. Thus insurgent citizenship relies on direct action as a means of claiming citizenship rights, where distinctions of legality/illegality are suspended and replaced with discourses of human rights and social justice.

Faranak Miraftab and Shana Wills have provided a striking account of insurgent citizenship through their study of the anti-eviction struggles in Cape Town, South Africa.[20] As a backdrop to their study, the authors highlight the conflict in South Africa between the constitutional rights of citizens to access housing and services with the prevailing neo-liberal agenda of privatizing the social housing stock and public utility infrastructures. This conflict illustrates the shift discussed in the previous chapter, as the welfare principles of the state providing its citizenry with the basic social requirements conflicts with a neo-liberal model of market provision. In the case of Cape Town, Miraftab and Wills describe how the process of privatization has led to a dramatic increase in evictions, as vulnerable members of economically deprived townships cannot afford to keep up with payment demands. Resisting this shift from citizens to consumers, the residents of the townships organized into a social movement, the Western Cape Anti-eviction Campaign, in order to protect their constitutional right to basic services. When threatened with police action, members of the Campaign gathered to physically prevent evictions and used their technical expertise to reconnect utilities in the event of plumbing and electricity disconnections. Though the members of the Campaign are *de jure* citizens of South Africa, they have lost faith in the formal channels of political participation to enact change and produce just outcomes. Thus, rather than pursue political change through *invited* spaces of participation (official meetings, voting or lobbying councillors), the residents of the townships are turning to *invented* spaces of action, to create their own opportunities and terms of engagement.[21]

But we must be careful in how we classify the spaces and subject positions of those involved in insurgent citizenship. Despite efforts by the Western Cape Anti-eviction Campaign to position their activities as socially just, Miraftab and Wills illustrate the antagonistic media responses to this insurgent activist politics. They suggest that mainstream media outlets represented the Campaign as indicative of 'inauthentic' civic action in contrast to 'authentic' participation which occurs through formal political channels. But the empirical material did not support such a rigid distinction. On the one hand, activists clearly attempted to use formal channels to voice their concerns, but these were perceived to be ineffectual. On the other, Miraftab and Wills document the collusion of individuals in the electricity and plumbing services in supporting their action through failure to fully implement the disconnection of services. While the representations of media institutions and elite politicians may rely on the casting out of insurgent citizens as 'inauthentic' in opposition to 'authentic' law-abiding citizenry, the reality in this case appears to be a more blurred and complex picture.

To understand the relationship between insurgent citizenship and the wider public we need to rethink our conceptions of political transformation. In particular, we need to think beyond state-based reformism or conventional models of liberal democracy. This has been a key aspect of recent work within areas of critical and radical geography. For example, Paul Chatterton, in a paper in the radical journal of geography *Antipode*, explores the question of how common conceptions of political change can be forged between protest groups and the individuals who are directly affected by their actions. To investigate this question, Chatterton, a committed environmental and social activist, joined a protest to mark a G8 meeting in the USA which involved barricading an oil depot in the UK town of Nottingham. He describes the tension that developed over the course of the three-hour protest between delivery drivers blocked by the action and the protestors attempting to draw attention to their political message. In order to better understand their position and defuse growing antagonism, Chatterton discussed the protest with the blocked drivers. Here he recounts his response to complaints about the tactics used by the protesters:

> There was also anger that we had stopped the whole of the local traffic system rather than just the gates to the oil depots. I suggested that the aim was to cause a high level of disruption for a short period of time to force discussion on crisis issues we all faced, like climate change, our dependency on oil and why Iraq was invaded. I went on to say that I do use other tactics, like lobbying MPs, but they didn't seem to bring about change as our government seemed unwilling to tackle root causes of climate change and war.[22]

Reflecting the findings of Miraftab and Wills, this excerpt highlights Chatterton's loss of faith in formal political channels and the subsequent need to invent new spaces of informal political participation. But underpinning Chatterton's research findings lies an anxiety concerning the position of protesters and the public as two 'sides' of a rigid (and antagonistic) binary. Chatterton argues that struggles for environmental, social or economic justice will only succeed if common ground is forged between activists and non-activists. This need not be a process of carving out political commonalities, but rather one of questioning the identity labels and spaces of political action through which such antagonisms thrive. Drawing on social and cultural theory, in particular the work of Sarah Whatmore,[23] Chatterton suggests that the binary between 'activist' and 'non-activist' can be transcended by highlighting the hybrid and socially negotiated nature of such positions. Rather than stressing stark political differences, such a process focuses on new scales and sites of political activity. Echoing the findings of other geographers examining new forms of democratic politics,[24] Chatterton highlights the considerable common ground that could be fostered through the micro-politics of everyday life and social encounters. This conception of democratic change clearly differs from conventional understandings of pluralist democratic governance, where changes in the political direction of the state are enacted through political parties competing for the popular vote (see below). In this case, Chatterton draws on the political theorist Chantal Mouffe in calling for a more radical conception of democracy labelled 'antagonistic pluralism', not based on liberalism and individualism, but on 'a reclaimed notion of global civil society, collective action and a questioning of state and corporate power'.[25]

This discussion of 'insurgent citizenship' unsettles our conception of citizenship as a relationship between an individual and the state in two ways. First, within these accounts the state is mistrusted as a reliable locus of social justice and political freedom. In a departure from other radical political projects, most notably Marxism, these accounts suggest fostering a conception of collective ethics that does not centre on state reform. Secondly, both accounts stress the importance of political processes operating 'above' the level of the state, either neo-liberalism in the South African example or environmental destruction and economic inequality described in Chatterton's paper. Struggles against such global concerns require new forms of solidarity that stretch beyond the borders of states. We will go on to develop these potential challenges through a discussion of 'cosmopolitan citizenship'.

Cosmopolitan citizenship

As we have seen, the concept of citizenship has a strong historical connection with the modern state. Citizenship is often defined as 'membership of a political community' and the state has long been understood by scholars as the pre-eminent manifestation of a political community. But this stable and rather unproblematic understanding of citizenship is coming under sustained scrutiny by both scholars and political actors. This scrutiny has focused on a perceived core problem of contemporary international governance. While citizenship focuses on the scale of the state, many of the most pressing political issues transcend state boundaries. As we can see in the case of global warming, international military action, financial crises or global terrorism, political issues do not fit neatly within state boundaries. While regulating such transnational political events could fall into the remit of intergovernmental organizations such as the United Nations and the European Union, commentators have questioned the extent to which such organizations represent the views and priorities of individual citizens. As Mary Kaldor, a political scientist at the London School for Economics, has explained:

> In the context of globalization, democracy in a substantive sense is undermined, however perfect the formal institutions, simply because so many important decisions that affect people's lives are no longer taken at the level of the state.[26]

In this excerpt, Kaldor is articulating a commonly heard refrain that democracy is failing on account of its state-based nature. Termed the 'democratic deficit', this criticism centres on the failure of the state-based system to allow citizens to participate politically at an international level. In this section, we will examine the prospects for transnational citizenship by outlining two potential conceptual frameworks for bridging the democratic deficit: global civil society and cosmopolitan democracy. Each of these frameworks builds on existing political practices and institutions to offer visions of alternative mechanisms of participation in the international sphere.

The concept of civil society has recently received increased scholarly attention.[27] Civil society is understood as social associations that are part of neither the state (the formal process of government) nor the market (operating with a profit motive). But civil society is a contested term, as political scientist Michael Bratton suggests, 'few social and political concepts have travelled so far in their life and changed their meaning so much'.[28] These shifts in the meaning of civil society are not surprising: historically, the term has formed a vital part of the vocabulary of political philosophers as they have considered how people can meet individual needs while also achieving collective ends. As Mary Kaldor has suggested,

> different definitions of civil society have reflected the different ways in which consent was generated, manufactured, nurtured or purchased, the different rights and obligations that formed the basis of that consent, and the different interpretations of that process.[29]

The renewed political and academic interest in civil society in the 1990s can be traced to the fall of Communism across Central and Eastern Europe in 1989. The power of dissident and pro-democracy groups to shape the institutions of Central and Eastern European states has been portrayed as a victory for 'civil society': the will of the people holding the state to account. Civil society has thus entered the discourses of international development agencies such as the United Nations Development Programme, since they are keen to draw on its role of encouraging 'genuine spaces of democratic politics'.[30] Such democratic aspirations may not relate to the formal practices of democratic participation, but rather the stimulation of more informal practices of deliberation, debate and consensus-building among social groups.

The growth in interest in the concept of civil society has also involved a profound rethinking of the term. Scholars have begun to explore what civil society means in an era of increasing interconnections, transnational flows and the associated questions over the primacy of the nation-state. This work has centred on the idea of *global civil society*; or networks of deliberation and communication operating across the borders of states. Pioneered by scholars such as Mary Kaldor and John Keane, the concept of global civil society focuses attention on the establishment and protection of norms and rights that are common to all humanity. Therefore, the concept of global civil society draws attention to the emergence of a global common consciousness in an era of purported globalization. Improvements in technology and transport have allowed disparate organizations and movements to unite on common issues: the examples of demonstrations against corporate-led globalization, the anti-war movement or environmental protests serve as key illustrations of a global civil society at work. But the presence of international action must not be uncritically assumed to represent global civil society at work, as conceived within theoretical models. In critically assessing the operation of global civil society we need to re-insert geography into our analysis, and we would identify three particular areas of spatial scrutiny.

First, the actions of global protest movements are often directed at the policy priorities of particular states. For example, the activities of the Free Tibet movement are now a global consciousness-raising movement, directed towards an increasing awareness of China's occupation since its invasion in 1950. This movement may be global but its politics remain directed towards particular territorial political actors. Similar effects may be seen in the environmental movement, which may be attempting to confront a global set of concerns but its protests are often directed at the polluting actions of individual states, such as the case of the USA's refusal to sign the Kyoto Protocol to the Framework Convention on Climate Change. Thus movements may be global but their targets are often highly localized and specific.

Secondly, acts of resistance are unequal across space – those with the appropriate time and technological resources are in the best position to be involved and set agendas. While studying global civil society, we must therefore be attentive to the spatially uneven field of power in which they operate. For example, in assessing the 'global' nature of an organization or movement, we must consider the location of its membership, the staffing of its headquarters, the sources of its funding and the content of its programs.[31] Amnesty International (AI), the human rights and freedom of expression non-governmental organization, can be examined using this spatial analysis. While promoting causes that are seemingly universal in their application, AI reflects a specific spatial organization. Its offices are located in 52 countries and these are primarily clustered in the wealthy states of the developed world. This does not mean that AI is not active in other areas, nor can it be used to naively suggest a 'Western bias' in AI's work. In many ways, this is a pragmatic decision to locate in close proximity to centres of power and influence. But the example of AI also serves to illustrate our broader point that global movements are rooted in particular geographies and that this often reflects established geographies of power.

In contrast to the notion of global civil society, theorists of cosmopolitan democracy seek a more formal model of political participation structured around a concept of global citizenship. Echoing the advocates of global civil society, scholars of cosmopolitan democracy argue that the increasing number of democratic states across the world is of little significance to democratizing the global world order. The increased prominence of environmental, financial and human rights concerns on a global scale has led to calls to grant the global citizenry a voice in shaping the practices of international organizations such as the United Nations (UN, see Figure 4.4), the World Trade Organization (WTO), the World Bank and the International Monetary Fund (IMF). As a key proponent of cosmopolitan democracy, Daniele Archibugi, argues:

> Why shouldn't the process of democracy – which has already had to overcome a thousand obstacles within individual states – assert itself beyond national borders, when every other aspect of human life today, from economy to culture, from sport to social life, has a global dimension.[32]

Figure 4.4   The Palais des Nations, the UN Assembly in Geneva © Matthew Bolton, 2005

Archibugi's calls for a cosmopolitan democracy have been criticized for being overly utopian, that is, they may be desirable in theory but they are unlikely to be realized in practice. There are both logistical and geographical reasons why a global democratic order would be challenging to establish. In logistical terms, the prospect of a single agency having the capacity to organize a global ballot seems highly questionable. The experience of domestic electoral logistics are often too challenging – to this end the chaos of different voting systems and technologies in the 2000 election in the world's richest country, the USA, is illustrative of the difficulties that would be faced on a global scale. In geographical terms, the idea of establishing a liberal- democratic government that operated 'above' the level of the state would require the consent of the existing state system. The current international order is structured to favour powerful states, such as through the privileged permanent membership of the United Nations Security Council for France, the UK, the USA, Russia and China. We cannot invent a cosmopolitan political order from scratch; we need to work with (and move beyond) the present system of unequally distributed power.

While noting this scepticism at the possibility of a complete realization of the vision of cosmopolitan democracy, we can observe some partial examples. The European Union would appear to present one such case.[33] Jürgen Habermas has been at the forefront of theorizing Europe as a cosmopolitan democractic form, suggesting that the challenge of Europe is not to '*invent* anything but to *conserve* the great democratic achievements of the European nation-state, beyond its own limits'.[34] Certainly, the EU does not seek to regulate capital in any meaningful way beyond smoothing the path for investment and trade through processes of product harmonization and the removal of tariff barriers.[35] Rather, the EU is designed as a form of democratic polity above the level of the nation-state. The roots of the EU are in peace-building; the inception of a European project at the Treaty of Rome in 1947 was directed towards moderating the egotistical ambitions of individual states following the Second World War and this remains a central objective of the European Union. As the EU has expanded, its institutions and structures have been increasingly called upon to adjudicate in complex territorial disputes, and the resolution of such disputes has often formed part of the conditionality of initiating EU accession (for example, in Northern Cyprus and Serbia and Montenegro).[36] Such progressive 'Europeanization' has included new democratic forms, where certain aspects of state sovereignty are ceded to the European level (through the pressure of conditionalities rather than direct instruments of government), while the state remains the central locus of political power. This has led political geographers to identify the emergence of multilevel citizenship in Europe, where individuals affiliate to a number of political authorities (region, the state and the supranational organization) simultaneously.

Electoral geographies

Electoral geography is a vital part of the history and practice of political geography, a sub-disciplinary field that explores the practice and organization of electoral competition. Elections vary greatly from state to state in their form and arrangement. Broadly speaking, all elections involve a popular vote where a predetermined selection of the populous identify their preference for political representation. This model can be described as *pluralist democratic governance*, since governments are elected following what is usually open competition among political parties which offer a range of alternative manifestos to rational, self-interested voters.[37] Despite struggles for universal suffrage and a broad trend of expanding enfranchisement (see above), all democracies exclude certain individuals from voting on account of specified grounds, such as incarceration in prison or immigration status.[38] A state's general election therefore offers scholars and politicians the chance to observe and map the political orientation, or at least voting preference, of a given population. But perhaps more importantly, the voting system is itself usually arranged into territorial units, thus the division of territory can play a significant part in the outcome of a popular vote. This nexus of territory and politics has proved a fertile area for political geographers and has led to a diverse range of scholarly research in the spatiality of elections.

The work of French geographer André Siegfried (1875–1959) is often cited as the first example of electoral geography, in particular his pioneering analysis of voter behaviour in his 1913 book *Tableau Politique de la France de l'Ouest*.[39] Siegfried's research in the French *department* of Ardéche was ground-breaking:

he studied census data and voting behaviour to attempt to map tendencies within the separate districts. There were two stages to Siegfried's analysis. In the first, he highlighted the mechanisms through which elections served to aggregate public opinions on either the political left (socially progressive/liberal) or the political right (traditional/conservative) through the voting process. Through a consideration of the political perspectives of elected officials, Siegfried was able to ascertain whether a particular district could be considered a 'left' or 'right' district. From this initial stage of analysis came the second and more fundamental question of why individuals were voting in these ways. Siegfried explained voter behaviour through 'direct and simple explanations', such as the division of property, occupation, submission to the priest or racial character. The district's physical, economic and cultural geography was therefore seen as an important structuring framework on the establishment of political priorities among voters.

Siegfried's work has been extremely influential though not without criticism, and scholars have identified two particular areas of concern. First, critics have questioned whether the range of political perspectives can be adequately accommodated on a single dimension between left and right. Political issues do not fit neatly on this scale and often individuals can hold apparently contradictory views on different political issues. Siegfried's model struggles to acknowledge this. Secondly, and perhaps more profoundly, Siegfried's study has since been accused of promoting an environmental determinism – or that the environment shapes social and political development and attitudes. Since its peak in popularity at the turn of the nineteenth/twentieth century, environmental determinism has been critiqued as a racist theory of human development that served to legitimize European colonial expansion (see Chapters 8 and 9). Though any trace of environmental determinism should be critiqued, we should not be surprised to see its explanatory systems at work in Siegfried's work considering the era (the early twentieth century) and the location (metropolitan France) in which he was working. Like all scholarship, Siegfried's work has its own political geography.

Following Siegfried's work, the trajectory of electoral geography in the nineteenth century mirrored the wider geographical discipline. We can imperfectly divide this into two areas. In the first, there was a shift away from a quest for grand explanatory narratives of voter tendencies towards a more empiricist and grounded approach that sought to measure and quantify voter behaviour. In the second, geographers have turned their attention to the study of geographies of representation – examining how the spatial organization of elections serves to shape the possible outcomes.

Voter behaviour

Over the 1950s and 1960s this quest for empirics was assisted by the prevalence of numerical data through which voter patterns could be mapped and projected. One early attempt to theorize the emerging quantitative data came in the form of the 'neighbourhood effect', an explanatory framework of voter behaviour which argued that:

> social interaction within locales, particularly though not only residential communities, affects people's political attitudes and voting behaviour. People are influenced by those they talk to – so that if the majority of a person's social contacts favour one political position and/or party, that person is more likely than otherwise to favour it also, even if her/his personal characteristics suggest a predisposition to favour another position/party.[40]

As with other areas of spatial scientific research, critics of the positivist approach of electoral geography felt that it lacked engagement with social theory and consequently failed to contribute to understanding the spatial politics of elections. For example, Fred Shelley, Ron Johnston and Peter Taylor, key figures in the sub-discipline, criticized early electoral geography for 'rampant empiricism', where analysis consisted of 'mere descriptions of the spatial patterns of votes with little or no concern for the wider issues'.[41]

Studies of voter behaviour have diversified their theoretical frameworks over recent years and drawn on a wider range of qualitative methodologies. Such theoretical and methodological insights have helped understandings of the interaction of space and voter behaviour by adopting more nuanced concepts of space and human agency. For example, greater attention has been paid to space as socially constructed, thereby drawing attention to the role played by human agents in a continual process of spatial production. Colin Flint demonstrates this approach in his study of party support in the German region of Baden between 1924–32, where he suggests that 'the Nazi party worked within the constraints and opportunities of existing spatial settings to create new locales of electoral support'.[42] The work of political geographer John Agnew has also been highly influential in developing a more theoretically sophisticated concept of the context of voter behaviour. For example, his work on Italian voter behaviour and political party formation has illustrated a more nuanced understanding of place:

> [R]ecent years have seen a dramatic falling off in electoral participation in Italy. But the character of the process of decreasing electoral participation is best understood contextually. Closer analysis reveals that the highest rates of abstention are among older voters (particularly women) in the metropolitan south and young voters in the largest metropolitan areas of the north. Different sets of reasons are at work in producing this pattern; a set that in the south give rise to increased alienation from politics in general, particularly among older women, and in the metropolitan north a set that produces a protest against the existing parties on the part of the least-affiliated, younger voters.[43]

But Agnew does not restrict the context of voter behaviour to this localized scale. Instead, he argues that context is relevant to the ways in which 'space across a range of geographical scales figures in the rhetorical strategies of parties, the nesting of influence processes, and the political geography of electoral choice'.[44] This work examining voter behaviour has therefore served to enrich our understanding of the historical specificity of voting patterns, connecting shifts in party support to economic and social transformations occurring at a range of geographical scales.

While significant advances have been made in electoral geography, we echo John Agnew's sentiment that electoral geography could go further in its adoption of socio-cultural theory to help understand the formation of party loyalties and voting patterns. While the use of archival data and longitudinal poll figures has helped to convey the social construction of place, individual identities remain trapped in terms of single characteristics such as occupational class, sex, ethnic origin or age. This approach reflects a residual attachment to the discontinuous data requirements of statistical models, but it does not cohere with the large body of socio-cultural studies that have highlighted the interrelation and social construction of such identity labels. The interpretation of specific historical contexts can help animate the interplay of these subject positions, but to understand their political effects in greater detail we need more qualitative engagement with the actors involved. Here electoral geography could productively engage with political anthropology, in particular, studies such as Douglas Holmes' account of the rise of extreme nationalist politics in Western Europe[45] or Donald Moore's detailed elucidation of political struggles over territory in Zimbabwe.[46] The ethnographic approach utilized in both these examples serves to highlight the importance of individual and collective testimonies in bringing to life the plural economic, social and cultural factors that shape political affiliation.

Geographies of representation

In addition to simple vote distribution, the spatial arrangement of elections has been a crucial concern for geographers. Every first-past-the post electoral system in the world – with the exceptions of the Netherlands and Israel – divides their electorate into geographically defined constituencies. Constituencies are not natural or predetermined territories; they are established over long periods and are subject to continual revision. Population decline, new towns or significant immigration are all factors that can lead to adjustments in the boundaries of constituencies. In the UK, an independent body, the Boundary Commission, undertakes this procedure. Their independence from the UK government is crucial, since the redrawing of electoral constituencies is a fraught and contested process. Just as the choice of electoral system favours certain parties over others, so the boundaries of constituencies can shape electoral outcomes. We can illustrate this point through the fictional example portrayed in Figure 4.5. In this case, the state consists of four towns, 4,000 inhabitants, two political parties and two constituencies. In the first configuration, Party A wins the constituency comprising Habourville and Newtown, while Party B wins the second

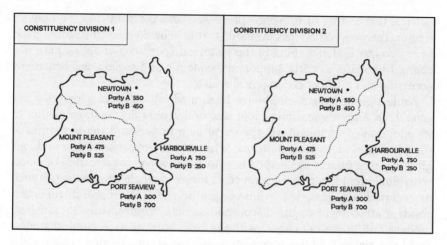

Figure 4.5   Maps of two fictional constituency divisions © Alex Jeffrey, 2008

constituency containing Port Seaview and Mount Pleasant. However, as the second example demonstrates, if the constituency division is altered, the electoral outcome is changed: Party A wins both seats.

The drawing of constituency boundaries – or redistricting – is therefore a key concern of electoral geographers. The potential for electoral bias in this process is illustrated in the examples of malapportionment and gerrymandering. Malapportionment refers to unequal representation, where constituencies vary in size, and is of particular relevance in cases where two parties are dominant (such as in the USA). If one party is dominant in small constituencies (let's call it Party A), while the other is stronger in larger constituencies (Party B), Party A will require fewer votes to claim the same number of seats. In this case, we can say that Party A has a lower vote: seat ratio than Party B. Since constituencies are not rigidly fixed in time and space, electoral geographers have charted the evolution of malapportionment in a number of geographical settings. Ron Johnston, a leading figure in this field, suggests that malapportionment can either occur through '*deliberate intent* if one party controls the districting process – creating larger constituencies in the areas where one's opponent is strong – or through *creeping malapportionment*, whereby changes in constituency size over time create smaller seats where one party is strong'.[47]

Gerrymandering refers to the practice of reorganizing the territory or population of a constituency in order to gain electoral advantage. This practice is named after the nineteenth-century Governor of Massachusetts, Elridge Gerry, who sanctioned the redrawing of county boundaries to bolster electoral support. A local newspaper represented the new territorial arrangements in a cartoon as resembling a salamander, or 'gerrymander' as it was labelled. Perhaps the best-known example of a gerrymander in the UK context is the case of Dame Shirley Porter's actions as the Conservative Party leader of Westminster Council (1983–91). Through an initiative entitled *Building*

Stable Communities, Porter and her colleagues offered council houses for sale to prospective Conservative voters in marginal wards within the Westminster Council District. In this case, it was the demographic constitution, rather than the geographical boundaries, that was altered in order to gain electoral advantage. Porter's actions had two outcomes: first, the Conservative Party won a landslide victory in the 1990 Westminster Council elections (the gerrymander worked); and second, subsequent investigations uncovered the extent of this electoral abuse and fined Dame Shirley Porter £27 million (though this figure was reduced to £12.3 million).

While gerrymandering has rightly become a central focus for electoral geographers and political scientists,[48] we need to offer a note of caution. The critical perspective offered by this book has highlighted the socially-constructed nature of political positions and, consequently, their plural and dynamic nature. There is clearly a tendency within electoral geography to reduce political attitudes to the preferences voters express on election days. Though our data may be fixed, we can never assume that the vote cast represents the nuanced and potentially contradictory politics of the individual. This is a point made by the political scientist Mark Rush in his study of the effects of gerrymandering in the US state of Montana.[49] Rush uses the term 'partisan fluidity' to draw attention to the changing nature of voter loyalty both over time and *as processes of redistricting take place*. Hence, processes of redistricting may themselves alter the preferences of voters as they lose trust in incumbent parties on account of their manipulation of electoral geography. Rush's argument highlights that individual political preference is not fixed and unchanging, but rather a fluid identification that is shaped through multiple social and geographical factors.

Case study: the US Electoral College

The US electoral system stands as a stark illustration of the centrality of geography to the outcome of elections. The US public vote for a President and Vice President every four years. Rather than simply count the total number of votes and decide the election accordingly, the election is decided through a system known as the Electoral College. The Electoral College comprises 538 presidential electors and it is these individuals who choose the President and Vice President after the counting of the public vote. The presidential electors are divided between the 50 states of the USA, roughly in proportion to the total population (see Figure 4.6). Therefore, California (with a population of around 37 million) has 55 presidential electors, while Wyoming (with a population of just 500,000) has three presidential electors. The important aspect of this arrangement is that it remains a first-past-the-post system: the presidential electors will give *all* their votes to whichever candidate wins the popular vote (regardless of the margin of victory). Each state therefore has a different voter: Electoral College vote ratio. Keeping with the examples named above, each presidential electoral vote in California corresponds to around 673,000 popular votes, while in Wyoming each presidential electoral vote only corresponds

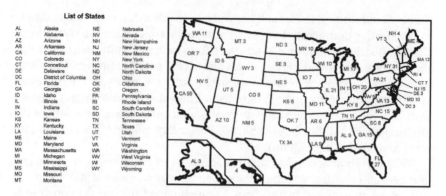

Figure 4.6   Map of the US Electoral College © Alex Jeffrey, 2008

to around 166,000 popular votes. This variability in state size and significance serves as a useful example of malapportionment in practice.

A group of cartographers from the University of Michigan has developed a series of maps that depict the geographical distortions of the Electoral College system.[50] In particular, their work confronts the question that is often posed concerning recent US elections: if the vote was so close between Republican and Democrats, why do the maps show a dominance of one party over the other? In the case of the 2004 election, George W. Bush (Republican) gained 50.73% of the popular vote while John Kerry (Democrat) won around 48.27%. Figure 4.7 (See colour plate section following p.100) illustrates how this result appears in terms of the destination of Electoral College votes.

This is a conventional depiction of the US election results though it is hard to understand why there was a narrow margin of victory when the majority of the states are in the Republican shade. In order to represent the level of the popular vote rather than geographical territory, the scholars at Michigan created a cartogram (Figure 4.8, see colour plate section following p.100). This device depicts each state by the size of its population rather than its territorial coverage. In doing so, this map represents spatially the differential weightings of the US Electoral College system.

But in constructing this cartogram, we remain locked in the boundaries of the US states and we therefore do not have a sense of the support for the Republican candidate in Democrat states, and vice versa. By breaking down the vote by county rather than by state, we have a better impression of the distribution of voter loyalty (Figure 4.9, see colour plate section following p.100).

But due to the fact that we are still representing first-past-the-post voting (albeit on a county scale) this map continues to represent the political attitudes of counties in absolute terms: either Democrat or Republican. We can begin to see the strength of political party support by texturing the map to display the margin of victory within each county, from bright red (100% Republican vote) through to bright blue (100% Democratic vote) (Figure 4.10, see colour plate section following p.100).

Finally, by redrawing the cartogram based on these weighted county results, we begin to see a clearer reflection of voter preference and aggregation (Figure 4.11, see colour plate section following p.100). Rather than reproducing the distortions of the Electoral College system, this map highlights the spread of voters for both parties across the US landmass. Abstracted from the Electoral College framework, we can ask ourselves, how else could the US electoral system be organized and with what consequences?

Conclusion

We set out in this chapter with two objectives: to examine the spaces of citizenship, democracy and elections and illustrate the role of socio-cultural theory in enriching our understanding of these concepts. We have met these aims through an exploration of the history of liberal democracy, the nature of theorizations of citizenship and the spatiality of elections. These discussions have illustrated that we cannot think of political practice outside its social and cultural context – politics is lived, and consequently it exists in space. In the following chapter we explore one site of contemporary political change in further detail: the city.

Notes

1. OSCE (2007) *OSCE Election Observation Mission. The Kyrgyz Republic Statement of Preliminary Findings and Conclusions*. Available at: www.osce.org/documents/odihr/2007/12/28916_en.pdf. p. 1 (accessed 10/01/08).
2. OSCE, *OSCE Election Observation Mission*. p. 11.
3. For a further discussion of the concept of modernity, see Berman, Marshall (1982) *All That is Solid Melts into Air*. London: Verso.
4. John Gray (1986) *Liberalism*. Milton Keynes: Open University Press. p. 82.
5. Christopher Pierson (1991) *Beyond the Welfare State*. Cambridge: Polity Press. p. 110.
6. White House (2002) 'The national security strategy of the United States of America'. Washington, DC: The White House. Available at: www.whitehouse.gov/nsc/nss.html. (accessed 03/02/08).
7. Huntington, S. (1991) *The Third Wave: Democratization in the Twentieth Century*. London: University of Oklahoma Press.
8. Fukuyama, F. (1992) *The End of History and the Last Man*. London: Penguin.
9. Bell, J. and Staeheli, L. (2001) 'Discourses of diffusion and democratization', *Political Geography*, 20(2): 175–95. p. 178–79.
10. Marshall, T.H. (1950) *Citizenship and Social Class*. Cambridge: Cambridge University Press. His arguments have been reprinted in a more recent edition: Marshall, T.H. (1991) 'Citizenship and social class', in T.H. Marshall and Tom Bottomore, *Citizenship and Social Class*. London: Pluto Press. pp. 3–51.
11. Dietz, M. (1985) 'Citizenship with a feminist face: the problem of maternal thinking', *Political Theory*, 13(1): 19–37. p. 20.
12. In line with recent social science literature on the topic, we use the capitalized 'Deaf' (with a capital D) to highlight that we are discussing a linguistic and cultural minority rather than 'deafness' as a medical or disability issue (see Valentine, Gill and Skelton, Tracey (2007) 'The right to be heard: citizenship and languages', *Political Geography*, 26(2): 121–40. p. 123).

13. Valentine and Skelton, 'The right to be heard.

14. Valentine and Skelton, 'The right to be heard'. p. 126.

15. Valentine and Skelton, 'The right to be heard'. p. 132.

16. Giddens, Anthony (1986) *Modernity and Self Identity*. Cambridge: Polity Press. Cited in Lister, R. (1997) 'Citizenship: towards and Feminist synthesis', *Feminist Review*, 57: 28–48. p. 35.

17. See Isin, E. (2002) *Being Political: Genealogies of Citizenship*. Minneapolis, MN: University of Minnesota Press.

18. See Itzigsohn, J. (2000) 'Immigration and the boundaries of citizenship: the institutions of immigrants' political transnationalism', *International Migration Review*, 34(4): 1126–54.

19. Account of WTO protests in Seattle source: www.zmedia.org/WTO/N30.htm (accessed 06/08/07).

20. Miraftab, Faranak and Wills, Shana (2005) 'Insurgency and spaces of active citizenship: the story of Western Cape Anti-eviction Campaign in South Africa', *Journal of Planning Education and Research*, 25: 200–17.

21. This distinction between invited and invented spaces of participation is developed in the work of Andrea Cornwall. See Cornwall, A. (2002) 'Locating citizen participation', *IDS Bulletin*, 33(2): 49–58.

22. Chatterton, Paul (2006) '"Give up activism" and change the world in unknown ways: or, learning to walk with others on uncommon ground', *Antipode*, 38(2): 259–81. p. 264.

23. See Whatmore, Sarah (1997) 'Dissecting the autonomous self: hybrid cartographies for a relational ethics', *Environment and Planning D: Society and Space*, 15: 37–53.

24. See Amin, Ash (2002) 'Ethnicity and the multicultural city: living with diversity', *Environment and Planning A*, 34: 959–80.

25. Chatterton, '"Give up activism"'. p. 272.

26. See Kaldor, M. (2003) *Global Civil Society*. Cambridge: Polity Press. p. 110.

27. See, for example: Dolhinow, Rebecca (2005) 'Caught in the middle: the state, NGOs, and the limits to grassroots organizing along the US–Mexico border', *Antipode*, 37(3): 558–80; Jeffrey, Alex (2007) 'The geopolitical framing of localized struggles: NGOs in Bosnia and Herzegovina', *Development and Change*, 38(2): 251–74; Mercer, Claire (2002) 'NGOs, civil society and democratization: a critical review of the literature', *Progress in Development Studies*, 2(1): 5–22.

28. Bratton, M. (1994) 'Civil society and political transitions in Africa', in J. Harbeson, D. Rothchild and N. Chazan (eds), *Civil Society and the State in Africa*. Boulder, CO: Lynne Rienner. pp. 51–82 p. 52.

29. See Kaldor, *Global Civil Society*. p. 1.

30. Isaac, J. (1996) 'The meanings of 1989', *Social Research*, 63(2): 291–344. pp. 293–4.

31. Willetts, P. (2002) *What is a Non-Governmental Organization?* Available at: www.staff.city.ac.uk/p.willetts/CS-NTWKS/NGO-ART.HTM (accessed 13/01/08).

32. Archibugi, D. (2003) 'Cosmopolitical democracy', in D. Archibugi (ed.), *Debating Cosmopolitics*. London: Verso. pp. 1–15. p. 10.

33. Velek, J. (2004) 'Jürgen Habermas and the utopia of perpetual peace', *Filosoficky Casopis*, 52(2): 231–56.

34. Habermas, Jürgen (2001) 'Why Europe needs a constitution', *New Left Review*, 11: 5–26. p. 6.

35. Barry, A. (2001) *Political Machines: Governing a Technological Society*. London: Athlone.

36. See Coppieters, Bruno, Emerson, Michael, Huysseune, Michel, Kovzidre, Tamara, Noutcheva, Gergana, Tocci, Nathalie and Vahl, Marius (2004) *Europeanization and Conflict Resolution: Case Studies from the European Periphery*. Gent: Academia Press.

37. For a further discussion of pluralism, see Johnston, R.J., Shelley, F.M. and Taylor, P.J. (1990) *Developments in Electoral Geography*. London: Routledge.

38. For a discussion of the legal debates surrounding prisoner enfranchisement in the UK, see Department for Constitutional Affairs (2006) *Voting Rights of Convicted Prisoners Detained within the United Kingdom*. Available at: www.Dca.Gov.Uk/Consult/Voting-Rights/Cp2906.pdf (accessed 04/02/08).

39. Siegfried, A. (1913) *Tableau Politique de la France L'Ouest*. Paris: Colin.

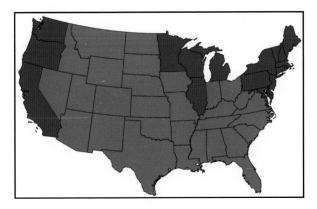

Figure 4.7   Map of the 2004 US election results by state © Michael Gastner,
Cosma Shalizi and Mark Newman

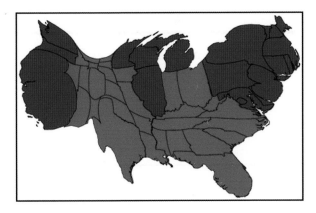

Figure 4.8   Cartogram of the US election results by state © Michael Gastner,
Cosma Shalizi and Mark Newman

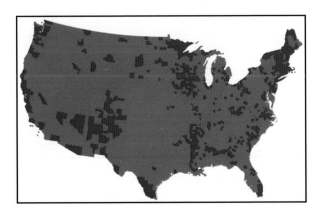

Figure 4.9   Map of the US election results by county © Michael Gastner,
Cosma Shalizi and Mark Newman

Figure 4.10   Map of the US election results by county with vote weighting
© Michael Gastner, Cosma Shalizi and Mark Newman

Source: www-personal.umich.edu/~mejn/election/

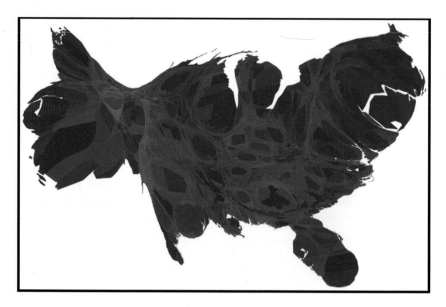

Figure 4.11   Cartogram of the US election results by county with vote weighting
© Michael Gestner, Cosma Shalizi and Mark Newman

Source: www-personal.umich.edu/~mejn/election/

40. MacAllister, I., Johnston, R.J., Pattie, C.J., Tunstall, H., Dorling, D.F.L. and Rossiter, D.J. (2001) 'Class dealignment and the neighbourhood effect: Miller revisited', *British Journal of Political Science*, 31: 41–59. p. 42.

41. Johnston et al., *Developments in Electoral Geography.* p. 1.

42. Flint, C. (2000) 'Electoral Geography and the Social Construction of Space: the example of the Nazi Party in Baden 1924–32', *Geojournal* 51: 145–156. p. 154.

43. Agnew, J. (1996) 'Mapping politics: how context counts in electoral geography', *Political Geography*, 15(2): 129–146. p. 132.

44. Agnew, 'Mapping politics'. p. 144.

45. Holmes, D. (2000) *Integral Europe: Fast-Capitalism, Multiculturalism, Neofascism.* Princeton, N.J: Princeton University Press.

46. Moore, P. (2006) *Suffering for Territory: Race, Place and Power in Zimbabwe.* Durham, NC: Duke University Press.

47. Johnston, R.J. (2000) 'Manipulating maps and winning elections: measuring the impact of malapportionment and gerrymandering', *Political Geography*, 21(1): 1–31. p. 7. Original emphasis.

48. See, for example, Johnston, R.J. (2002) 'If it isn't a gerrymander, what is it?', *Political Geography*, 21: 55–65.

49. See Rush, M. (2000) 'Redistricting and partisan fluidity: do we really know a Gerrymander when we see one?', *Political Geography*, 19: 249–60.

50. These maps were drawn by Michael Gastner, Cosma Shalizi and Mark Newman at the University of Michigan. Details and further maps are available at www-personal.umich. edu/~mejn/election/.

Further reading

For a theoretically sophisticated account of the development of state citizenship, see:

Isin, E. (2002) *Being Political: Genealogies of Citizenship.* Minneapolis, MN: University of Minnesota Press.

There has been a series of important papers in recent years that have studied the distinction between *de facto* and *de jure* citizenship, and between 'invented' and 'invited' spaces of political action:

Chatterton, Paul (2006) '"Give up activism" and change the world in unknown ways: or, learning to walk with others on uncommon ground', *Antipode*, 38(2): 259–81.

Miraftab, Faranak and Wills, Shana (2005) 'Insurgency and spaces of active citizenship: the story of Western Cape Anti-eviction Campaign in South Africa', *Journal of Planning Education and Research*, 25: 200–17.

Valentine, Gill and Skelton, Tracey (2007) 'The right to be heard: citizenship and language', *Political Geography*, 26(2): 121–40.

The field of electoral geography has produced a wealth of high-quality empirical work. For two examples, see:

Agnew, J. (1996) 'Mapping politics: how context counts in electoral geography', *Political Geography*, 15(2): 129–146.

Johnston, R.J. (2000) 'Manipulating maps and winning elections: measuring the impact of malapportionment and gerrymandering', *Political Geography*, 21(1): 1–31.

For a broader survey of the field of electoral geography, see:

Johnston, R.J., Shelley, F.M. and Taylor, P.J. (1990) *Developments in Electoral Geography*. London: Routledge.

FIVE

Politics and the City

It is August 1988. In Manhattan's Lower East Side police clad in riot gear prepare to enforce a 1:00am curfew in Tompkins Square Park. The curfew has been imposed by the city authorities in an effort to rid the square of drug dealers and the homeless people who were using it as a place to live. Groups of protestors and local residents joined those living in the square to confront the police and defend the park. Numerous eye witness reports and still and video photography testified to the excessive violence used by the police in their ultimately unsuccessful efforts to clear the protestors from the area. Shortly before dawn the police gave up and the park was reoccupied by the protestors. The shelters used by homeless people were rebuilt and Tompkins Square became a focus for anti-gentrification campaigners throughout the city and beyond.[1]

In June 1991, after nearly three years of intermittent skirmishes between the authorities and the protestors, the city finally closed the park. Access thereafter was closely regulated. The more than 200 homeless people who had been living in the park were evicted. No alternative accommodation was provided for them. According to the 2008 edition of the *Time Out* guide to New York, the park has since been 'renovated to suit the area's increasingly affluent residents' and 'now boasts lovely landscaping'. During the riots in 1988, protestors had attacked the Christodora building, the most prominent symbol of the area's gentrification. In 2006, a two-bedroom apartment in the same building would have cost you a cool $1.6 million. The changes in Tompkins Square are particularly dramatic, but cities across the world have been affected by similar processes. In this chapter we unpick the politics of some of those urban transformations.

OVERVIEW

The chapter begins by discussing the surprisingly tricky question of how to define cities and their politics. We then look at the worldwide growth of cities and the emergence of 'world cities'. Although the special characteristics that define 'world cities' are important, we follow the geographer Jennifer Robinson in focusing on the ordinary aspects of cities

(Continued)

and urban life. The chapter then uses the work of three geographers to examine three themes that lie at the core of urban politics today: urban infrastructures, gentrification and the public sphere. We explore the politics of urban infrastructure in Mumbai, India, through attempts to provide toilet facilities for its poorest residents. Gentrification has grown from small beginnings in New York and London in the 1960s and 1970s to shape the social and physical landscape of hundreds of cities worldwide, often in highly controversial ways. We illustrate this with a particularly divisive example from Sydney, Australia. Finally, we consider how the changing character of the public sphere is related to access to urban public space.

What is Urban Politics?

In Chapter 1 we discussed some of the challenges of defining what politics is, and suggested that it is a more complex matter than it sometimes seems at first sight. The same is also true (perhaps even more true) of cities. Although we all 'know' what a city is and can probably summon up a mental image of cityness fairly easily, it is surprisingly tricky to produce watertight definitions of the terms 'city' and 'urban'. In large measure, this is because of how cities have changed over time. Although the origins of urban living go back several thousand years,[2] it is probably the city as it developed in medieval Europe that exerts the most powerful pull on our imaginings of what a proper city should look like. The medieval European city was small by modern standards. A typical city might be home to around 10,000 people, though the largest were five or ten times as big as that. The city functioned as an administrative, political and economic centre for its rural hinterland, along the lines of Johann Heinrich von Thünen's model of land use. Agricultural goods flowed from the surrounding farmlands into the city's markets. More food was produced than was required to feed the farming families who produced it, and that surplus could thus sustain a non-agricultural, urban population. The city was home to elite groups. These might include an aristocratic ruler and his (such people were usually men) court or administrators, a class of religious teachers and leaders, wealthy traders and military officers. A middle-ranking group consisted of artisans, producing craft goods such as clothes and furniture, and smaller traders. The lower ranks of servants, slaves and labourers complete the picture. The emergence of cities, then, is a product of changing geographies of production and consumption.

We tend to imagine this stereotypical medieval city as a functioning organic unit, politically independent (relatively) both from other cities and from 'higher' authorities, like the monarch, the emperor or the Pope. This picture of an integrated, fairly autonomous, neatly bounded (often walled) settlement with a clear unified cultural identity has influenced popular understandings of cities up to the present, even though contemporary cities are quite different in many important respects.

Today, almost all cities are tied economically not to their immediate hinterlands, but to wider networks of trade, investment and labour migration that reach over long distances within and beyond the national territory. The von Thünen model no longer applies. They are usually embedded in a complex political and administrative hierarchy in which the national state exerts huge influence over urban affairs and the minutiae of urban life. And instead of the compact layout and supposedly organic, integrated community of the medieval city, modern cities are large, sprawling, increasingly fragmented (both spatially and socially), geographically dispersed and socially and culturally diverse. In some senses, the world of discrete, unified cities has given way to a generic 'urbanism'. We can see this in the geographically scattered character of many new urban developments, such as out-of-town shopping malls and suburban, 'edge city' office complexes.

These characteristics make it difficult today to define precisely where the boundary of the city lies, both geographically and conceptually. If you live in a rural village, but work, shop and socialize in a nearby city, returning home mainly to eat and sleep, are you really a country person? In industrialized countries, the distinction between urban and rural can seem pretty blurred or arbitrary.

All of this can make it rather hard to define urban politics. If it is difficult to identify what is distinctively urban and what is not, how can we specify the distinctively urban aspects of politics? One important starting point for an answer is that we should not see all the politics that takes place in cities as urban politics. For example, a candidate in a national election campaigning for votes in a city is not necessarily engaging in urban politics, nor are people marching through a city protesting against an unpopular war. If 'urban politics', or 'politics of the city', is to mean anything, it must refer to politics that is 'about' urban issues. Also, urban politics is not the same as urban government. Formal electoral politics and the political decisions of elected officials are important, but they are only part of the urban political mix.

One way to approach the question of definition is to look at the relationship between urban function and urban form. In an important essay first published in 1985, geographer David Harvey sought to establish a rigorous conceptual basis for understanding the distinctiveness of urban politics. Harvey's approach uses Karl Marx's analysis of capitalist production as its starting point, and he aims to demonstrate the value of that analysis for the interpretation of the often turbulent world of urban politics. He states that 'urbanization should be understood as a process rather than as a thing', a process that 'necessarily has no fixed spatial boundaries, though it is always being manifested within and across a particular space'.[3] The starting point for the analysis is the urban labour market, defined in terms of the daily commuting range. In medieval cities most people either lived and worked in the same building or walked to their place of employment. This is one reason why medieval cities were rarely bigger than five kilometres across: roughly an hour's walk. Modern motorized transport means that today the possible commuting range extends well beyond the core of the urban area. It is not uncommon for workers to travel 50 or 80 kilometres by car to get to work or up to 150 kilometres by rail.

Harvey argues that employers have to adapt to the availability of labour power within the spatial constraints of each urban region. If a shoe factory runs short of leather and cannot find a local source, it is relatively straightforward to buy in additional supplies from outside the city, even from overseas. If there is a shortage of labour power, on the other hand, employers cannot so easily import a fresh supply at short notice, since labour power, as Harvey points out, following Marx, is embodied in the human beings who produce it.

Over longer timescales, the possibility of labour migration into the city, of population growth or of relocating production to another region or country mean that the constraints are not permanently insurmountable. In the short term, however, employers must work with the labour resources to hand. The qualitative character of the labour force is important here. Training workers takes time and money so again, in the short term, the mix of skills and attributes available in the urban workforce acts as a constraint. Workers with skills in high demand may be able to command higher wages, for example, while trade unions and labour organizations may be able to bid up the wages of lower-skilled workers through collective action. The result, Harvey suggests, is a complex mix of struggles and alliances between business, other urban elites (who may have their own agendas), and workers and their families. In addition, the wages of the workforce are largely spent locally, first and foremost on housing, food, clothing and transport. Each urban labour market thus supports a distinctive blend of consumption practices shaped by the distribution of wages among different social groups.

On the employers' side of the equation, Harvey argues that capitalist competition is also subject to spatial constraints. While the restless search for new sources of profit imparts considerable 'geographical dynamism to production, exchange and consumption', this is not unlimited. There are countervailing pressures. Once a capitalist firm has found a desirable (that is, profitable) location, it will seek to protect its advantage and may:

> push to consolidate monopoly powers, move to prevent the infiltration of competition, try to seal in access to special qualities of labor supplies, lock up flows of inputs by exclusive subcontracting, and monopolize market outlets by equally exclusive franchises, dealerships, and the like.[4]

As a result, 'they necessarily become deeply embroiled in the totality of political-economic processes operating within a particular labor market'[5].

According to idealized models of the operation of perfectly competitive market economies, geographical constraints are supposed to be easily overcome by the laws of supply and demand. Labour shortages would be quickly filled by migration, and competition is supposed to lead to the most efficient allocation of resources between sectors, firms and places. In practice, as Harvey shows, things do not conform to that model. Geographical constraints, notably at the urban scale, influence both labour and capital, with two results. The first is what Harvey calls the tendency towards the 'structured coherence' of urban regions, reflecting the mix and pattern of wage earning and consumption sketched above and reinforced by the physical and social infrastructures of the city. In the case of physical infrastructures, the availability of public transport, for example, affects the ability of workers to take up new employment opportunities, while on the social side, the extent and quality of childcare provision influences the ability of parents (in patriarchal societies usually mothers) to enter the labour market.

The second is the development of coalitions of social and economic interests that arise from all the struggles and compromises over wage rates, consumption practices, the safeguarding of competitive advantage and the provision of physical and social infrastructures. Under the (mythical) state of pure competition there would be no basis for political alliances and all conflicts would be resolved by market forces. In the more realistic, geographically constrained world described by Harvey, urban politics is inevitable as all kinds of collaborations between vested interests, political negotiations and power struggles over resources, service provision and social issues develop within the urban region.

These processes do not establish 'the city' as a wholly unified political actor: class and other alliances shift and the mix of constraints and opportunities may result in contradictory pressures. Overall, though, the effect is to form the urban region as a space within which a 'relatively autonomous' urban politics can emerge. On the one hand, this means that urban politics is not simply a direct reflection of national politics – cities develop distinctive political traditions and place-based political interests. On the other hand, the content of urban politics cannot be derived directly from economic logic, although Harvey insists that 'while there are aspects of urban life and culture which seem to remain outside the immediate grasp of the contradictory logic of accumulation, there is nothing of significance that lies outside its contest, not embroiled in its implications'.[6]

Some urban political geographers, including Harvey himself, take the story forward by seeking to investigate exactly how the diversity of urban political practices is 'embroiled in the implications' of capital accumulation. Others seek to explore the extent and scope of urban politics' relative autonomy from economic processes. In this chapter, we will look at applications of both approaches. First, though, we want to put those examples in context by looking at some key features of contemporary urbanization.

An Urban Species

According to the United Nations, 2007 was the year in which, for the first time in history, a majority of the world's population was living in towns and cities. That raw fact hides considerable diversity, however. At one end of the scale are the world's mega-cities. Twenty sprawling urban agglomerations each accommodate over 10 million people. Many of these are in Asia, including the largest, the Tokyo metropolitan area, with 36 million people, alongside Mumbai, Delhi, Shanghai, Kolkata and Dhaka. Latin America is also well represented, with Mexico City, Rio de Janeiro, Sao Paolo and Buenos Aires all making the cut. European cities only get a look in at the lower end of the top twenty: Moscow, Istanbul and Paris fill places 18, 19 and 20, respectively.[7] The list of largest cities looks a little different (and the cities appear smaller) if we take administrative definitions of city boundaries, but that reflects the fact that rapid growth has seen urban populations overspill formal city limits. The agglomerations mentioned above accord better with David Harvey's notion of functional urban regions. They also testify to the shift we mentioned from *cities*, as clearly defined discrete places, to a more generalized *urbanism*.

Size of population is not the only measure of the significance of specific urban areas, nor necessarily the best (though size does affect urban politics, as we shall see). Political geographer Peter Taylor and his colleagues at Loughborough University's Globalization and World Cities (GaWC) programme place much more importance on the relative functions of cities and the linkages between them. Taylor argues that cities have been shaped over time by their changing international roles. In this approach, processes of globalization are central to any understanding of cities and their politics. On the basis of detailed statistical and other research, GaWC has identified 55 'world cities' grouped into three major and eight minor categories.[8] At the top of the category are the ten 'alpha' world cities, divided in two sub-groups. The most important are London, New York, Paris and Tokyo. These are all very large cities, to be sure, but they do not appear at the top of the GaWC list on account of their size as such, but because of their functions within the world economy. In particular, the GaWC approach takes account of the 'global capacity' of cities, defined by the services (particularly business services) that cities provide. These include accountancy, banking, advertising and legal services. The ranking reflects the concentration of firms providing these services in each city. Below the top four are other 'alpha' cities, including Frankfurt and Singapore, 'beta' cities, including Sydney, Stockholm and Seoul, and 35 'gamma' cities, including Boston, Beijing and Budapest.

The GaWC approach is helpful because of the focus on the functions and global roles of cities. But it is also important to recognize that while mega-cities such as Los Angeles, London and Lagos exert great economic, political and cultural influence and channel vast flows of money, people, goods and information, most urban-dwellers live in smaller, more ordinary cities. There are around 50 cities in the world with populations above 5 million. Taken together, they are home to some 500 million people – a large number, to be sure, but equivalent to only 15% of all city-dwellers worldwide. Most of us urbanites live in towns or in small or middle-sized cities. If we map our urban futures by looking only at vast, iconic mega-cities we risk missing much of the picture. Moreover, it is evident that there is no one pattern to urban growth and development. A compact city of half a million inhabitants faces different challenges from a sprawling metropolis with ten times as many people. An old industrial city like Cleveland, Ohio, with a declining downtown and burgeoning new suburbs beyond the city limits, is urbanizing differently from many cities in developing countries where rural to urban migration and the rapid construction of informal housing accounts for much of urban growth. Each city reflects its own particular biography. Ancient religious centres, market towns and cities of commerce, seats of learning, industrial metropolises, commuter towns, administrative capitals – no one paradigm can capture this variety of urban forms.

Geographer Jennifer Robinson argues that we should pay more attention to ordinary cities (and to the ordinariness of city life).[9] Indeed, she argues that it is useful to think of all cities as ordinary:

> Rather than categorising and labelling cities as, for example, Western, Third World, developed, developing, world or global, I propose that we think about a world of ordinary cities, which are all dynamic and diverse, if conflicted, arenas for social and economic life. Whereas categorising cities tends to ascribe prominence to only certain cities and to certain features of cities, an ordinary-city approach takes the world of cities as its starting point and attends to the diversity and complexity of all cities.[10]

This perspective accords with the approach we are adopting in this book. Urban politics is just as much about the everyday conflicts and disputes that arise through the mundane practices involved in getting by and making a life in urbanized spaces and places, as it is about the drive to, for example, maximize urban economic growth. Moreover, policies to promote urban economic growth are also 'ordinary' – they have effects in our daily lives and they too involve all kinds of mundane practices: meetings, drawing up plans, running advertising campaigns, lobbying governments and investors, designing, building and maintaining roads, houses, offices and shops and so on. In the next section, we examine in more detail the politics of some of the most mundane of these urban 'infrastructures'.

Urban Infrastructures

The term 'infrastructure' conjures up images of major constructions: roads, bridges, railways and perhaps of things buried in the ground – sewers, cables, water mains and gas pipelines. These are the things we take for granted, until they fail or breakdown; in some ways, they are only really made visible when they are no longer working. Although professional planners have always taken them very seriously, until recently they have not attracted much attention from academic geographers. It is said that for many years the British classified telephone directory (*Yellow Pages*) featured the entry 'Boring – see civil engineering'. Such jokes have worn thin and a growing awareness of the importance of the material structures that hold cities together has seen the study of urban infrastructures emerge from the geekier reaches of transport geography and urban planning to take centre-stage in urban geography.

There are several reasons for this development. For one thing, in many cities dramatic urban growth has placed more and more strain on the material networks on which daily life depends. Even where infrastructure provision has managed to keep pace with population growth (in Western cities), larger cities mean more complex infrastructure systems and pose more difficult management challenges. Secondly, networks are increasingly *inter*dependent.

Gas companies rely on electricity companies to power their distribution networks. Road maintenance involves the negotiation of a seeming tangle of buried pipes and lines, each vital to someone's daily life. And everything depends on computers and the networks of satellite transmissions, fibre optic cables, telephone lines and wireless transmissions that enable them to work. Thirdly, the vulnerability of urban life to the disruption of infrastructures has been dramatically illustrated by some high-profile breakdowns. In August 2003, the largest electricity outage in American history brought a blackout to large parts of the northeastern USA and parts of Canada. Roads were jammed as traffic controls failed. Streets thronged with commuters trying to get home on foot after subway trains stopped running. Times Square went dark and ice cream was handed out free of charge as freezers failed. Despite the party atmosphere that reportedly took hold in some areas, the outage revealed the serious and sometimes life-threatening consequences of infrastructure failure.

The technical infrastructures themselves are part of the picture, but they are entwined with social and political practices too. Within geography and urban studies there is a long tradition of work focusing on the politics of the collective provision of services. In the 1970s and 1980s, the leading urban sociologist Manuel Castells proposed that political conflicts over 'collective consumption' constitute the very core of urban politics.[11] While both the form and content of such conflicts may have changed over the years (in the 1970s no one was talking about the digital divide, for example), they remain central to urban political life. A telling example of this is provided by the current struggles over sanitation in Mumbai (formerly Bombay), India's largest city and the capital of Maharashtra state.

Despite its vast size, Mumbai, on India's west coast, does not figure in GaWC's list of 55 world cities. It is, though, identified by the GaWC researchers as one of 13 cities that show 'relatively strong evidence' of world city formation. In the language of the music charts, it is bubbling under. From Jennifer Robinson's perspective, it is also an ordinary city, and it is certainly home to millions of 'ordinary people' – for Robinson, of course, we are all ordinary and the term should not be seen as disparaging – living ordinary (if frequently materially impoverished) lives.

And one of the most ordinary activities for any human being is defecation. None of us has a choice in the matter. When we have to go, we have go. Those of us living in wealthy countries can in most cases count on having clean and functioning sanitation facilities. This is certainly true when we are at home and usually also at work, though even in some of our richer-than-ever Western cities there are concerns about the poor and/or declining provision of fully public toilets in urban centres, especially for parents with young children, people with disabilities and homeless people.

The situation in Mumbai is rather different. Geographer Colin McFarlane has studied the provision of sanitation in Mumbai's informal settlements, often termed 'slums'.[12] McFarlane reports that over half the city's population lives in informal settlements occupying just 8% of the land. The settlements consist of anything from flimsy shelters on a pavement to reasonably solid (but unregulated and usually unserviced) houses in shantytowns like Dharavi, the world's largest slum. Living conditions in such areas are poor:

> Most people in informal settlements lack security of tenure, live in poor-quality housing vulnerable to monsoon rains, suffer from frequent bouts of state or private demolition, lack access to sufficient and clean water and sanitation facilities, and live in highly polluted environments vulnerable to illness and disease. As the informal population continues to grow, the task of providing adequate infrastructure becomes more challenging.[13]

For residents, gaining access to basic services such as water, sanitation, electricity, transport and schooling involve major challenges (see Figure 5.1). According to one survey reviewed by McFarlane, 63% of those living in informal settlements rely entirely on public toilets, and there is considerable geographical variation across the city. Public toilets are often poorly maintained and serviced, and also have to be paid for by users, for example through a

Figure 5.1   Poor infrastructure is a feature of Mumbai's informal settlements
© Colin McFarlane

monthly subscription. Faced with such poor access, many resort to individual solutions, or simply have to go without. Of particular interest from the point of view of urban politics, though, are the efforts made by some groups to fight for the collective provision of services, whether provided by public bodies or community organizations. And for slum-dwellers, such struggles may have wider significance. As McFarlane notes, 'people living in informal settlements are not treated on a par with "proper citizens"'.[14] They are frequently seen not as people with equal rights to public services, but as problems.

The Mumbai Slum Sanitation Programme (SSP) is a new attempt by the city authorities to provide decent toilet facilities for the residents of informal settlements. According to Colin McFarlane, it is the 'most ambitious urban sanitation intervention in Indian history'.[15] Under the programme, the municipal corporation uses credit from the World Bank and matching funds from the Maharashtra state government to pay for the land for the toilet blocks and connections to water, sewers and electricity network (Figure 5.2). The blocks are built, and for the first year managed, by a contractor (a non-governmental organization or an engineering firm). After the first year they are handed over to a local community organization which then manages the block using funds raised from the users of the facility.

McFarlane argues that the SSP represents a shift from state provision of urban services to a 'partnership' approach, involving a network of private, public and non-governmental organizations. The programme is also supposed to work through community 'participation'. Ideas of partnership and participation

Figure 5.2   SSP toilet block, Khotwadi, Mumbai © Colin McFarlane

have become mantras for new forms of local infrastructure and service provision all over the world, in rich countries as well as poor ones. In the case of the SSP, a participatory approach was a condition of World Bank funding. McFarlane notes that, in practice, 'partnerships' have usually ended up involving just one non-governmental organization, rather than a diverse network of groups, while participation 'has been translated into well-connected individuals or groups' rather than ordinary residents.[16]

Moreover, it has also been difficult to put the material, technical infrastructure in place. At least in the early stages of the programme, water connections were not made in many cases because of the cost. The toilet blocks will only function properly if there is water for flushing, electricity and effective maintenance. It is sometimes easier to build the structure than to manage and maintain it. The ongoing costs of cleaning and maintenance are supposed to be borne by the community through charging users. According to McFarlane, this works well in some cases. Indeed, in one relatively better off settlement, the leaders of the community-based organization managing the toilets were rumoured to be making undeclared profits from the toilets. This was apparently of limited concern to residents, provided the toilets were clean and accessible. In the poorest areas, though, where many residents cannot afford even the most modest user charges, residents may be more concerned about the misappropriation of funds. In line with the prevailing orthodoxy of community participation in service provision, the allocation of toilets under the SSP is supposed to be driven by 'demand' from residents. McFarlane questions whether it is realistic to expect the poorest not only to demand the provision of toilets, but also to 'demand' the right to pay for them.[17]

McFarlane argues that state policy towards informal settlements oscillates between elimination and regulation. The better established and relatively wealthier settlements are well connected, both politically and infrastructurally. They are subject to regulation via, for example, the SSP. Less stable, poorer settlements are subject to periodic attempts at demolition, interspersed with more benign phases when efforts are made to regularize them through such things as toilet provision. As the case of sanitation in Mumbai's 'slums' reveals, urban politics and urban infrastructures are intimately connected.

This example reveals several key features of contemporary urban politics. First, there is the emphasis on the state as a 'facilitator', rather than a direct provider of public services and facilities. This became a familiar theme in the UK during the government of Margaret Thatcher, when local councils were encouraged to employ external contractors to provide a wide range of city services. The ostensible aim of the policy was to reduce waste and cut costs, but it was also intended to provide business opportunities for the private sector and to reduce the power of the public sector trade unions. Secondly, the requirement to organize 'partnerships' linking organizations in the public, non-governmental and private sector has been a prominent characteristic of the restructuring of urban governance in many places. Thirdly, the concern with community participation has also become a standard feature of efforts to reform the way services are provided in cities worldwide. 'Community participation' is invoked as an essential ingredient in fields as diverse as planning, policing, education, environmental protection, housing management, to name but a few. Finally, McFarlane's Mumbai research draws attention to fundamental conflicts over access to the city: are the urban poor legitimate citizens, or a problem to be eliminated? The next section examines such conflicts further, through the lens of 'gentrification'.

Gentrification: Urban Renaissance or Urban Revanchism?

As the example of sanitation indicates, much of Mumbai's politics is linked to struggles over urban space between rich and poor. These struggles have intensified in recent years as Mumbai has become ever more closely intertwined with the international economy. Shortage of space, exacerbated by the fact that the city is built on an island, means that land is in high demand. The cityscape has been transformed as a result of new investments in apartments, shopping facilities and offices for the growing middle class and the economic elite.

This is hardly unique to Mumbai. Cities all over the world are experiencing such 'gentrification' as the process has become known. Initially, the term 'gentrification' applied principally to housing. It referred to the movement of middle-class households into working-class or former industrial parts of the city, especially the inner city. In many European and North American cities, the middle years of the twentieth century saw a strong trend towards suburbanization. Growing affluence and the spread of car ownership made suburban living an affordable aspiration for many. Poor housing and environmental conditions in many inner urban areas contributed additional push factors. The ideal suburban lifestyle, with a detached house and garden, a nuclear family (with stay-at-home mother) and a car, came to seem a desirable alternative to the grimy, overcrowded city. One outcome was the further deterioration of inner-city neighbourhoods coupled to a decline in land values. This made housing in the inner city comparatively cheap and affordable by poorer social groups and a marked social division emerged between poorer inner urban areas and the more affluent suburbs.

But from the 1960s a counter-trend emerged. Although suburbanization continued, areas such as London's Islington and New York's SoHo began to see the return of the middle classes, a process that became known as 'gentrification'. Early gentrification worked in one of two ways. In some cases, housing in poorer neighbourhoods and inner-city industrial premises, such as warehouses, were bought up by property developers, renovated, and resold for a profit. In others, individuals would buy a single property to live in and do it up themselves (generating what became known as 'sweat equity' – property wealth produced by the sweat of the owner's brow). In both cases, the market value of the property went up and over time the social composition of these neighbourhoods was transformed. In rented properties, poorer tenants were displaced, often reluctantly, to other areas through rent increases or evictions. In owner-occupied neighbourhoods, some working-class householders took advantage of the new middle-class demand and sold up. As the supply of existing buildings suitable for renovation was used up, property

Figure 5.3   Luxury riverside apartments in central London © Joe Painter

developers began to build new housing in the urban core, often in the form of apartment blocks and condominiums (Figure 5.3).

Geographer Neil Smith explains the process of gentrification using the concept of the 'rent gap'. The rent gap refers to the difference between the rental value of a property in its existing (pre-gentrification) use and the potential rent the property could attract under its 'highest and best use'.[18] Smith argues that the renovation of dilapidated inner-city housing only makes sense (and will only be undertaken) if a sound economic return on the investment involved can be expected. So gentrification will only take place where the gains to be made from exploiting the rent gap exceed the costs of the refurbishment required to allow the property to fulfil its 'highest and best use'. Smith insists, therefore, that gentrification is driven principally by an economic logic.

Other writers have taken a different view, suggesting that the driving force behind gentrification is the changing tastes and aspirations of consumers. According to geographer David Ley, the city is being remade by the 'new middle class'. It is their preference for living in the centre of the city, rather than in the suburbs where they may have grown up, that has created a demand for up-market housing and fuelled the process of gentrification.[19] The term 'service class' is also sometimes used for this group, reflecting the importance of employment in business and professional services for such people. More populist terms range from the 'yuppies' of the 1980s to today's 'metrosexuals'.

During the 1990s, the relative importance of the supply side (the urban economy, property developers, the land market, and so on) and the demand side (cultural trends, consumer tastes and preferences) in understanding gentrification was hotly debated in geography. More recently, most researchers recognize that both elements are important.[20] What is clear, though, is that gentrification has had profound implications for urban politics.

From the point of view of city planners, urban managers and many commentators, gentrification is usually seen in very positive terms: as an 'urban renaissance'. The term 'urban renaissance' dates back at least to the 1970s. According to Dennis Judd and Todd Swanstrom, it came to prominence with the redevelopment of Quincy Market in downtown Boston.[21] Old buildings in the inner-urban core, the most visible part of the city, are repaired or replaced. Vacant lots are filled with new buildings, catering for the affluent. 'Signature' architects are employed to add lustre to the changing skyline. Mega-events, such as international sports competitions – especially the Olympic Games – and world exhibitions, provide opportunities to redevelop large swathes of land at a stroke. Wealthier residents generate economic demand for shops, restaurants and high-value services. The city's cultural life appears to benefit as these same residents and growing numbers of tourists patronize art galleries, concert halls and theatres. Gentrification, it seems, results in a virtuous cycle of investment, improvements to the built environment, in-migration, and rising living standards, and a veneer of prosperity that, it is hoped, will encourage further investment. And as the process of gentrification has continued, it has expanded from its origins in the housing market to affect a variety of other aspects of city life. Use of the term has been extended accordingly, so that it is now not uncommon to hear talk of the gentrification of public space, retailing and employment, as well as of housing.

However, as numerous geographical studies have shown, gentrification is not wholly (some would say not at all) a benign phenomenon. Many argue that at the heart of the process is displacement. For the new middle-class urban-dwellers to move in, poorer groups have to move out. Sometimes the displacement is deliberate and targeted, involving evictions and demolition and, for the homeless, forced clearances of streets and parks. In other cases, it is the outcome of the apparently politically neutral operation of market forces. Rents go up and poorer people move on to cheaper areas. Property developers make offers that cannot be refused. Either way, the end result is much the same. The supply of low-cost housing in the central city declines, long-standing social ties are ruptured, and communities are broken up and dispersed. And displacement does not affect only those who are displaced. In some cities (London is a good example), a lack of affordable housing makes it difficult to recruit workers for a wide range of lower-paid occupations, including public service jobs such as school teaching, firefighting and nursing.

For Neil Smith, gentrification and displacement cannot be separated from a range of other conflicts over urban space, including the intensive policing of public behaviour, crackdowns on the presence of homeless people, and anti-immigrant discrimination in the provision of services. This potent mixture of social change, economic transformation and state regulation has given rise, in Smith's view, to the 'revanchist' city. *Revanche* is French for 'revenge'. The original *revanchists* were a group of political reactionaries in late nineteenth-century

France who espoused 'traditional values' and 'organized a movement of revenge' against the working class which had had the effrontery to establish a commune in Paris in 1870–1.[22] Smith argues that gentrification is, in effect, a vengeful 're-taking' of the city by the middle class, the affluent and the powerful from the working class, the poor, and the marginalized.

Class is not the only axis of social division that connects with gentrification. Gender is important and so, in many cases, is race. Geographer Wendy Shaw has studied the impact of gentrification in central Sydney on the lives of indigenous Australians living in the inner-city neighbourhood of Redfern.[23] Gentrification has proceeded apace in Sydney. Shaw documents how the city has been remodelled in ways strikingly reminiscent of Manhattan to a greater extent than most other cities outside North America. This has included the construction of a series of dramatic tall office buildings in the downtown core (see Figure 5.4). It has also seen a growing demand for period 'heritage' housing in the inner suburbs. Victorian row houses which were built for industrial workers in the nineteenth century, and subsequently housed many of Australia's European immigrants in the twentieth, are now being bought up by affluent professionals and renovated to 'restore' them to what their new owners imagine to be their former glory. This process, which bears all the hallmarks of classic gentrification, has seen the cost of housing in Sydney's inner suburbs soar. Inflation has fuelled further, sometimes speculative, investments. It has also encouraged would-be gentrifiers to move into other areas.

Figure 5.4   Downtown Sydney © Joe Painter

One of the new sites of gentrification since 2000 has been the area of Redfern to the south of the Central business district (CBD), not far from Sydney University. For many years, a number of streets near Redfern railway station (known locally as 'The Block') have been home to a fluctuating number of Aboriginal people. In 1973, the federal government under Labor Prime Minister Gough Whitlam provided funds for the purchase of 70 terraced houses to provide housing for the Aboriginal community of inner Sydney. Many services for Aboriginal people, including medical and educational facilities, are also located in the area. Like Aboriginal communities throughout urban and rural Australia, the Block has more than its fair share of social and health problems. It has long been a highly stigmatized place within the dominant (white) understanding of the city as well as a focus of protest and resistance by Indigenous Australians against discrimination (Figure 5.5).

Figure 5.5   Graffiti in support of Redfern residents, Canberra © Joe Painter

Recently, the rapid progression of gentrification through Sydney's inner suburbs has led to greater pressure on the Aboriginal community and on the public authorities to 'do something' about the Block. Why? Because, according to Shaw, the presence of indigenous people is an impediment to further gentrification. Many 'early' gentrifiers expect the value of their properties to rise once the Block has been 'dealt with'. Others, who have been holding back, are ready to move in when the problems of crime and drug use that are popularly associated with the area have been alleviated.

Shaw argues that there is more going on here than the class-based displacement seen in other cases of gentrification across the world. Gentrification in

Sydney is highly racialized. It is as much about whiteness as it is about middle classness. According to Shaw (and many other writers on Australian history), since its inception in the late eighteenth century, white Australia has been marked by both fear and hatred of its Indigenous 'other'. In addition, elements of (white) working-class life form an important, if stylized, component of gentrification – this is evident in the industrial aesthetic of many 'loft' and warehouse developments, for example. Indigenous culture, on the other hand, seems to have no place in the gentrification script. Shaw's research shows that this combination of fear of the other and a narrative of contemporary urban living that takes its whiteness for granted, lies behind the growing efforts by gentrifiers and local political actors to displace the Aboriginal community from Redfern.

It is notable that policy-makers rarely talk about gentrification directly, preferring the more positive-sounding and apparently neutral language of renaissance, regeneration and revitalization. When Tony Blair's 'New Labour' government came to power in 1997, one of its first acts was to commission a report on urban regeneration from a newly established 'Urban Task Force' chaired by the leading modernist architect Richard Rogers. The report was entitled 'Towards an Urban Renaissance',[24] but as Loretta Lees, Tom Slater and Elvin Wyly point out in their book *Gentrification*, the report's recommendations amounted to the promotion of gentrification throughout urban England.[25]

Gentrification allows us to identify several key aspects of contemporary urban politics.[26] In line with the arguments of Chapter 1, it demonstrates that the politics of cities is not solely or even mainly about what happens in the formal institutions of urban government – the city council and the mayor's office, for example. Power relations and conflicts of interest are played out for the most part away from City Hall, in neighbourhoods and housing estates, workplaces and parks. Gentrification also reveals the shift in most cities away from public provision towards private and market-based approaches to urban development. Proponents of this shift highlight the large amounts of capital investment in previously dilapidated areas that this has produced and assert that the benefits will 'trickle down' to more deprived households and neighbourhoods. Critics point to the growing inequalities that result from an over-reliance on market solutions and argue that there is very little evidence of a meaningful trickle-down effect. Most agree that gentrification seems set to continue and will expand its scope and its geographical reach.

Public Cities and City Publics

We began this chapter with conflicts over the use of a public park in New York. We then discussed the provision of public toilet facilities in Mumbai. The previous section on gentrification highlighted trends towards the privatization of the city – with an emphasis on market, rather than public, provision. The concept of 'public' thus seems to be a central issue in urban politics, so to conclude the chapter we want to consider the idea of urban publics and their relationship to urban space.

Many commentators have linked the changes associated with gentrification to a shift from public to private. Public housing may be replaced with private housing. Retailers move from the public street to private malls. Public open spaces may remain, but they are more intensively regulated. In most of these accounts, the meaning of public and private is often taken for grant – public is equated with being open to all or being owned by the government, private is equated with restricted access or being owned by individuals or business. On further examination, however, it becomes clear that the concepts of public and private are rather more complicated.

In his book *Publics and the City*, geographer Kurt Iveson has looked at this problem in detail.[27] He begins by making an important distinction between 'topographical' and 'procedural' approaches to public space. The most common definition of urban public space is a topographical one. It refers to 'particular places in the city that are (or should be) open to members of "the public". Here, we are talking about places such as streets, footpaths, parks, squares and the like'.[28] In short, topographical public spaces are ones that you could colour in on a map. Iveson suggests there are two problems with this approach. First, many arguments about better access to public space are framed in terms of loss and reclamation. They tend to suggest that there was a past golden age, a time before property developers and riot police, when public space was freely accessible to all, and urban citizens could rub shoulders with one another in an expression of democratic freedom and tolerance.

In practice, of course, such a golden age did not exist. Access to public space has always been circumscribed and a source of conflict. And often the conflict has been between different sections of the public themselves – which is why Iveson always refers to multiple publics rather than 'the public' in the singular. The second problem with the topographical approach is that, even when narratives of loss and reclamation are avoided, it tends to equate being part of a public with being in public space. Iveson sums up the problems with the topographical approach by suggesting that it conflates three distinct aspects of publicness: a context for action (public space), a kind of action (public address) and a collective actor (a/the public).[29] This suggests that the public/private distinction is not cut and dried. As Iveson points out, one can undertake public activities in a private space – participating in a radio phone-in from a private house, for example. One can also do private things in public, such as conducting a personal conversation with one other person.

Some of this complexity is evident in London in relation to protests against the war in Iraq. During 2003, many cities, including London, saw very large public protests against the planned invasion of Iraq. These protests combined Iveson's three aspects of publicness. They took place in public space, they involved public address and thousands of members of the public took part. Nearly two years earlier a lone protestor, Brian Haw, had established a continuous peace vigil in Parliament Square in central London (see Figure 5.6).

Initially, Haw was concerned with the impact of economic sanctions on the Iraqi people. He then broadened the focus of his action to protest against the US-led invasion and occupation of Iraq. Haw's protest involves public address

Figure 5.6   Parliament Square peace protest, London © Joe Painter

and took place in public, but involves action by a private individual (albeit one with considerable public support). It has also brought him into conflict with agencies of the British state, which sought to restrict the protest in various ways, culminating in a police raid on the vigil on 23 May 2006. In a further twist, however, the entire display was recreated by artist Mark Wallinger in London's Tate Britain art gallery under the title 'State Britain', a work for which Wallinger won the prestigious Turner Prize for contemporary art. In this way, the original protest was incorporated into a new form of public address. But is the space of the art gallery in which it was installed public or private. Tate Britain is open to the public, but a fee is charged for entry to the exhibition for the Turner Prize. These reconfigurations of what on the surface might seem an unambiguously public activity – a peace protest outside Parliament – highlight some of the limitations of the topographical approach that Iveson identifies.

The alternative procedural approach defines public space as any space, in which a certain kind of action – public address – takes place. 'Public address' involves communication through text, speech, imagery or performance with 'a public'. Examples include writing a letter to a newspaper, making a speech on TV, chanting slogans on a street corner, engaging in a theatrical performance in a town square, and so on. There is a curious, but important, circularity here, a kind of chicken and egg paradox that Iveson highlights: the public being addressed only comes into being because it is being addressed as a public.

The difficulty with the procedural approach, though, is that it downplays the importance of the materiality of public space. Iveson suggests that its proponents tend to assume that *any* space can become equally and unproblematically as public as any other simply by being used for public address. Iveson's work shows how different kinds of material spaces can become public in different kinds of ways and for different groups of people.

To illustrate this, we can apply Iveson's ideas to the example of sanitation in Mumbai discussed above. You will recall that the slum sanitation programme involves the construction of 'public' toilet blocks. But in most cases they are not open to all and sundry. Access is restricted to specific categories of people – to particular publics in Iveson's terms – such as residents of a specific area, or those who pay the monthly subscription. But the materiality of the blocks also affects their publicness. For instance, blocks that are well maintained and clean are more usable and thus in some senses more public than dilapidated or dirty blocks. In some cases, the buildings provide additional public spaces, such as classrooms or meeting areas, allowing the coming into being, at least in modest ways, of potential new publics. Toilet blocks may not be the kind of iconic public spaces of street activism and protest, but their construction and use in Mumbai both expresses and constitutes a certain kind of urban publicness nonetheless.

The Mumbai example shows that conflict is endemic in even the most mundane aspects of urban service provision. More generally, urban politics is centrally concerned with public debate and disagreement and with debate and disagreement between different publics. Iveson argues that there is no direct relationship between these activities and specific types of urban space, such as parks and squares. Rather, there is a dynamic relationship between the actions associated with being public and different kinds of spaces and places in the city. The city, for Iveson, is not a stage on which 'being public' is performed. Instead, the 'public city' has to be produced through the 'particular political labours which seek to make particular publics'.[30]

Notes

1. For a fuller account, see Smith, Neil (1996) *The New Urban Frontier: Gentrification and the Revanchist City*. London: Routledge. pp. 3–12.
2. Soja, Edward W. (2000) *Postmetropolis: Critical Studies of Cities and Regions*. Oxford: Blackwell.
3. Harvey, D. (1989) *The Urban Experience*. Oxford: Blackwell. p. 127.
4. Harvey, *The Urban Experience*. p. 137.
5. Harvey, *The Urban Experience*. p. 137.
6. Harvey, *The Urban Experience*. p. 156.
7. United Nations (2008) *World Urbanization Prospects*. New York: United Nations.
8. See: www.lut.ac.uk/gawc/citylist.html (accessed 18/07/08).
9. Robinson, Jennifer (2006) *Ordinary Cities: Between Modernity and Development*. London: Routledge. See also Amin, Ash and Graham, Stephen (1997) 'The ordinary city', *Transactions of the Institute of British Geographers*, 22: 411–29.
10. Robinson, *Ordinary Cities*.
11. Castells, Mannel (1977) *The Urban Question: A Marxist Approach*. London: Edward Arnold.

12. McFarlane, Colin (2008) 'Sanitation in Mumbai's informal settlements: state, 'slum', and infrastructure', *Environment and Planning A*, 40: 88–107.
13. McFarlane, 'Sanitation'. p. 91.
14. McFarlane, 'Sanitation'. p. 91.
15. McFarlane, 'Sanitation'. p. 88.
16. McFarlane, 'Sanitation'. p. 97.
17. McFarlane, 'Sanitation'. p. 104.
18. Smith, *The New Urban Frontier*.
19. Ley, David (1996) *The New Middle Class and the Remaking of the Central City*. Oxford: Blackwell.
20. Lees, Loretta, Slater, Tom and Wyly, Elvin (2008) *Gentrification*. London: Routledge.
21. Judd, Dennis R. and Swanstrom, Todd (1994) *City Politics: Private Power and Public Policy*. New York: HarperCollins. pp. 335–8.
22. Smith, *The New Urban Frontier*. p. 45.
23. Shaw, Wendy S. (2007) *Cities of Whiteness*. Oxford: Blackwell.
24. Urban Task Force (1999) *Towards an Urban Renaissance*. London: Department of Environment, Transport and the Regions.
25. Lees, Slater and Wyly, *Gentrification*. p. xviii.
26. Atkinson, Rowland (2003) 'Misunderstood saviour or vengeful wrecker: the many meanings and problems of gentrification', *Urban Studies*, 40(12): 2343–50.
27. Iveson, Kurt (2007) *Publics and the City*. Oxford: Blackwell.
28. Iveson, *Publics and the City*. p. 4.
29. Iveson, *Publics and the City*. p. 8.
30. Iveson, *Publics and the City*. p. 208.

Further reading

David Harvey's important arguments about urban politics can be found in:

Harvey, David (1989) *The Urban Experience*. Oxford: Blackwell. pp. 125–64.

Another key essay by Harvey highlights the shift from managerial to entrepreneurial urban governance that has facilitated several of the developments we have discussed in this chapter, including privatization, the role of partnerships and gentrification:

Harvey, David (1989) 'From managerialism to entrepreneurialism: the transformation of urban governance in late capitalism', *Geografiska Annaler*, 71B(1): 3–17.

A somewhat different approach to understanding the geographies of the urban is offered by:

Amin, Ash and Thrift, Nigel (2002) *Cities: Reimaging the Urban*. Cambridge: Polity Press.

An important study by Neil Brenner links new entrepreneurial forms of urban governance to the changing spatialities of the state:

Brenner, Neil (2004) *New State Spaces: Urban Governance and the Rescaling of Statehood*. Oxford: Oxford University Press.

A useful survey of the debates around gentrification is:

Lees, Loretta, Slater, Tom and Wyly, Elvin (2008) *Gentrification*. London: Routledge.

Geographer Don Mitchell provides a somewhat different approach to questions of urban citizenship and the urban public sphere from that developed by Kurt Iveson:

Mitchell, Don (2003) *The Right to the City: Social Justice and the Fight for Public Space*. New York: Guilford Press.

SIX

Identity Politics and Social Movements

In 1955, an African-American woman named Rosa Parks was working as a seamstress in a department store in Montgomery, Alabama. On 1 December she finished work for the evening and boarded a bus to go home. At that time in Montgomery, African Americans were required under the racist 'Jim Crow' segregation laws to sit in a separate section at the back of the bus. When the 'white' seats at the front of the bus were full, the driver, James F. Black, moved the sign indicating the start of the 'colored' section back one row and asked four passengers, including Rosa Parks, to move to allow the extra white passengers to sit. Rosa's fellow passengers complied, but Rosa refused to move. She was arrested by the city police for 'refusing to obey the orders of a bus driver'.

After Rosa Parks' arrest and refusal any longer to accept the humiliation of racial segregation, African Americans in Montgomery began a boycott of the city's bus system. They formed a new organization, the Montgomery Improvement Association, to co-ordinate the protest and elected a young pastor, one Martin Luther King Jr, as its leader. The boycott lasted for over a year and the campaign led directly to the ending of racial segregation on public buses in Montgomery. It also fuelled the nascent civil rights movement across the USA that campaigned vigorously throughout the 1960s for equal rights for all American citizens, regardless of race.

OVERVIEW

The chapter begins by defining 'identity', 'identity politics' and 'social movements'. We then outline different approaches to understanding social movements and the connections between social movements, social difference and identity politics. The main part of the chapter then examines the geographies of social movements through three case studies: the trade unionism and the labour movement, feminism and women's movement, and the newer forms of grassroots mobilization and resistance associated with 'DIY politics'.

Introduction

What is your identity? You probably have a sense of what you mean when you talk about your identity – it is what makes you you. But once you begin to look into it in detail, identity turns out to be quite a complicated matter. In recent years, fear of terrorism and of identity theft have turned questions of identity into highly political issues. Identity cards, databases and registers are all based on the idea that an individual has a unique identity. At the same time there has also been a lot of interest in notions of *shared* and *common* identities – of membership of a group being defined in terms of common social or cultural characteristics, such as gender, race, ethnicity, religion or place. You are also probably familiar with the idea of multiple, or at least multi-sided, identities. An individual's overall identity might be seen as a composite of their gender, class, ethnic and other identities. We need to think about whether identity is the unchanging 'essence' of our being or something that changes with the changing circumstances of our lives. Is identity an objective phenomenon determined by our position in society or a subjective 'sense of self' that we can only experience from within? Is our identity something we passively express or is it a chosen persona, even a performance, that we might be able to shape and change?

We can speak of identity *politics* when group identity difference is a source of conflict or becomes the focus of efforts to bring about social change. For instance, the problem of discrimination against disabled people becomes a form of identity politics when it is tackled by disabled people organizing around a shared sense of identity as disabled people and expressing the concern that discrimination was based on (possibly unconscious) prejudice against disabled people.

Identity politics is an important foundation for many social movements. In the past, political geographers had relatively little to say about social movements, preferring to focus on the geographies of formal political processes and institutions. That has now begun to change, but there are still few systematic accounts of the political geography of social movements. This is a bit of a paradox, since many geographers have espoused the notion, originally put forward by Karl Marx, that people make history, but not under conditions of their own choosing. While much work has been done on the 'conditions not of their own choosing', rather less attention has been paid to the role of people in the making of their own history (and, we would add, geography). Social movements are one of the most important mechanisms which people have to enable them to 'make history'. This chapter will consider how that making of history both depends on and creates geographies, but first we need to look at what we mean by 'social movements' in a bit more detail.

What are social movements?

Social movements may be defined as groups of people pursuing shared goals that require social or political change. Examples include peace movements, civil rights movements, labour movements, anti-globalization movements, women's movements and environmental movements. These are all 'collective enterprises to establish a new order of life'.[1] They may of course vary in the extent of change sought and in the elements of society in which change is thought necessary. A revolutionary movement may seek the wholesale over-throw of the existing social order, while a movement for voting reform may be concerned more narrowly with the extension of political rights within the *existing* political framework. Social movements are also *oppositional*, or as geographer Walter J. Nicholls puts it, 'contentious'.[2] That is, they are opposed to one or more elements of the existing social and political order. This means that they are in *conflict* with other groups or institutions in society who wish to preserve the *status quo*.

Some social movements are concerned with a single issue because they focus on and organize around one axis of conflict within society. For this rea-son, political parties are sometimes seen as different from social movements because they try to offer a broad appeal across a wide range of issues. However, it would be a mistake to draw too rigid a distinction here. Social movements can become political parties, and some political parties do appeal to very particular interest groups. Moreover, the beliefs of social movements that seem to be 'single issue' can in fact involve a broad view of society as a whole and form the basis for policy proposals in a wide range of fields. A good example is the women's movement, which may appear at first sight to be a sin-gle issue ('rights for women') movement, but which contains within it a vari-ety of traditions of feminist thought which involve a critical perspective on many aspects of social and political life.

We have suggested in this book that the practice of politics always involves strategies, and this is particularly true of social movements, as they seek to bring about change. According to the sociologist Anthony Giddens, all of social life involves the 'reflexive monitoring of action'.[3] In our daily lives we all observe ourselves and our actions, and adjust our future actions in the light of the knowledge we gain of ourselves, others and our surroundings. Giddens argues that we generally don't think about this very much, we just do it. In social movements, on the other hand, the process of reflexive self-regulation is more explicit and developed than in daily life. The participants in social movements want to have a particular effect on the wider society, and this implies a deliberate attempt to steer the activities of the movement in the light of its past successes and failures.

There are two other important characteristics of social movements, accord-ing to Walter J. Nicholls.[4] First, they are networks of organizations and indi-viduals, rather than single institutions. This means their geographies may be more diffuse than formal organizations that tend to operate within 'fixed locales'.[5] Secondly, they use 'non-traditional means' – protests, boycotts, vig-ils, rallies, demonstrations, civil disobedience and public campaigns – rather than conventional electoral politics. Social movements blur the distinction we set out in Chapter 1 between the formal politics of official institutions and the informal politics of everyday life. They link formal and informal politics by placing issues from the informal arena on the formal political agenda. They also involve direct, active participation by ordinary people in the political process.

Many social scientists believe that social change is the result of social struggle. Historically, improvements in the lives of ordinary people are rarely handed down from the top, but have to be fought for from below. By studying social movements we can understand how such struggles take place in more concrete terms – and how they affect and are affected by geography.

Since the late 1970s an important focus for geographers studying social movements has been the concept of 'urban social movements', developed by Manuel Castells.[6] Castells argued that the city is the arena of social reproduction of the labour force. With the development of capitalism, more and more of the means of social reproduction, such as housing, health care and education, had come to be provided by the state. The city was thus also the site of struggle and conflict over the state provision of these services, and urban governments were frequently the focus of campaigns by 'urban social movements' to improve the provision of public services. In his later work, Castells broadened the focus away from the specific issue of the reproduction of the labour force to include a variety of new social movements.

The term 'new social movements' refers to movements that rose to particular prominence in the 1960s and 1970s, including the women's movement, the environmental movement and the civil rights movement. These movements gathered pace in response to the breakdown of traditional communities with the development of large cities; the rapid growth of technological development and the consequent threats to environmental and military stability; and the failure of the state to resolve the contradictions between economic growth and development and its social, cultural and environmental effects.[7]

Understanding social movements

'Objective' and 'subjective' approaches

There are two broad approaches to interpretations of social movements: those that stress the 'objective' conditions which give rise to social movements, and those that concentrate on the 'subjective' experiences which prompt people to join and participate in them. Objective inequalities may provide the basis for social mobilization. For example, the development of the labour movement was prompted by entrenched class inequalities. Alternatively, a subjective sense of group belonging or group disadvantage may be important. In the case of the labour movement, this might relate to the emergence of class-consciousness.

There is some truth in each of these perspectives. Clearly, the social and economic conditions in which social movements develop and operate are likely to have important influences on their strategies and success. Equally, as political movements comprise committed individuals, the politics of social movements must be seen in part as the consequence of the views, emotions and perceptions of the people who make them up. On the other hand, taken separately, both perspectives have their limits. If we emphasize objective conditions, it is difficult to explain why social movements arise in some situations, but not in others which appear, 'objectively', to be similar. Conversely, it is difficult to account for the development of similar kinds of movements in very different circumstances. If nationalism (for example) were driven by objective economic disadvantage, how can we explain its greater strength in Scotland than in Wales when Scotland has the stronger economy? Indeed, there seems to be no consistent relationship between socio-economic conditions and the rise of nationalist movements (see Chapter 7). In the past, economic problems have resulted in socialist revolutions in some contexts and nationalist uprisings in others.

An emphasis on subjective experience seems, at first glance, to offer the solution to this conundrum. Perhaps different responses to similar circumstances are the result of different people being involved with different ideas and perceptions, interpreting their situations in different ways. The problem with this is that it fails to address how those ideas and perceptions are formed in the first place. Since it seems likely that they will be heavily influenced by the circumstances in which they develop, we are back where we started.

It may help to combine the insights of both points of view. Yes, social and economic circumstances are important, but while they influence the development of consciousness on the one hand, they are also interpreted by consciousness on the other. This interaction between social conditions and human perceptions is important. However, we want to develop the argument in a slightly different direction, by focusing on what seems to be 'political' about social movements, in the sense of politics as it was set out in Chapter 1. Stressing socio-economic conditions on the one hand, or individual consciousness on the other, to some extent neglects the *political* nature of social movements. That is, we need to focus on how and why particular human feelings or group attachments become mobilized in a political movement and how the contexts in which social movements are *used by them* in developing political strategies.

Identity politics and social difference

Many social movements are closely associated with the personal identities of their participants and with the politicization of those identities. Feminism involves a politicization of women's identities as women, social movements of black people work because their participants are conscious of a particular ethnic identity, and so on. With some movements, the link with personal identity is more diffuse. For example, the environmental movement is not obviously organized around an element of personal identity. On the contrary, in many ways it tries to appeal to a shared sense of humanity, and seeks to be universal. However, although it is less stark, there are notions of identity here too, in so far as environmentalists challenge the basis of industrial society and thus the sources of people's identities as producers and, especially, consumers.

The tension between universalism, on the one hand, and a stress on different identities, on the other, is discussed in detail in the work of American political thinker Iris Marion Young. Young outlines two contrasting approaches to dealing with the problems of inequality and social oppression. These 'competing paradigms of liberation' are an 'ideal of assimilation' and an 'ideal of diversity'.[8] The ideal of assimilation argues that liberation from oppression will be achieved when social differences cease to have political significance. Thus, human beings can be divided into groups according to the colour of their eyes, but no society or political system in the world makes any distinction at all between people on the basis of eye colour. The assimilationist ideal works for a society in which all social group differences have ceased to have any significance. Drawing on ideas from Richard Wassertrom, Young outlines the assimilationist perspective as follows:

> A truly nonracist, nonsexist society, [Wassertrom] suggests, would be one in which the race or sex of an individual would be the functional equivalent of eye color in our society today. While physiological differences in skin color or genitals would remain, they would have no significance for a person's sense of identity or how others regard him or her. No political rights or obligations would be connected to race or sex, and no important institutional benefits would be associated with either. People would see no reason to consider race or gender in policy or everyday interactions. In such a society, social group differences would have ceased to exist.[9]

Young accepts that the ideal of assimilation has been very important in politics by stressing, among other things, 'the equal moral worth of all persons, and thus the right of all to participate and be included in all institutions and positions of power'.[10] It also challenges the still widespread popular assumptions that certain groups in society are inherently inferior. However, Young herself prefers the alternative 'ideal of diversity'. She notes that although the assimilationist position has its attractions, it remains something of a distant utopia, and that in the present climate social groups have turned to the distinctive aspects of their identities as sources of strength. The ideal of diversity stresses respect for difference rather than its erasure, and also insists that certain social differences require different treatment (for example, treating men and women exactly the same might result in neglecting women's particular needs during pregnancy and childbirth).

Writing of the situation in the USA, Young outlines the move towards political movements based on social difference. This has involved a variety of social movements:

- The 'Black Power' movement, which argued, for example, that 'Black English is English differently constructed, not bad English' while 'Afro-American hairstyles pronounced themselves differently stylish, not less stylish'.[11]
- The 'Red Power' movement, which asserted the right of native Americans to self-determination and distinctive cultural practices.

- The gay and lesbian liberation movements, which reject the dominant assumption that a heterosexual lifestyle is 'normal' or 'more healthy', and stress pride in gay and lesbian sexual identities and sexualities.
- The feminist movements, many of which have turned away from the stress on improving the position of women in existing institutions and seek to challenge the patriarchal assumptions around which the institutions are built. They also stress the positive aspects of qualities understood as feminine, such as caring, nurturing and co-operation.

For Young, the importance of a continued emphasis on social difference arises both because of continuing oppression of some groups by others, and because of the political and cultural strength which comes from group identity. Difference is thus a positive aspect of society that need not be the basis of systematic discrimination.

Some writers argue that too great an emphasis on social difference risks being 'essentialist'. That means that identity differences are seen as inherent and enduring features of society. Stressing the differences between men and women and between masculinity and femininity suggests that there is some essence or ultimate core of femininity and masculinity, which makes men and women inevitably different from each other. Essentialism might imply an uncomfortable choice between permanent oppression or separatism. Geographer Gillian Rose has linked this to an ambivalence in feminist thinking.[12] On the one hand, feminists want to assert that women and men are alike and that women can and should have access to rights and privileges currently accorded to men. On the other hand, they want to assert that women are different from men in so far as masculine traits are seen as socially oppressive. A similar ambivalence about essentialism is present in many examples of identity politics.

Iris Marion Young insists that emphasizing difference does not mean adopting an essentialist notion of identity. She defines difference in terms of the relations between groups, rather than the essential characteristics of groups. Group formation is not a rigid and objective process, in which individuals can be assigned to groups on the basis of established and enduring identities. Rather, social movements based on identity groupings are porous and not exclusionary:

> Membership in a social group is a function not of satisfying some objective criteria, but of a subjective affirmation of affinity with that group, the affirmation of that affinity by other members of the group, and the attribution of membership in that group by persons identifying with other groups. Group identity is constructed from a flowing process in which individuals identify themselves and others in terms of groups and thus group identity itself flows and shifts with changes in social process.[13]

Young's conception of difference and identity confirms that, as we suggested at the start of this chapter, we all have multiple sources of identity. We are not just men and women but also working-class and middle-class, able-bodied and disabled, healthy and sick, rich and poor and members of different ethnic and national groups. Each individual is at the centre of a web or network of potential multiple identities. This raises a further question, however. If identities are multiple, then why do some identities and not others form the basis of political movements? The answer is that different identities are *politicized* in different ways, at different times and places. To consider this issue we need to move from the social and cultural bases of social movements to their more explicitly political characteristics.

Discourses and resources

We can think about how some socio-cultural identities become politicized while others do not by considering the relationship between *discourses* and *resources*. The development of a social difference into a social movement involves the *discursive construction* of that difference as being of political importance. But the ability of a social movement to capitalize on that politicization will depend in part on the mixture of *resources* which it is able to mobilize.

The discursive constructions surrounding a social movement may develop in a number of different ways. In the case of nationalist movements (see Chapter 7), ethnic elites may play a central role. Ethnic elites are often the guardians of key symbols of the national culture that can be used to generate support for nationalism. Often an iconic event (such as Rosa Parks' arrest in Montgomery) provides the spark that ignites a movement. This illustrates how a protest with limited initial objectives can gain momentum and organization leading to the formation of a wider social movement.

Once a movement has got going, it needs to be sustained through further discursive development. Movements develop narratives about their own history, their 'great thinkers', important activists, tragic defeats and glorious victories. They also typically promote representations of the movement as a struggle against oppression or discrimination. Labour movements invoke rhetorical figures such as 'the bosses' and 'the workers', environmental movements use metaphors such as 'spaceship earth' or 'Gaia' and might describe the biosphere as 'fragile' or 'vulnerable'. Nationalist movements often rely heavily on 'patriotic' symbols of the national culture, and so on.

For social movements, ideas and stories are central to success or failure, but they are only part of the picture. Success also depends on the resources that the movement draws on to promote its ideas. *Resource mobilization theory* aims to explain the success of social movements in terms of the availability of resources.[14] There are many different kinds of resources, including money and material resources, symbolic resources, organization capacity and people's time and commitment. Ideas and discourses can be seen as forms of symbolic resources.

The resource mobilization approach was grounded in *rational choice* theory. Rational choice theory assumes that people act on the basis of rational calculations about the costs, benefits and likely outcomes of different courses of action. Critics point out that human behaviour can often be impulsive, emotional or habitual, and in any case we often have too little information to calculate accurately all the costs and benefits of actions in advance. Incomplete information means that our actions have unintended and unpredictable consequences. However, the success and impact of action still depends partly on the resources we can mobilize in the pursuit of our goals. So access to resources, such as time, symbols, and money, is still likely to be important in explaining the success or failure of social movements, even if their use cannot necessarily be planned rationally in advance. Sydney Tarrow, a leading writer on social movements, argues that political opportunities are also central to the growth or decline of social movements. Tarrow suggests that social movements operating in a favourable political environment can expect to grow as the risks associated with participation in the movement are reduced.[15]

The geographies of social movements

Space, place, scale and social movements

Most studies of social movements pay little attention to geography. Walter J. Nicholls suggests that they 'have conceived social movements as developing on the head of a pin'.[16] The growing body of work by geographers on social movements shows this to be a problem because the geography of social movements profoundly affects their development and outcomes. There are several reasons for this:

(1)   There are geographical differences and variations in the development of social groups and group identities. This may be partly as a result of the rise specifically of identities which are associated with particular places, sites, or use of space, and partly because the formation of identity is always conditioned by the geographical context in which it occurs.

(2)   There are geographical variations in the distribution of the resources which groups mobilize in trying to achieve their goals.

(3)   There are geographical variations in the distribution of other social movements, political institutions, economic circumstances and cultural understandings which influence the impact that particular social movements have in particular places.

(4)   Different social movements operate (or aspire to operate) at different geographical scales. Some may be highly localized – a campaign against a specific road project, for example. Others may operate nationally, such as a civil rights campaign, at a continental scale (for example, European Nuclear Disarmament (END)) or aspire to be global (for example, many forms of environmentalism). Geographical scale has an impact both on the objectives of the social movement as a political entity and on its organizational requirements and capacities. Few are genuinely worldwide in scope, but several social movements have had an impact in diverse parts of the world.

Thus every social movement has a geography. Each operates at a particular geographical scale or combination of scales, and is likely to be unevenly developed with stronger and more successful elements in some places and not in others. Moreover, social movements are also constituted geographically, in at least three ways.

First, every social movement develops in a particular geographical context, which provides the resources and opportunities for its development. The context need not be highly localized. Many resources and opportunities are available across a wide area, but none of them is entirely ubiquitous. For example, the distribution of skills for publicity and fundraising is uneven. Some social movements will find it easier to get access to publicity and fundraising skills than others. Equally, certain discourses resonate more in some places than in others. An environmental discourse about the threat to ecological stability from industrialization may receive short shrift in a country that has yet to see many of the benefits of industrial development.

Secondly, there are considerable variations in the characteristics of social movements in different regions of the globe. The new social movements that developed in the West in the 1960s and 1970s did not have direct counterparts in Eastern Europe and the former Soviet Union. Social movements in those countries developed in the late 1980s and early 1990s to challenge state socialism. One of their objectives was to create the kind of public arena and civil society missing because of tight state control. In the West, it was the presence of such a public arena that provided the space within which new social movements could develop. In the Global South, social movements have been particularly influenced by the context of colonization and decolonization. Initially, social movements developed around the national liberation struggles in colonized areas. Since independence, many social movements have been concerned with the problems of poverty and the inability of the state to fulfil promises to produce rapid development.

Finally, recent research in geography has begun to examine how social movements 'use' geography to further their objectives. This might involve explicit efforts to scale up their activities (from local to national to global), to form spatially extended networks with activists in other contexts, or to root their work in local, place-based concerns.

In the rest of the chapter we illustrate the relationship between geography and social movements through three case studies: trade unionism and the labour movement, feminism and the women's movement, and new forms of radical grassroots activism.

The geographies of labour movements

Class, identity and trade unionism

Trade unions, which make up labour movements, are collective organizations of workers acting together to further their interests *as workers*. Although industrial action in general and strikes in particular are often the main reasons many people hear about trade unions (particularly through the media), most of the work of trade unions is much more mundane. In addition to representing workers who have individual problems at work (such as difficulties over sickness, accidents or pensions), the main function for many trade unions is bargaining with employers over wages and terms and conditions of employment.

In the West, modern trade unions are highly institutionalized, with their own staff, elected officers, bureaucratic procedures and internal politics. In some ways they are becoming like other member organizations, such as clubs and societies, in which services are provided in exchange for a subscription. However, the origins of trade unions lie in a social movement made up of workers. Elsewhere, trade unionism can be rather less formal and the 'social movement' nature of the labour movement is much clearer.

The labour movement is based on identities linked to employment and social class. Like other identities, class identity emerges in relation to other classes. It is also partly the product of discursive constructions. Because our identities are multiple, we do not always develop a strong *sense* of our class identity. On the other hand, most paid workers do have a strong sense of their occupational identity. It is common to hear people describe themselves in terms of their jobs ('I'm a teacher' or 'I'm a secretary', and so on).

Participation in the labour movement depends on at least a minimum sense of occupational identity. For some people it may be linked to a sense of class identity too. Alternatively, a sense of class identity may develop through participation in the labour movement. In all these cases, what class 'is' (and indeed what the labour movement 'is') is partly the product of discursive construction. Some unions deploy a rhetoric and discourses which stress working-class solidarity. Others emphasize occupational skills and traditions. As with all discourses, labour movements have their heroes, heroines and villains, their narratives of victories and defeats and their symbols of tradition and unity. And these discourses do not develop in a vacuum, but intersect with others. For example, some rhetorics of class solidarity and working traditions are linked to cultural norms of masculinity.

Space, place and labour movements

Labour movements have both histories and geographies. With the emergence of factories, industrial production and capitalist economies, new kinds of social relations were formed. Traditional ways of life in settled rural communities were disrupted and new working practices, wage relationships and forms of management and business control were developed. This began in Britain in the eighteenth century, developing and spreading internationally through the nineteenth and early twentieth century and forming a global network of capitalist activity in the present day.

Trade unionism developed as part of these changes, and in relation to the changing character of the state. States sought to regulate the development of trade unionism, channelling it into consideration of economic questions, rather than allowing it to challenge the political order (although it did this too from time to time). States often sought accommodation with labour movements, leading to the development of welfare states and, in some cases, incorporation into state decision-making (corporatism). Esping-Andersen's concept of welfare state regimes (discussed in Chapter 3) describes how the labour movement was included in different ways in different welfare states.

There is a complex geography to trade unionism, which has become an important focus of research for geographers[17] within the relatively new and expanding field of labour geography.[18] Today we commonly speak of labour movements in national terms: the British or American labour movement, for example. This reflects the political significance of the modern nation-state and the desire of trade unions to influence government policy, leading them to operate at a national level.

In its early stages, though, trade unionism was a much more local affair. In Britain, craft unions, with their roots in the medieval artisanal guilds, were often based in particular towns or cities, where a specific craft was practised. At this time, the prospect of alliances between workers in different places was one of the things about which both the government and employers were most worried, but tentative steps to broaden the geographical base of support for trade unions were made. The emergence of 'industrial' unions with membership drawn from all trades in a particular industrial sector (coal mining, shipbuilding, engineering) produced further geographical integration. Many of the frequent mergers among trade unions in the same industry were between unions representing different geographical areas. The twentieth century saw the rise in many countries of large 'general' unions representing workers not only in different trades and professions, but also in different production sectors. There has also been a large increase in the size of the public sector in many countries and in the proportion of its workforce which belong to trade unions. Both of these trends helps to establish 'national' labour movements.

There have also been developments at the international scale. In the late nineteenth and early twentieth centuries, many socialists argued that the working class should be united across national boundaries. A number of attempts were made to establish socialist 'internationals' which could draw together the strength of different labour movements. More recently, the development of a single market for goods, capital and labour in Europe has led to attempts to establish effective European-wide labour organizations.[19] Trends in the opposite direction are also apparent, with many governments and employers seeking to introduce greater 'flexibility' into the labour market by encouraging, or forcing, trade unions and employees to bargain at a firm, plant, work team or individual level, rather than at a national or industry-wide level.

There are complex geographies to trade unionism within individual countries, industries and union organizations. In Britain, for example, trade union membership rates vary widely around the country even within the same industry. Research by economic geographers Ron Martin, Peter Sunley and Jane Wills suggested that within a pattern of overall decline in trade union membership, some regions of Britain had proved markedly resilient, while others had lost members much more quickly.[20] Such a pattern cannot be accounted for wholly by the socio-economic conditions of different regions, but depends in part on variations in the political strategies, resources and discourses of union organizations in different places. Research by one of us into trade unionism in the British public services found that trade union responses to the threat of privatization were very different in different parts of the country.[21] These differences were partly a result of the geographically uneven pattern of privatization, but were also heavily influenced by the local availability of resources. These included commitment and time on the part of trade union members, representatives and officials, financial resources, organizational infrastructure and local traditions of trade union activity and labour movement culture. In some places, it was possible to draw on narratives that referred to past activities and represented them as 'the way we do things here'. In other places, with little or no history of campaigning and trade union organizing, there were fewer 'discursive resources' on which local trade unionists could draw. These findings support Andrew Herod's argument in his book *Labor Geographies* that social movements of workers are actively involved in shaping the landscapes of capitalism, but in geographically uneven ways.[22]

Geographies of feminism and the women's movement

Feminism in geography

The 1960s and 1970s saw the rise of the civil rights movement, the environmental movement, the peace movement and the women's movement, among others. Together they became known as 'new social movements'. In fact, this label is something of a misnomer, and it probably applies least of all to the women's movement, which can trace its roots back at least to the late eighteenth century and Mary Wollstonecraft's classic text *The Vindication of the Rights of Woman*, published in 1792. Feminist writers have shown how women have struggled for civil, social and political rights and equality with men throughout human history and not just since 1960! Nonetheless, the years following the 1960s saw an upsurge of activity in support of women's rights and in opposition to continuing gender discrimination and inequality.

Geographers have made important contributions to feminist ideas and practice. An initial concern was to 'make women visible' in geographical scholarship. Geography had been concerned primarily with the spaces and places of men and had ignored how the geographical experiences of the two halves of humanity are systematically different, most often to the advantage of men.

Geographers have also explored how spatial relations, the character of places and geographical landscapes both express and constitute unequal gender relations. This means that inequalities between men and women 'show up' in the geography of the world (in the social patterning of city life, for example, or in the dominant symbolism of landscapes), but are also influenced by that geography (so that the design and planning of cities has an impact on gender relations, for example).[23]

A related strand of feminist geography considers how geographical knowledge itself is gendered. Mona Domosh has shown how the experiences of nineteenth-century women travellers were ignored by the geographical establishment, while those of their male counterparts were elevated to the status of 'scientific' geographical knowledge.[24] Gillian Rose has suggested that the whole tenor of geographical thought is based on characteristically masculine assumptions about what 'knowing the world' as a geographer involves.[25] Such critiques have prompted geographers to develop distinctively feminist approaches to geographical research.[26]

There has been a lot of research on both the geography of gender and the gendering of geography. Rather less attention has been given to the geographies of feminism and the women's movement. There are some good reasons for this. Many feminist geographers have placed more stress on *participating* in the women's movement than on writing about it. And for many feminists, research into the lives and experience of women and their geographies is necessarily concerned with women's strategies of resistance to gendered inequalities and masculine oppression, whether that is formalized as a political movement or not. Some feminists argue that it is in any case inappropriate to judge women's political activity by a masculine norm of what political participation and political organizations involve. While these are important arguments, a study of the geography of social movements should certainly include the women's movement. It was, after all, one of the most influential social movements of the twentieth century.

Geography, difference and feminist politics

Like many grassroots movements, feminism grew unevenly. The rapid growth in women's movements during the 1970s began in Western industrial countries. It was organized around campaigns for women's rights and gender equality in a variety of fields, including employment, access to public services, the unequal distribution of childcare and domestic work, and women's control over their own bodies with regard both to fertility and male violence.

In the former state socialist countries, women were accorded many of the formal rights which their Western counterparts were struggling for, but such rights only rarely brought gender equality in practice. In the former Soviet bloc, independent women's movements faced similar problems to other efforts to pursue political strategies separately from the state. The absence of an effective 'civil society' significantly restricted their sphere of operation. In the poorer countries of the world, women's movements developed around some of the same themes as in the West, but were also particularly concerned with the role of women in 'development', and with the particular impacts on women of severe poverty.

Another (related) set of geographical variations reflect the different experiences of women in different social and cultural systems around the world. Variations in the role of the family, in childcare practices, in cultural attitudes to women and work, and in the view of women in different religious traditions has led to important differences in the ways in which women's movements have developed in different places.

In the 1980s and 1990s, these differences in women's experiences gained greater recognition. In particular, black feminists argued that women of colour are subject to a 'double' discrimination in societies which are racist as well as patriarchal.[27] They also argued that previous feminist thinking had not given enough weight to the ways in which women in different ethnic, religious and cultural communities experienced 'being women' differently. This heightened awareness of differences between women (including differences of sexuality, able-bodiedness and class, as well as ethnicity) raised important questions. For example, should women's movements stress the shared oppression of all women as women or emphasize sensitivity to the particular experiences of groups of women with a variety of identities?

The political theorist Nancy Fraser has related these changes in feminist politics to wider geographical shifts. According to Fraser, the period since the '9/11' attacks in the USA in 2001 have seen 'a major shift in the geography of feminist energies'.[28] She suggests that there have been three phases to the development of feminism since the 1960s. The first 'new social movement' phase involved a radical critique of the 'normalizing structures of post-World War II social democracy'. The second phase (referred to in the previous paragraph) focused more on identity politics, while the current third phase involves a more transnational form of politics. Each of these phases involved a distinctive geography:

> the first (new social movements) phase encompassed North American and Western European feminisms – and possibly currents elsewhere as well. In contrast, the second (identity-politics) phase found its fullest expression in the United States, although it was not without resonance in other regions. Finally, the third phase is most developed, in transnational political spaces, paradigmatically those associated with 'Europe'.[29]

Fraser argues that these shifts cannot be understood as changes internal to feminism, but are linked to wider political and economic transformations. In particular, the shift to 'Europe' reflects both the new opportunities for transnational alliances arising from European integration, and the hostile climate feminists have faced in US political systems since 9/11. While Fraser's analysis seems to underestimate the importance of feminist contributions from outside Europe and North America, her approach does highlight the importance of the relationship between the character of a social movement and its geographical context.

That context can be local too. There are notable geographical differences in the strength and activities of the women's movement within countries. Susan Halford investigated initiatives to promote the role and position of women in British local government during the 1980s.[30] She found that there were very marked variations in the extent and character of such initiatives. All the initiatives had been undertaken by local councils controlled by the Labour Party. However, only a minority of Labour councils had developed initiatives. The distribution of women's initiatives was related not only to formal political control, but also to the character of the local Labour Party, the number of women in electorally secure council seats and the social and economic geography of the local area, with women's initiatives more likely in large urban areas, possibly on account of the relatively high proportion of young single women and women in professional occupations.

Women's activism can also relate to highly localized contexts. During the 1980s the women's movement became closely associated with the peace movement, and in particular with the campaign to end the nuclear arms race and the threat of nuclear war. Research by geographer Tim Cresswell showed how the activities of women peace activists at the Greenham Common missile base in Britain involved transgressing social norms (for example, to do with 'feminine' behaviour).[31] Cresswell argued that this transgression was also a geographical one, which involved undertaking particular activities in the 'wrong' places, such as holding a peace carnival at the gates to the missile base.

One of the most important political effects of the women's movement has been to broaden the conception of politics to include the sphere of the personal and private. Traditionally, the public realm has been gendered masculine and the private realm feminine. Geographer Hilda Kurtz has examined the involvement of women in the environmental justice movement in the USA.[32] She studied a community protest by mainly working-class women of colour against the siting of a chemical plant in Louisiana. Kurtz found that as the women drew on their personal experiences of rearing children and trying to protect the health of their families, they subverted and blurred the conventional geography of public = masculine and private = feminine.

These examples begin to reveal something of the complex geographies of the women's movement: the historical shifts in its international centre of gravity, its uneven development within a national political system, its transgressing of the social norms associated with particular places, and its subverting of the public–private divide. In the final section of the chapter we revisit these themes in relation to some of the most recent developments in social movements: the radical activism of DIY politics and the anti-globalization protestors.

From social movements to DIY politics?

The labour movement and many of the new social movements that grew up in the 1960s and 1970s are highly organized and have become part of the institutional landscape of contemporary politics. When we speak of *the* women's movement or *the* environmental movement it almost sounds as if we are speaking of formal organizations. And of course many social movements involve formal organizations. There are political parties (such as the Green Party in Britain), pressure groups (such as the National Organization for Women in the USA), and numerous voluntary groups and non-governmental organizations that began life as part of one social movement or another.

For people who are interested in promoting political change, this formalization has advantages and disadvantages. For those who are willing (or who prefer) to work within the mainstream political system, establishing formal organizations can promote legitimacy and increase access to decision-makers and resources. Others may be concerned that such access comes at a cost and may involve compromising the movement's aims, objectives and principles. The liberal-democratic state is often adept at accommodating protest movements by offering to meet some of their demands in return for a willingness to work within the existing system. Within most social movements you will find a spectrum of attitudes to joining the mainstream from those who reject

incorporation on principle, through those who accept it for tactical or pragmatic reasons to those who embrace conventional politics wholeheartedly.

As existing social movements have matured (or ossified, depending on your
point of view) novel forms of political mobilization have sprung up around the
edges of formal politics or sometimes wholly outside 'the system'. Eco-warriors,
anti-capitalist protestors, direct-action campaigners, civil disobedience organiz-
ers, flash-mob instigators, guerrilla gardeners, community activists, graffiti
artists and many others have taken over when the radicalism of the 1960s new
social movements has sometimes run out of steam (see also Chapter 4).

Geographer Paul Routledge has worked with and written about global resistance movements.[33] His work provides striking insights into the politics of radical grassroots activism. In one notable contribution, he published the text of an
interview he conducted with 'General Unrest' of the Clandestine Insurgent
Rebel Clown Army (CIRCA).[34] Whatever its name may suggest to the contrary,
the Clown Army takes its work very seriously.[35] Loosely modelled on a conventional military organization, CIRCA aims to recover some of the original sub-
versive spirit of clowning using pastiche, comedy and slapstick in street protests
and direct actions. Looking back at the CIRCA operations to protest at the 2005
summit meeting of the G8 group of leading capitalist countries, General Unrest
offered a deadpan parody of the political strategy of G8 governments. In place
of the 'war on terror', the General said that the Clown Army was waging a 'war
on error'. The G8 was led by notorious 'errorists' who needed to be kept under
house arrest to protect the world from the consequences of their errorism. So
the Clowns decided to try to imprison the G8 leaders in their five-star hotel. The
'house arrest' action was accompanied by other similarly satirical actions,
including deploying clowns as 'weapons of mass distraction'. This activity aimed
to lampoon and highlight the failure to find any weapons of mass destruction
(WMDs) in Iraq following the US-led invasion of 2003, despite the claim that
the invasion was justified by the existence of Iraqi WMDs (Figure 6.1).

The geographies of activist movements like the Clown Army are as distinctive as their political tactics. More formal political organizations tend to operate within a specified spatial domain or territory. As we saw above, labour
movement organizations nowadays tend to be national in scope, and their
local branches, though important, operate within a hierarchical structure.
Grassroots activist organizations, by contrast, often work through more hori-
zontal networks. As the Clown Army itself puts it, 'CIRCA works horizontally,
we have no leaders, no centralized command – everyone is an officer, a general and a private'.[36] Moreover, 'we are insurgent because we have risen up
from nowhere and are everywhere ... we are approximate and ambivalent, neither here nor there, but in the most powerful of all places, the place in-
between order and chaos'.[37] Radical protest networks also seek explicitly to
link the local and the global. In fact, Routledge and his co-authors, Andrew
Cumbers and Corinne Nativel, have argued that the label 'anti-globalization
movement' is a misnomer since many grassroots movements for justice are
trying to propagate an alternative form of globalization.[38]

There are also implications here for how we understand the geographies of
power. CIRCA draws explicitly on clowning's radical origins. Historically,

Figure 6.1   Clown Army on manoeuvres © Paul Routledge

clowns, jesters and tricksters were not part of the 'entertainment industry' or 'leisure sector', but acted as anarchic disrupters of the *status quo*. In many of Shakespeare's plays, for example, the character of the fool plays a vital role and speaks many truths that the more straight-laced characters are unable to articulate. There are sound academic arguments to support the thinking behind the Clown Army's actions. Geographer John Allen has written extensively on the 'whereabouts of power'. According to Allen, different modes of power have different geographies.[39] For example, a mode of power such as authority can be exercised most effectively at close quarters. A 'weaker' form of power, such as seduction, by contrast works well at a distance (think of the seductive power of advertising). These different modes of power and their diverse geographies are subject to different forms of resistance. For Allen, one of the most effective forms of resistance to authority is laughter. The Clowns may be on to something after all.

Notes

1. Blumer, Herbert (1951) 'Collective behaviour', in Alfred M. Lee (ed.), *Principles of Sociology*. New York: Barnes and Noble. pp. 167–222. p. 199.
2. Nicholls, Walter J. (2007) 'The geographies of social movements', *Geography Compass*, 1(3): 607–22.
3. Giddens, Anthony (1984) *The Constitution of Society*. Cambridge: Polity Press. pp. 5–6.

4. Nicholls, 'The geographies of social movements'.
5. Giddens, *The Constitution of Society*. p. 204.
6. Castells, Manuel (1977) *The Urban Question: A Marxist Approach*. London: Edward Arnold; Castells, Manuel (1983) *The City and the Grassroots: A Cross-cultural Theory of Urban Social Movements*. London: Edward Arnold; Lowe, Stuart (1986) *Urban Social Movements: The City after Castells*. London: Macmillan.
7. Camilleri, Joseph and Falk, Jim (1992) *The End of Sovereignty?* Aldershot: Edward Elgar.
8. Young, Iris Marion (1990) *Justice and the Politics of Difference*. Princeton, NJ: Princeton University Press. p. 158.
9. Young, *Justice and the Politics of Difference*. p. 158.
10. Young, *Justice and the Politics of Difference*. p. 159.
11. Young, *Justice and the Politics of Difference*. p. 160.
12. Rose, Gillian (1993) *Feminism and Geography: The Limits of Geographical Knowledge*. Cambridge: Polity Press. pp. 11–12.
13. Young, *Justice and the Politics of Difference*. p. 172.
14. McCarthy, J. (1996) 'Mobilizing structures: constraints and opportunities in adopting, adapting, and inventing', in D. McAdam, J. McCarthy and M. Zald (eds), *Comparative Perspectives on Social Movements*. Cambridge: Cambridge University Press. pp. 141–51.
15. Tarrow, Sydney (1998) *Power in Movement: Social Movements and Contentious Politics*. Cambridge: Cambridge University Press.
16. Nicholls, 'The geographies of social movements'. p. 610.
17. Massey, Doreen and Painter, Joe (1989) 'The changing geography of trade unions', in J. Mohan (ed.), *The Political Geography of Contemporary Britain*. Basingstoke: Macmillan, pp. 130–50; Martin, Ron, Sunley, Peter and Wills, Jane (1996) *Union Retreat and the Regions: The Shrinking Landscape of Organised Labour*. London: Jessica Kingsley/RSA; Herod, Andrew (ed.) (1998) *Organizing the Landscape: Geographical Perspectives on Labor Unionism*. Minneapolis, MN: University of Minnesota Press; Sadler, David and Fagan, Bob (2004) 'Australian trade unions and the politics of scale: reconstructing the spatiality of industrial relations', *Economic Geography*, 80(1): 23–43.
18. Herod, Andrew (2001) *Labor Geographies: Workers and the Landscapes of Capitalism*. New York: Guilford Press; Hale, Angela and Wills, Jane (eds) (2005) *Threads of Labour: Garment Industry Supply Chains from the Workers' Perspective*. Oxford: Blackwell.
19. Sadler, David (2000) 'Organizing European labour: governance, production, trade unions and the question of scale', *Transactions of the Institute of British Geographers*, 25(2): 135–52.
20. Martin, Sunley and Wills, *Union Retreat and the Regions*.
21. Painter, Joe (1991) 'The geography of trade union responses to local government privatization', *Transactions of the Institute of British Geographers*, 16(2): 214–26.
22. Herod, *Labor Geographies*.
23. McDowell, Linda (1999) *Gender, Identity and Place: Understanding Feminist Geographies*. Minneapolis, MN: University of Minnesota Press; Nelson, Lise and Seager, Joni (eds) (2004) *A Companion to Feminist Geography*. Oxford: Blackwell.
24. Domosh, Mona (1991) 'Towards a feminist historiography of geography', *Transactions of the Institute of British Geographers*, 16: 95–104.
25. Rose, *Feminism and Geography*.
26. See, for example, Moss, Pamela (ed.) (2002) *Feminist Geography in Practice: Research and Methods*. Oxford: Blackwell.
27. hooks, bell (1981) *Ain't I a Woman: Black Women and Feminism*. Boston, MA: South End Press; bell hooks (1984) *Feminist Theory: From Margin to Centre*. Boston, MA: South End Press.
28. Fraser, Nancy (2005) 'Mapping the feminist imagination: from redistribution to recognition to representation', *Constellations*, 12(3): 295–307. p. 295.
29. Fraser, 'Mapping the feminist imagination'. p. 297.
30. Halford, Susan (1988) 'Women's initiatives in local government: where do they come from and where are they going?', *Policy and Politics*, 16(4): 251–9.
31. Cresswell, Tim (1994) 'Putting women in their place: the carnival at Greenham Common', *Antipode: A Radical Journal of Geography*, 26: 35–58.

32. Kurtz, Hilda (2007) 'Gender and environmental justice in Louisiana: blurring the boundaries of public and private spheres', *Gender, Place and Culture*, 14(4): 409–26.

33. For example, Routledge, Paul (2006b) 'Protesting and empowering: alternative responses to global forces', in Ian Douglas, Richard J. Hugget and Chris Perkins (eds), *Companion Encyclopaedia of Geography: From Local to Global*. London: Routledge. pp. 927–40.

34. Routledge, Paul (2005) 'Reflections on the G8: an interview with General Unrest of the Clandestine Insurgent Rebel Clown Army (CIRCA)', *ACME: An International E-Journal for Critical Geography*, 3(2): 112–20.

35. See: www.clownarmy.org (accessed 02/04/08).

36. See: www.clownarmy.org/rebelclowning/councils.html (accessed 02/04/08).

37. See www.clownarmy.org/about/about.html (accessed 02/04/08).

38. Routledge, Paul, Cumbers, Andy and Nativel, Corinne (2007) 'Grassrooting network imaginaries: relationality, power, and mutual solidarity in global justice networks', *Environment and Planning A*, 39(11): 2575–92.

39. Allen, John (2003) *Lost Geographies of Power*. Oxford: Blackwell; Allen, John (2004) 'The whereabouts of power: politics, government and space', *Geografiska Annaler*, 86B(1): 19–32.

Further reading

For a more extended discussion of identity politics have a look at:

Kenny, Michael (2004) *The Politics of Identity*. Cambridge: Polity Press.

A comprehensive general introduction to social movements is provided by:

Della Porta, Donatella and Diani, Mario (2006) *Social Movements: An Introduction* (2nd edition). Oxford: Blackwell.

The diverse field of social movement studies is mapped by the contributors to:

Snow, David A., Soule, Sarah A. and Kriesi, Hanspeter (eds) (2004) *The Blackwell Companion to Social Movements*. Oxford: Blackwell.

For an overview of the geographical aspects of social movements, see:

Nicholls, Walter J. (2007) 'The geographies of social movements', *Geography Compass*, 1(3): 607–22.

Alison Blunt and Jane Wills discuss the links between ideas and the geographies and practices of social movements in:

Blunt, Alison and Wills, Jane (2000) *Dissident Geographies: An Introduction to Radical Ideas and Practice*. Harlow: Pearson.

The geographies of grassroots transnational action are explored in more detail in:

Featherstone, David (2008) *Resistance, Space and Political Identities: The Making of Counter-global Networks*. Oxford: Blackwell.

SEVEN

Nationalism and Regionalism

Alizee Poulicek took her place on a high silver throne, *faux*-diamond tiara perched on her head and red and gold sash with 'Miss Belgium' placed over her shoulder. This victory in the December 2007 beauty pageant represented the culmination of years of ambition for Poulicek, who had recently moved to Belgium following an upbringing largely spent in the Czech Republic. But the mood in the auditorium changed when the presenter of the show began the post-pageant interview in Flemish (a Belgian dialect of the Dutch language). Clearly uneasy with the interview, the newly-crowned beauty queen asked the interviewer to repeat the questions in French. As the audience became aware that Poulicek could not speak Flemish they began to boo and wolf-whistle. Regardless of her looks, sections of the audience clearly felt that Poulicek was not qualified to represent Belgium if she could not speak both the main languages: Flemish and French.[1]

This event draws attention to the significant divisions that exist between Flemish-speaking Belgians in the northern region of Flanders (comprising around 59% of the Belgian population) and the French-speaking population living in the region of Wallonia (comprising 40% of the Belgian population) (see Figure 7.1). Since the beauty pageant was held in Antwerp, a town in Flanders, it is perhaps no surprise that the audience reacted with animosity towards a Belgian beauty-queen who could not speak Flemish. But the antagonistic response from the audience highlights a broader public concern with the integrity of the Belgian state – and in particular the growing division between the different language communities in Belgium. This concern was reflected in the 2007 general election results. Following the 10 June vote, no single political party received the necessary electoral majority to govern Belgium, leading to six months of political stagnation as the largest single party, Christen-Democratisch & Vlaams (the Christian Democratic and Flemish Party), failed to establish a ruling coalition. In addition, there was a significant vote for right-wing parties such as the Vlaams Belang (Flemish Interest), which campaigned for Flemish independence. Until the establishment of an interim government in December 2007 there was a significant threat of the fragmentation of Belgium into opposing sub-state territories according to linguistic grouping. Following the post-election political stagnation, a number of Belgian commentators came forward to criticize the federal arrangements in the state's constitution, arguing that the existing structure fails to accommodate adequately the differences between the two main communities.[2]

Figure 7.1   Map of regional divisions in Belgium © Alex Jeffrey, 2008

OVERVIEW

The Belgian example illustrates the common desire for an alignment between collective identity and political territory. It also serves to emphasize the importance of language in constructing political communities. In this chapter, we will be exploring one such collective form: nations, and how such common groupings have shaped the power and organization of nation-states. In particular, the accommodation of more than one nation within a single state (as is the case in Belgium) has brought into focus the importance of regional identities and territories operated at both scales 'above' and 'below' the state. We will therefore focus on both nationalism and regionalism and how these processes have been assessed by political geographers.

This chapter explores the power and ambiguities of nationalism as both a concept and a political movement. In the first section, we explore the concepts of the nation and national identity. Though these terms are challenging to define, we locate an underlying exclusionary impulse in their make-up: the definition and construction of a sense of ethnic identity comes about through marking differences between different ethnic groups. In the second section, we explore nationalism as a social movement, exploring how the membership of a nation can translate to particular political objectives and mobilizations. In the third section, we explore the relationship between nations and states through the example of Basque nationalism.

Introduction

Nationalism is a powerful and ambiguous political force in the contemporary world. Its power is derived from its ability to mobilize individuals towards collective goals, including protecting the nation from potential threat or struggling to secure an exclusive national territory. In these cases, the survival and well-being of the individual is mapped on to the survival and well-being of the collective: the nation. Its ambiguity stems from the conceptual uncertainty as to the philosophical or political nature of nationalism. As a reflection of this ambiguity, the scholar Tom Nairn identifies nationalism as the 'modern Janus'.[3] This reference to the two-faced Roman God is common in writing on nationalism and attempts to capture something of the conflicts, and even contradictions, of the idea. Nationalism is seen as facing two ways because it has both emancipatory and repressive elements. On the one hand, it has been the motive for struggles of liberation from colonial oppression, while on the other, it has motivated extreme hatreds culminating in genocide.

In addition to this political variability, there are very marked geographical and historical variations in nationalist movements and conflicts. The Indian nationalism which led to independence was different from that which has generated conflicts between ethnic and religious groups in modern-day India. The German nationalism mobilized by the fascist Nazi Party in the 1930s is different from the patriotism of the democratic government of 1990s Germany. The left-of-centre nationalism of the Scottish National Party or Plaid Cymru ('Party of Wales') is different from the exclusionary, xenophobic nationalisms which prised apart the communities of the former Yugoslavia. All of these phenomena are called nationalism. What is common to them that they can share the same label?

Nations and national identity

One of the earliest and most often cited definitions of national identity can be found in the 1882 essay *'Qu-est-ce qu'une nation?'* by French philosopher Ernest Renan (see Figure 7.2):

> A nation is a soul, a spiritual principle. Only two things, actually, constitute this soul, this spiritual principle. One is in the past, the other is in the present. One is the possession in common of a rich legacy of remembrances; the other is the actual consent, the desire to live together, the will to continue to value the heritage which all hold in common.[4]

Renan's definition centres attention on the shared nature of national identity – that a group of people share particular cultural traits and historical memories. Nations therefore constitute a cultural grouping, aspects of cultural practice shared between members of a human community. While there is little disagreement over the basic tenets of this definition, there has been sustained debate among scholars as to the historical and geographical origins of nations. This debate has led to an almost unlimited number of classifications of

Figure 7.2   Etching of Ernest Renan

national identity, each focusing on the different political, cultural, demo-graphic and social criteria of nationhood. One of the simplest ways to navigate these blurred and contested categorizations is to explore one fundamental question: when did nations first emerge? By exploring this question, we begin to see the fault lines of the political and philosophical debates surrounding nations and nationalism.

Primordial perspective

The first response to the question posed is that nations have always been part of human experience. Certain commentators and political figures have argued that nations are an intrinsic aspect of human nature, to be human is to be part of a nation. This position is often referred to as *primordialism*, since it is an argu-ment that nations have existed since the beginnings of humanity. Within this framework, national identity is often represented as a biological trait, a state of being that is determined by human genetics. Such a primordial vision of national identity is prevalent among extreme nationalist political movements, where leaders have attempted to demonstrate the biological (and hence unques-tionable) truth of a particular national identity. This idea was perhaps most vio-lently enacted in the case of the Nazi philosophies of a Germanic Aryanism during the 1930s and early 1940s. This violent ideology was structured around the belief in the existence of an Aryan race that needed to be protected from the supposed impurity of other groups and communities (such as Jews and the

Roma). Within this view, national identity is not a construct but rather is a real and tangible phenomenon that divides the human population.

While a recurrent image in nationalist political campaigns, primordialism is a vision of national identities that has been largely rejected by scholars working in the field of nationalism. One key problem with the primordial perspective is that it makes it very difficult to explain the dramatic variations in national feeling and nationalist activity. If 'human nature' is the cause, then how can we account for some humans who will happily kill or die for nationalist sentiment and others who express only weak national identity, or none at all? In place of primordial theories scholars have argued that national identity is connected to the emergence of the modern state, in particular in Western Europe in the late eighteenth and early nineteenth centuries (see Chapter 2). Therefore, rather than treating nations as an inevitable part of human existence, scholars have viewed national identity as a consequence of specific social, cultural and economic developments. But this does not mean that nationalism is simply regarded as a modern phenomenon without historical precedent. Within this framework we can identify two positions: the ethno-symbolist and modernist conceptual frameworks.

Ethno-symbolist perspective

An exposition of the ethno-symbolist approach can be found in the work of Anthony Smith. He argues that 'most nations, including the earliest, were based on ethnic ties and sentiments and on popular ethnic traditions, which have provided the cultural resources for later nation-formation'.[5] The term 'ethnic' carries connotations of kinship and common genetic ancestry. These connotations are very important in the discourse of national identity, but it is important to emphasize that they are discursive constructions. Of course some members of a particular ethnic group are related to one another genetically, but the idea that all the members of the group are related is a myth which helps to define the group culturally, but which need not (and almost certainly does not) have any real biological basis. In suggesting an ethno-symbolist approach, Smith does not wholly reject the notion of some aspect of national identity existing prior to the formation of the modern state, though he dismisses the idea that such formulations could be referred to as 'nations'. Instead, Smith argues that national identities develop around ethnic identities, given particular social, economic and political changes. He suggests that for an ethnic group to become a nation there must be a stronger, more physical and immediate connection between the group and 'its' territory, and while an ethnic group may exhibit common cultural 'markers', a nation has a common public culture. Smith believes that present-day nations draw their sustenance from ties to earlier communities, which he refers to as *ethnies*. According to Anthony Smith, there are six characteristics which define an ethnie:

(1) A collective proper name.
(2) A myth of common ancestry.

(3) Shared historical memories.
(4) One or more differentiating elements of common culture.
(5) An association with a specific 'homeland'.
(6) A sense of solidarity for significant sectors of the population.

Smith's work provides a wealth of historical examples of ethnies, each placing a different weighting on one or more of the characteristics listed above. In the example of ancient Greece, Smith highlights the identification of a distinct homeland around the Aegean, attachment to historical memories centred on the Homeric canon and the common pantheon of Greek deities.[6] Though Smith's research suggests a preoccupation with historical identity formations, he is keen to draw out the many examples of the ethnies of the past becoming (or at least legitimizing) nations of the present. Smith talks of the celebration of a mythical past, or 'golden age', on which present-day national identities are founded and enriched. For example, Smith talks of nation-building in Finland structured around the recovery of a Finnish ethnie differentiated from neighbouring Swedes and Russians. This past ethnie was celebrated by intellectual and cultural historians in the nineteenth century, though according to Smith these cultural artefacts 'bore only a very partial resemblance to earlier Finnish society, particularly its pagan era in the later first millennium AD'.[7] These potential historical 'inaccuracies' are not of issue since the purpose of these cultural performances was to recover an ancient but 'lost' period of Finnish history and culture on which modern claims to nationhood may be based.

     While not adopting the other modernist perspectives outlined below, certain political geographers have found Smith's concepts useful in explaining contemporary claims of nationhood. For example, in *Nation-building in the Post-Soviet Borderlands* (1998) Graham Smith et al. use the concept of ethnies to explain resurgent nationalism in Georgia following the fragmentation of the Soviet Union.[8] The history of Georgia testifies to the country's previous incorporation into the Persian, Ottoman and finally Russian empires. But following the break-up of the Soviet Union in 1991, nationalist activists drew on the existence of the Georgian language in the fifth century AD as evidence of a distinct Georgian history and identity. The existence of a distinct language provides the cultural resources for nationalists to identify a pre-modern ethnie, and the existence of the ethnie in turn legitimizes present-day claims to nationhood. Consequently, Anthony Smith uses an economic metaphor of a fund of cultural myths, symbols and values on which claims to national identity are based.[9]

     The ethno-symbolist approach can be relatively flexibly applied to empirical examples of national identity. The recourse to a 'golden age' of national identity is an almost omnipresent aspect of claims to nationhood. The final example we will use to highlight the ethno-symbolist perspective is the rise of Serbian nationalism in 1980s Yugoslavia. Perhaps the best-known moment in this emerging political movement was Slobodan Milosevic's speech in 1989 marking the 600th anniversary of the Battle of Kosovo Polje (the Field of the Blackbirds) in 1389. At this time Milosevic was the President of Serbia, one of six republics within the Federal Republic of Yugoslavia. Within Serbia there

existed two autonomous regions, Kosovo and Vojvodina. The Battle of Kosovo
Polje is a central theme in tales of Serbian nationhood and is portrayed as a
moment when the Serbian kingdom on the Balkan Peninsula fell to invading
Ottoman troops, in the process claiming the lives of the Ottoman Sultan
Murad and the Serbian Prince Lazar. Serbian national discourses mythologize
the battle as a turning-point in Serbian history, and particularly a moment
where Prince Lazar chose an eternal 'kingdom in heaven' over a temporal
'kingdom on earth'. In 1989, Milosevic made a direct reference to the role of
the Battle of Kosovo and crucially its historical connection to the essence of
Serbian nationalism:

> The Kosovo heroism has been inspiring our creativity for six centuries, and
> has been feeding our pride and does not allow us to forget that at one time
> we were an army great, brave, and proud, one of the few that remained
> undefeated when losing.[10]

The importance of the battle to narratives of Serbian nationhood is further
illustrated in the oral tradition of Serbian epic poetry collated by Serbian
writer and historian Vuk Stefanović Karadžić (1787–1864). Among other
Serbian imagery and myths, this poetry draws on the themes and images of
the Battle of Kosovo in order to commemorate the significance of the battle.[11]
Reflecting Anthony Smith's characteristics of an ethnie, this body of cultural
resources illustrates the power of the Battle of Kosovo to unite the Serbian
people through common emotional reference points. Figure 7.3 shows a bicy-
cle rally in the Bosnian town of Brčko organized to commemorate the battle
and celebrate Serb Orthodox culture. This is not restricted to simple narratives of the battle. The territory of Kosovo has become a wellspring for Serbian
national pride and identity, illustrated by the mass demonstrations in
Belgrade as a response to Kosovo's declaration of independence in February
2008.[12] While we cannot make an easy assessment of the nature of Serbian
group identification in the fourteenth century, we can observe the ability of
Serbian cultural artefacts to energize and mobilize political forces in the present day. This, for Smith, is the power of the ethnie.

   The ethno-symbolist concept of nationalism clearly differs from primordial
understandings. Ethno-symbolism questions the primordial claims that
national identity is an intrinsic part of human existence. Smith suggests that
nationalism is a modern phenomenon, stating that nations have emerged in
the modern era 'with its specific modes of domination, production and communication'.[13] But he draws our attention to the strategies and techniques
through which nations forge connections with pre-modern collectivities, cultural artefacts and events. Smith finds it difficult to conceive a modern nation
maintaining itself as a distinct identity without such mythology, symbolism
and culture. Smith therefore draws our attention instead to the discursive
construction of national identity, that particular concepts and ideas carry
political power to change perceptions, attitudes and group identifications.
This is particularly important for scholars of political geography as it draws
our attention to the power of imaginative geographies of the 'homeland'. As

Figure 7.3   Serb Orthodox Cycle Rally in Brčko, 2003 © Alex Jeffrey, 2008

we shall see below, we should not dismiss such techniques as 'mere' myths or 'untruths', but rather focus on their political power.

Modernist perspectives

In contrast to primordial and, to a lesser extent, ethno-symbolist perspectives, modernists believe that nations did not exist prior to the emergence of the modern state. Rather than holding the view that states reflect pre-existing human communities, the modernist perspective holds that nations emerged after the establishment of state sovereignty. Therefore, this position (or, more accurately, set of positions) identifies nations as the product of a particular era of the historical development of humanity associated with modernity. Political geographers have been at the forefront of theoretical and empirical work exploring the relationship between national identity and modernity, since this approach draws our attention to the spaces and scales through which national identity is produced.

This perspective has a number of foundational scholars. Perhaps the most famous is Ernest Gellner (1925–95), a philosopher and anthropologist who taught in London, Cambridge and Prague. Gellner debunks ideas of nations as a natural, God-given way of classifying humans. Instead, Gellner argues that we need to explore nations through the conditions which brought such a phenomenon into being, that is, their social and economic context. As we outline below, this is a recurrent refrain among modernist scholars of nations and nationalism. For Gellner, the key point of differentiation was between agrarian and industrial societies. Gellner argues that within agrarian societies the majority of the population were embedded within localized cultural groupings, while ruling elites operated at a level above and removed from these local affiliations.[14] This localized and two-tier organization militated against the formation of a coherent national identity. In contrast, Gellner sees the onset of industrial society as heralding a convergence in occupations and technical norms that fostered a greater sense of national identity. This argument serves to undermine the significance that the ethno-symbolist approaches (discussed earlier) placed on pre-modern formations and cultural artefacts:

> The connection between nationalism and the situation in which fully human men [*sic.*] can only be made by education systems, not by families and villages, underlines an amusing fact – the inverse relationship between the ideology and the reality of nationalism. The self-image of nationalism involves the stress of folk, folklore, popular culture etc. In fact, nationalism becomes important precisely when these things become artificial.[15]

As this quotation suggests, Gellner saw the development of mass education as crucial to the establishment of national identities in the industrial age. In this framework, education systems develop the sense of a national language that can be communicated effectively to all participants. The language of an education system (and here Gellner is using language in both the literal sense and a broader medium through which life is interpreted) produces a uniform human community: the nation. By developing a particular national language or 'medium of expression', as Gellner terms it, individuals are disposed to take jobs and build a life within a particular national context, since transfers between language areas is not straightforward. Gellner's modernist approach therefore draws our attention to the creation of nations out of practical necessity, rather than some mythic attachment to a golden age, citing the needs of the industrial age in terms of a mass-educated population.

We can see evidence of Gellner's chronology in the work of Eric Hobsbawm, a British Marxist historian who has written widely on the topic of nations and nationalism. Hobsbawm exhibits his modernist credentials in locating the origins of national identity in the emergence of the modern state, and specifically in post-Revolution France at the end of the eighteenth century. Through this historical lens Hobsbawm advances a Marxist critique of practices of national identity formation, drawing attention to their role in what he termed the 'deliberate ideological engineering'[16] of nation-building. Instead, Hobsbawm seeks to expose the hidden economic relations that underpin nation-building manoeuvres – in particular the creation of 'national' allegiances by wealthy elites as a means through which to establish the loyalty and consent of the general population. Rather than Gellner's industrialism, Hobsbawm identifies the rise of capitalism as the catalyst to the formation of nations and the invention of traditions. At certain points under the capitalist system, Hobsbawm argues that national identity serves as a form of 'false consciousness' masking 'real' social relations: economic class.[17]

An influential application of Gellner and Hobsbawm's modernist ideas can be found in Benedict Anderson's *Imagined Communities* (1991).[18] This work has proved an important text in the social scientific study of nationalism and provides a number of key insights for political geographers. The book builds on a modernist perspective to argue that nations are imagined communities since 'the members of even the smallest nation will never know most of their fellow-members, meet them, or even hear of them, yet in the minds of each lives the image of their communion'.[19] Crucially, Anderson is not using the term 'imagined' to imply that nations are without consequence or 'merely' imaginary. Indeed, part of his approach is a critique of the work of Gellner and Hobsbawm, who, he suggests, have conveyed the impression that nations are a fabrication in relation to 'true' human communities. Anderson questions this binary, suggesting that all human communities (outside the family) should not be discerned by their falsity/genuineness, but rather by the 'style in which they are imagined'.[20]

Anderson's text draws attention to the need for regular cultural practices to produce and reproduce the significance of national identities. Since nations are not pre-existing, there is a need for their constant re-imagining and, for Anderson, the rise of the print media was particularly influential in communicating collective national identities. As scholars of political geography, this orients our attention to the spaces and places through which national identity is celebrated and performed. Anderson himself draws attention to the role of museums, maps and censuses in fulfilling this function. Picking up this theme, Michael Billig, in his text *Banal Nationalism* (1995), explores the mechanisms through which the nation is communicated to a citizenry – a process he terms 'flagging'. Through everyday activities, such as posting a letter or reading a newspaper, the nation is 'flagged' by symbols (such as the Queen's head on a stamp or the flag positioned above the post office door) and linguistics (such as the use of the pronouns 'we' and 'us' in the speeches of political leaders) (see Figure 7.4 and 7.5). Of course, flags are not simply used in banal ways by the state to subconsciously convey the idea of a particular national identity; they are also used by citizens to communicate their support for a particular national project (see Figure 7.6 for an example of the use of flags by Greek football fans). But Billig's point is directed at the academy. He feels that there has been a tendency to study nations through extreme cases where violent separatist movements have emerged. Billig argues that this has led to a tendency to view nations and nationalism as exotic and marginal – phenomena that occur outside the West. In contrast, Billig is keen to identify the 'complex habits of thought that naturalize, and thereby overlook, "our" nationalism, while projecting nationalism, as an irrational whole, on to others'.[21]

While offering a diverse set of explanations for the emergence of nations, modernist perspectives draw our attention to the causal connection between the emergence of state sovereignty and national identity. This position clearly holds that nations do not exist, they are made – and we need to be attentive to the politics involved in this process of production. But by fusing nations with a particular historical period (modernity), this perspective simultaneously raises the prospect of a period when nations could cease to be an

Figure 7.4   Flagging the nation: Boston Public Library, Massachusetts
© Alex Jeffrey, 2008

important configuration of individual identity. If nations were 'made' through the establishment of territorial states, could nations be 'unmade' in an era of increasingly globalized forms of institutions, practices and solidarities? This question has preoccupied certain political geographers concerned with what has been termed postmodern approaches, since it explores new relationships in an era when the significance of the nation-state is argued to be waning. Sociologist Mike Featherstone sets out this argument:

In effect [national identity], the tendency towards centralization that accompanied the state formation process, in which attempts were made to eliminate differences in order to create a unified integrating culture for the nation, has given way to decentralization and the acknowledgement of local, regional and subcultural differences in the Western world.[22]

Figure 7.5   Flagging the nation: Boston Harbour, Massachusetts © Alex Jeffrey, 2008

There are two points we would highlight in relation to Featherstone's argument of the acknowledgement of sub-national identities and groupings. First, this approach should not be viewed as a marked break from the work undertaken by modernist scholars (such as Anderson, Billig and Hobsbawm). The approaches they identify are structured around the creation and performance of particular identities and this focus on the production of the nation has as its starting point the principle that no identity is complete, unquestioned and unitary. Rather, this work has illustrated the important point that national identities are in a constant process of revision and reproduction through the actions of individuals and institutions. Any nuanced attempt to examine such processes would highlight that national identity is differentiated over space and time and need to be addressed in their empirical context. Secondly, the postmodern perspective highlights the plural nature of identity, namely that

Figure 7.6   Greek football support during the European championships, 2004
© Sara Fregonese, 2004

individuals hold local and regional identities in addition to (or in replacement of) national identities. This is a crucial point – territorially configured identities are fluid and contested. We will explore this point in greater detail through the discussion of regionalism below. But in addition, and as we discussed in Chapter 6, the observation regarding the plurality of identity highlights that *national* identity is one of the many possible social identities that we have. As we have seen, it is based on the formation of a social group (the *nation*) which is differentiated from other groups (other nations) and from other sources of identity (gender, religion, sexuality, and so on).

Nationalism as a social movement

Just as there is a varied set of beliefs regarding the origin of nations, there are a number of different scholarly interpretations of the practice of nationalism. The commonly understood goal of nationalism is the establishment of a political community (usually a state) with the same territory of the nation such that the nation can achieve political sovereignty, and control over its own affairs. Put simply (and in the words of Ernest Gellner), political nationalists believe the national and the political unit should be congruent.[23] From this basic definition scholars have identified two broad categories of nationalism: *ethnic* and *civic*. Civic nationalism refers to state-led practices of nation-building. Civic nationalism suggests a form of patriotism or citizenship that celebrates the existence of a given state. We could identify the recent attempts by the UK to introduce a citizenship test as a means of strengthening British civic nationalism. In contrast, ethnic nationalism as a social movement marks a transition from the belief in the existence of an ethnic and national group to a political process and political activity organized around it.[24] This may constitute a separatist movement where a minority group within a state seeks independence, such as the case of the Tamil struggle to create an independent state (*Tamil Eelam*) in northern Sri Lanka. In contrast, an 'irredentist' ethnic nationalism represents a special case in which a national minority on the border of one state seeks to join with co-nationals in a neighbouring state. As we shall see below, Basque nationalism represents an example of such an irredentist cause since the Basque homeland is divided between northern Spain and southern France.

While the distinction between civic and ethnic nationalism seems a convenient basis through which to analyze the practices of nationalist politics, we would urge a note of caution on two counts. First, the distinction between civic and ethnic nationalism is often presented in popular and media accounts as a division between the Global North and the Global South. Where 'we' have patriotism and citizenship (civic), those elsewhere have primordial identity politics (ethnic). We must therefore critically examine the nature of claims to civic nationalism and assess the extent to which they draw on the same discourses of belonging and exclusion as ethnic nationalism. Secondly, when examined in empirical detail, the distinction between civic and ethnic nationalism appears hard to sustain. Nationalist movements outside the state are deemed 'ethnic', while those supported by state bureaucracies are legitimized as civic practices. Therefore, we would argue that these titles serve as indicators of the relative power of different nationalist movements rather than reflecting any aspects of their essence.

Rather than attempting to discern the civic or ethnic character of a given nationalist movement, we would encourage a perspective that views all nationalist movements as socially constructed in order to fulfil particular political objectives. We agree with Eric Hobsbawm and Terrence Ranger that nationalism necessitates the 'invention of tradition'.[25] Nationalism involves a discourse of antiquity. It argues that nations have ancient networks of kinship and cultural belonging. In practice, most nations are modern phenomena and in many cases what appear to be ancient cultural traditions are actually remarkably recent arrivals. Therefore Hobsbawm and Ranger argue that nations are constructed through *invented traditions*: 'practices ... governed by overtly or tacitly accepted rules and of a ritual or symbolic nature, which seek to inculcate certain values and norms of behaviour by repetition, which automatically implies continuity with the past'.[26] As Hugh Trevor-Roper shows in his discussion of Scotland, many of the distinctive markers of 'Scottishness' (to outsiders as much as to Scots) are quite modern inventions, including kilts and bagpipes.[27] Moreover, they were often developed after the Act of Union in 1707 which joined Scotland politically to England, and form in part a protest against it. While there is very much more to Scottish nationalism than this, the example serves to illustrate how significant elements of nationalist discourse can be constructed quite deliberately as part of particular political strategies.

Many writers on nationalism have stressed the social and economic conditions which can promote the development of nationalism. Nationalist movements are subject to significant geographical variation in their development, intensity and success. Geographers and others have often sought to explain such variation in terms of the uneven spread of social and economic processes. Regions that remain peripheral to economic growth, or excluded and remote from the sources of state power, for example, may develop nationalist movements. While such preconditions are very important, there is no universal rule about which kinds of economic, social or political problems will produce nationalist responses. There is no observable trend as to whether nationalist movements emerge in relatively rich or poor areas.

The ambiguity of economics to nationalist movements is illustrated in the case of the fragmentation of Yugoslavia. Yugoslavia was a federated state created after the First World War. It consisted of six republics and two autonomous regions (see Figure 7.6). Independence claims by Croatia and Slovenia (two of Yugoslavia's six republics) in 1991 were, in part, a consequence of the economic disparity across the six Yugoslav republics. Since the 1960s there had been lingering resentment towards the redistributive policies of the federal government among the Croatian economic elite. Croatia had benefited from tourism remittances from the Dalmatian coast and the historic Habsburg links to markets in Germany and Austria. The Croatian government felt it was 'milked of the fruits of its economic success in order either to support economically dubious projects in the underdeveloped regions or to subsidize government profligacy in Belgrade'.[28] These concerns solidified into wider calls for greater autonomy for the Croatian people and accusations of the subjugation of Croats under the political control of what was perceived to be a Serb-dominated Yugoslavia. The Yugoslav president, Marshal Tito, crushed this 1971–2 movement, known as the 'Croatian Spring', and its principal participants (mainly Croat scholars and academics) were imprisoned. As a response to these latent threats to Yugoslav integrity, Tito produced a new Yugoslav constitution in 1974. This document established a regimented pyramid hierarchy with Tito at its head. The nominal decentralization of power in the new constitution did little to appease Slovenian and Croatian complaints over the redistribution of state funds. This discontent was exacerbated during the late 1970s and 1980s. Economic conditions deteriorated with reductions in foreign capital investments and the fragmentation of the federal economic system. The relative economic affluence Yugoslavia had enjoyed as a key member of the 'Non-Aligned Movement' was replaced with stagnant national income growth and a debt crisis peaking at $22 billion.[29] In 1991, Croatia and Slovenia declared their independence from the Yugoslav state, sparking a series of conflicts and further secessionist movements across the remaining Republics. At the time of writing, Yugoslavia has now divided into seven states (Slovenia, Croatia, Bosnia and Herzegovina, Serbia, Montenegro, Macedonia

Figure 7.7   Map of Yugoslavia in 1990 © Alex Jeffrey, 2008

and Kosovo), though the independence of Kosovo is not universally recognized following its declaration of independence in February 2008.

The example of the fragmentation of Yugoslavia highlights three important factors concerning the rise of nationalist political movements. First, economic factors can play an important part in nationalist movements, but we must be attentive to their historical specificity. The example from Yugoslavia demonstrates that it was not (primarily) the economically disadvantaged republics (such as Macedonia and Montenegro) that sought to gain independence. Rather, it was two of the wealthiest republics that felt they were disproportionately funding the redistributive policies of the Yugoslav state. Secondly, the perceived economic cross-subsidies from Slovenia and Croatia were not presented by nationalist politicians as purely economic matters, but rather as symptoms of a longer historical lineage of oppression of national identities and traditions. Therefore the political platforms of nationalist politicians were not built on quantitative assessments of individual economics, but rather the economic factors served as tangible signposts to cultural subjugation. Thirdly, the perceived solution by nationalist politicians in both Slovenia and Croatia was the establishment of independent, sovereign states. Thus we see an illustration of Gellner's maxim that nationalist politics holds that the national and political unit should be congruent. In both Slovenia and Croatia (and later in Bosnia-Herzegovina), nationalist political parties argued that national identity and political territory should be linked through the creation of ethnically derived nation-states. This imagination of national 'purity' deviated from the reality of heterogeneous communities in the republics of Yugoslavia (particularly in cities), thus leading to the violence and horror of nationally motivated population expulsions and massacres.

The Yugoslav example demonstrates that a whole variety of circumstances *can* provide a foundation for nationalism, but it is impossible to predict on the basis of such circumstances alone which *will*. It is perhaps more appropriate to think of nationalism as a political strategy, and once we focus on the realm of politics the picture becomes a little clearer. Once nationalism is understood as a political project which is pursued by certain individuals and social groups within the nation on the basis of the resources they are able to mobilize, we can begin to explain its emergence and geography.

One line of reasoning stresses the role of ethnic elites in this process. The 'cultural intelligentsia' within a nation can be important because it often controls, or at least has good access to, resources for communication and political mobilization. The ethnic elites are likely to be well educated, articulate and familiar with the sources of cultural identity around which the ethnic group and the nation are discursively constructed. It is this ability to create the discourse of the nation that was evident in the case of the Croatian Spring discussed above. Furthermore, they may well have particular vested interests in achieving national autonomy, since it is the ethnic elite which would be likely to staff any new state apparatus, and benefit particularly from new sources of economic growth. For example, the greater development of ethnic elites in the Baltic Republics of Latvia, Lithuania and Estonia helps to explain why nationalism developed there much more strongly than in Soviet Central Asia. The argument about resources is also important in this case. Because the Baltic Republics had experienced a period of political independence between the two world wars, nationalists had particular resources on which to draw in making their case, in the forms of historical memories and in a discourse of lost statehood. Such resources were not available in the same way in other parts of the former Soviet Union.

Regionalism

Our discussion of nations and nationalism has centred upon the emergence of territorially configured identities (nations) and the political projects that have been conducted in their name (nationalism). As we have seen, these processes of identity formation and territorialization have been closely connected to the rise of the state as the primary unit of political life. However, there is a growing body of scholarship in political geography and beyond that is examining identity formation and political processes at a different level of analysis: the region. A basic definition of the region would present it at an intermediate territorial level, between the state and the locality, though this gives little idea of its territorial reach, since some regions in this sense are larger than states.[30] Therefore we should not think of regions in simple spatial terms but understand them as a territorial configuration set in relation to the governance and identity formation exercised by states. In this sense, regions have risen to particular prominence in the case of the establishment and expansion of the European Union, where new configurations of governance are changing the ways in which regions relate to the state, to the EU and to other regions both within and beyond the boundaries of their own state.

Regions therefore are perceived to offer a more flexible spatial unit through which to explore political, social and economic change, when the state may no longer be suitable for analysis. Some scholars have viewed this new regional focus as a natural reaction to the waning significance of state-level analysis in an era when global capital flows generate specific regional differences and accentuate the importance of sub-state processes.[31] The economist Kenichi Ohmae outlines this position in uncompromising language:

> The nation state has become an unnatural, even dysfunctional, unit for organising human activity and managing economic endeavour in a borderless world. It represents no genuine, shared community of economic interests; it defines no meaningful flows of economic activity.[32]

The solution for Omhae and others is to focus instead on the region. As a concept, the region is suitably supple to allow for multiple territorializations set by economic, political or cultural interests. For Omhae, the benefit of the region is that political interests do not fix its boundaries, but rather they are 'drawn by the deft but invisible hand of the global market for goods and services'.[33] This definition of the region as a space bounding particular economic relationships and processes has become a particularly influential aspect of economic geography.

But regions can also be conceived in cultural terms, for example the territorial delimitation of a particular language group. This chapter opened with two examples of such sub-state language regions: the cases of Wallonia and Flanders in Belgium. But cultural factors do not need to be distinct from economic preoccupations. For example, the Champagne region in France is a culturally defined area that has adopted identical practices of viticulture to produce the world-famous sparkling wine. But this also has an economic concern since champagne is a highly profitable commodity and is currently in short supply on the global market due to rising consumption. Following extensive lobbying by 38 local vineyard owners outside the boundaries of the Champagne region in March 2008, the French government decided to extend the region to include a larger number of vineyards. This has had profound economic implications: if your vineyard is located on the non-Champagne side, it is said to be worth €5,000 (£3,800) a hectare; on the Champagne side, they are worth over €1 million a hectare.[34]

In addition to providing a brief glimpse of the entanglement of economic and cultural concerns in the creation of regions, this example serves to highlight the political aspects of regionalism. Regions are not simply naturally emerging economic or cultural collectivities. In many countries, regions are politically defined territories through which practices of sub-state governance are enacted. Such explicit regional divisions are often the starting-point for analysis, though we need to adopt extreme caution in assuming these to be pre-existing and natural divisions of a state. In particular, we need to ask how these divisions were created, are they the result of top-down state reorganization or a case of a bottom-up struggle by civil society actors keen to establish a recognized regional identity?

The diversity of approaches to studying regions leads to a wide-ranging set of perspectives within regional geography. From a political geography perspective, we need to explore how regions are produced and struggled over, and what territorial divisions are dominant and why. As with the discussion of nationalism, this makes us particularly attentive to the role of power in shaping particular regional configurations. In order to better understand this process, the geographer Anssi Paasi has identified three predominant ways in which regions have been understood with geographical scholarship:[35]

- Pre-scientific perspectives
- Discipline-centred perspectives
- Critical perspectives.

Pre-scientific perspectives

The pre-scientific approach is a pragmatic disposition that views regions as simply a given spatial unit required for collecting and representing data but serving no further conceptual role. This idea of the region as a neutral container is evident in comparative work where statistics from different regions are compared without consideration of the varied social processes and histories that have been implicated in the production of the regional contexts. This pre-scientific perspective is common in applied studies of regional contexts for policy purposes, where different regional experiences are brought into comparison in order to attempt to resolve regional inequalities.

Discipline-centred perspectives

This perspective views regions as objects or results emerging out of the research process rather than natural or pre-existing phenomena. This perspective therefore views regions as an outcome of academic socialization and power/knowledge relations, where regions are created through the academic process for their ability to capture geographical relationships. This perspective suggests that research creates regions as knowable divisions of a given state, and through such practices new spatial imaginaries are established which have the power to change political realities. Paasi uses the example of school and university textbooks, where the presentation of naturalized connections between identities and territories can act as formative devices in shaping a given population's geographical imaginations.

Critical perspectives

Much of the recent work on regions within political geography could be brought under the banner of a critical perspective towards regionalism. As with other critical approaches to human geography addressed in this book, a critical regionalism suggests that regions are social constructs. As Paasi outlines, '[r]egions, their boundaries, symbols and institutions are hence not results of autonomous and evolutionary processes but expressions of perpetual struggle over meanings associated with space, representation, democracy and welfare'.[36] The focus on struggles draws our attention to the complex performances, institutions and ideas that sustain particular regional configurations over other competing visions. Just as Benedict Anderson's work draws our attention to the practices that sustain 'imagined communities', so a critical perspective on regionalism forces us to consider the processes and positions that reproduce what we could term 'imagined territories'. In short, regional classifications – statements concerning what regions and regionalization are – 'are orientated towards the production of social effects and are impregnated with power'.[37]

We can see this critical perspective at work in a number of recent studies of the politics of regional geographies. For example, in *Territory and Terror* (2005), Jan Mansvelt Beck explores the territorial dimensions of the Basque conflict, in particular, through an analysis of patterns of identification and the role of the local environment in shaping the emergence of politically motivated violence.[38] Through a detailed historical analysis of Basque politics, Mansvelt Beck seeks to explore the differences in identity formation and political behaviour in the contexts of the Basque regions of Spain and France (see Figure 7.9). While Euskadi Ta Askatasuna (ETA) has established an active campaign in northern Spain, the book considers the lack of equivalent paramilitary action in the Basque region of southern France. Mansvelt Beck's analysis suggests that regional identity formation is a product of the relationships between regions and states. While Basque nationalists claim the existence of a common Basque territory across southwest France and northwest Spain, Mansvelt Beck argues that this does not coincide with his observation of a more fragmented Basque identity between French and Spanish regions. In the case of France, centuries of nationalization from above has led to the 'Frenchification' of Basque lifestyle. The region was tightly integrated into French national culture and politics, literally through better infrastructure connections but also symbolically through French cultural traditions. Consequently, Mansvelt Beck suggests that France has only engaged in 'cosmetic decentralization', suggesting that little authority has been devolved to regional contexts. The French example is contrasted with the experiences of Spain, where, he suggests, the Basque region has played a prominent role in identity formation on account of the superficial nature of Spanish nationbuilding. Ironically, then, the Basque region in Spain enjoys greater devolved power but also a more extreme and militaristic form of Basque separatism.

Therefore, for Mansvelt Beck, we can only understand the role of the French and Spanish states in mediating Basque ethnonational violence

Figure 7.8   Map of the Basque Region © Alex Jeffrey, 2008

through a historical examination of broader processes of nation-building. This acknowledgement of the spatially varying claims to state legitimacy between France and Spain contributes to a nuanced understanding of the production of regional politics. In terms of our wider discussion of regions, Mansvelt Beck's work illustrates a number of important points. First, we need to study regions within their geographical and historical contexts. This is not an idle plea for broader understandings of the motivations for conflict, but rather an attempt to highlight the dynamic, shifting and incomplete nature of the formation of regions and identities. Secondly, we must be wary of comparing political practices in different regional settings. Though regions provide an important insight into the nature of identity politics, these discussions need to be framed in terms of the wider geopolitical dramas of states and interstate relations. Simply focusing on regions does not circumvent an appreciation of the role of states in the production of political space and identities. Finally, the Basque case study highlights the enduring significance of the discursive construction of regional geographies. Despite division between two states, a mountain range and distinct cultural practices, the idea of a unified Basque homeland continues to resonate within both Spanish and French political and cultural life. The performance of traditions and the creation of appropriate cultural artefacts has established the Basque region as a distinctive political territory despite being at odds with the existing state boundaries.

The study of regionalism is a complex arena that spans a number of different sub-disciplines of human geography. In keeping with the approach of this book, we would urge political geographers to adopt a critical stance towards regional geography. Regions are often fragile formations, poorly defined, and contained within them are complex social divisions. There is a constant danger of reification, attributing to the region characteristics proper to its constituent elements. A related trap is anthropomorphism, in which regions are endowed with wishes, interests and strategies, as if we can speak for an entire region. Some movements adopt a language of nationalism, others a regionalist vocabulary struggling for a reorganization of the state to allow increased pluralism and differentiation. Consequently, we must understand regions as partial social systems linked functionally to other levels, rather than as global societies encompassing the totality of social relationships that are the traditional aspiration of the nation-state.

Conclusion

In this chapter we have brought a critical perspective to the study of nations, nationalism and regionalism. Nations are a powerful concept in contemporary politics, though by acknowledging their power we should not assume they constitute natural human communities. We echo the arguments of modernist scholars in exploring nations as the product of modern states, and in particular of new forms of technology and knowledge production associated with the rise of capitalism in the nineteenth century. In connecting nationalism with the modern state, we support Billig's argument that nationalism should not be conceived as a political force experienced in parts of the Global South. As Billig's work demonstrates, modern states in the Global North utilize nationalist techniques (in everyday and banal ways) to stimulate affiliation and belonging among their citizenry. We explored the concept of nationalism through a similar critical framework. Nationalist movements are created to fulfil particular political ends. While nationalists highlight the authentic and archaic nature of their struggles, we must contextualize each movement within its political context. Through the example of the fragmentation of Yugoslavia, we identified how the role of multiple geographical and historical struggles, related to state power, were subsumed under the banner of nationalist antagonism. Finally, we examined the new geographies of regionalism, an area that has sought to explore the production of regional geographies operating at a number of scales. Again, we would urge a perspective that examines regions as lived places, such as the Basque region, and explores their production of regional territories and identities accordingly.

Notes

1. In addition to Flemish and French speakers, there is also a small German-speaking community of around 75,000 in the Eastern part of Wallonia.
2. See BBC News (2007) 'Viewpoint: Belgian crisis', *BBC News*. Available at: www.news.bbc.co.uk/1/hi/world/europe/6995511.stm (accessed 08/03/08).
3. Nairn, Tom (1975) 'The modern Janus', *New Left Review*, 94: 3–29.
4. Renan, Ernest (1996 [1882]) *'Qu-est-ce qu'une nation?'*, in Geoff Eley and Ronald Grigor Suny (eds), *Becoming National: A Reader*. New York and Oxford: Oxford University Press, pp. 41–55. p. 41.
5. Smith, Anthony D. (1998) *Nationalism and Modernism*. London: Routledge. p. 12.
6. Smith, Anthony D. (1989) 'The origins of nations', *Ethnic and Racial Studies*, 12(3): 340–67. p. 345.
7. Smith, 'The origins of nations'. p. 358.
8. Smith, G., Law, V., Wilson, A., Bohr, A. and Allworth, E. (1998) *Nation-building in the Post-Soviet Borderlands*. Cambridge: Cambridge University Press.
9. Smith, 'The origins of nations'. p. 353.
10. Milosevic, Slobodan (1989) 'St. Vitus Day Speech'. Available at: www.slobodan-milosevic.org/spch-kosovo1989.htm (accessed 10/03/08).
11. See Locke, Geoffrey (2002) *The Serbian Epic Ballads: An Anthology*. London: The Association of Serbian Writers Abroad.
12. Hawton, Nick (2008) 'Serbian fury erupts in Belgrade', *BBC News*. Available at: www.news.bbc.co.uk/2/hi/europe/7258373.stm (accessed 08/03/08).
13. Smith, 'The origins of nations'. p. 361.
14. Day, Graham and Thompson, Andrew (2004) *Theorizing Nationalism*. Basingstoke: Palgrave Macmillan. p. 45.
15. Gellner, Ernest (1994) 'Nationalism and modernization', in J. Hutchinson and Anthony D. Smith (eds), *Nationalism*. Oxford: Oxford University Press. pp. 55–62 p. 58.
16. Hobsbawm, Eric (1990) *Nations and Nationalism since 1780*. Cambridge: Cambridge University Press. p. 92.
17. Day and Thompson, *Theorizing Nationalism*. p. 27.
18. Anderson, Benedict (1991) *Imagined Communities*. London: Verso.
19. Anderson, *Imagined Communities*. p. 6.
20. Anderson, *Imagined Communities*. p. 6.
21. Billig, Michael (1995) *Banal Nationalism*. London: Sage. p. 38.
22. Featherstone, Mike (1991) *Consumer Culture and Postmodernism*. London: Sage. p. 142.
23. Gellner, Ernest (1983) *Nations and Nationalism*. Oxford: Blackwell. p. 1.
24. Geographers' writings on national identity and nationalism include: Bell, James (1999) 'Redefining national identity in Uzbekistan: symbolic tensions in Tashkent's official public landscape', *Ecumene*, 6(2): 183–213; Jones, Rhys and Desforges, Luke (2003) 'Localities and the production of Welsh nationalism', *Political Geography*, 22(3): 271–92; Kuus, Merje (2004) 'Europe's eastern expansion and the inscription of Otherness in East–Central Europe', *Progress in Human Geography*, 28(4): 472–89; Mansvelt Beck, Jan (2005) *Territory and Terror: Conflicting Nationalisms in the Basque Country*. Abingdon: Routledge.
25. Hobsbawm, Eric and Ranger, Terrence (eds) (1983a) *The Invention of Tradition*. Cambridge: Cambridge University Press.
26. Hobsbawm, Eric and Ranger, Terrence (1983b) 'Introduction: inventing traditions', in Eric Hobsbawm and Terrence Ranger (eds), *The Invention of Tradition*. Cambridge: Cambridge University Press. pp. 1–14. p. 1.
27. Trevor-Roper, Hugh (1983) 'The invention of tradition: the Highland tradition of Scotland', in Eric Hobsbawm and Terrence Ranger (eds), *The Invention of Tradition*. Cambridge: Cambridge University Press. pp. 15–42.
28. Lampe, John R. (1996) *Yugoslavia as History: Twice There was a Country*. Cambridge: Cambridge University Press. p. 90.
29. Bojicic, Vesna (1996) 'The disintegration of Yugoslavia: causes and consequences of dynamic inefficiency in semi-command economies', in David A. Dyker and I. Vejvoda (eds),

Yugoslavia and After: A Study in Fragmentation, Despair and Rebirth. Harlow: Longman. pp. 28–7.

30. Keating, Michael (1998) *The New Regionalism in Western Europe*. Cheltenham: Edward Elgar. p. 9.

31. See Paasi, Anssi (2002) 'Place and region: regional worlds and words', *Progress in Human Geography*, 26(6): 802–11.

32. Omhae, Kenichi (1993) 'The rise of the regional state', *Foreign Affairs*, 72(2): 78–87.

33. Omhae, 'The rise of the regional state'. p. 248.

34. Bremner, C. (2008) 'Champagne region expanded to meet world demand', *The Times Online*, 14 March, www.timesonline.co.uk/tol/life_and_style/food_and_drink/wine/article 3548465.ece (accessed 16/03/08).

35. Paasi, 'Place and region'. p. 804.

36. Paasi, 'Place and region'. p. 804.

37. Paasi, 'Place and region'. p. 805.

38. Mansvelt Beck, Jan (2005) *Territory and Terror*.

Further reading

There are a number of key texts that provide a foundational knowledge in the study of nationalism. These will be invaluable to the student of nations and nationalist political practices:

Anderson, Benedict (1991) *Imagined Communities*. **London: Verso.**

Billig, Michael (1995) *Banal Nationalism*. **London: Sage.**

Gellner, Ernest (1983) *Nations and Nationalism*. **Oxford: Blackwell.**

Hobsbawm, Eric and Ranger, Terrence (eds) (1983) *The Invention of Tradition*. **Cambridge: Cambridge University Press.**

We would encourage students to move beyond these canonical texts to engage with the wide range of recent empirical work on nationalism, much of it by political geographers. We would particularly draw attention to:

Jones, Rhys and Desforges, Luke (2003) 'Localities and the production of Welsh nationalism', *Political Geography*, **22(3): 271–92.**

Mansvelt Beck, Jan (2005) *Territory and Terror: Conflicting Nationalisms in the Basque Country*. **Abingdon: Routledge.**

While there is a large body or work in economic geography on the nature of contemporary regionalism, there has been markedly less in the field of political geography. We would encourage students to explore the work of Anssi Paasi and Michael Keating:

Keating, Michael (1998) *The New Regionalism in Western Europe*. **Cheltenham: Edward Elgar.**

Paasi, Anssi (2002) 'Place and region: regional worlds and words', *Progress in Human Geography*, **26(6): 802–11.**

EIGHT

Imperialism and Postcolonialism

In February 2008 the Australian Prime Minister Kevin Rudd offered an apology to Australia's indigenous population.[1] Rudd was voicing his regret to the 'Stolen Generations', a group of victims of a government procedure of forcibly removing indigenous children from their families. This policy lasted from the Aboriginal Protection Act in 1869 through to the early 1970s and is thought to have involved the removal of more than 100,000 children from their families.[2] The Australian government justified these actions at the time as necessary steps to provide protection to indigenous children, though others have since suggested that it was motivated more by a desire to retain Caucasian racial purity. Over the course of the 1990s and 2000s there have been concerted efforts by indigenous groups and their supporters to receive a government apology and economic compensation. While there has been an apology and some piecemeal compensation (usually as a result of individual legal claims), there has yet to be state-level economic redress of the injustices experienced by the Stolen Generations.

In order to understand and critique the practices of the Australian government in the case of the Stolen Generations we need to examine this policy in the broader geographical and historical context of the conquest of Australia. The relationship between the Australian state and indigenous communities has been premised on the concept of *terra nullius* – a Latin expression derived from Roman law that means 'empty land'. When the British began settling the Australian landmass in the eighteenth century they treated it as *terra nullius*, a land that was devoid of inhabitants and served as a 'clean slate' for British colonial rule. Of course, this was not the case and estimates suggest that there were as many as 350,000 indigenous peoples living in Australia at the time of European conquest. The designation of *terra nullius* served to exclude the indigenous population from territorial rights and political participation. It was not until the 1960s that indigenous Australians were able to vote in Australian elections.

The case of the plight of indigenous Australians raises three issues that relate to our discussion of political geography. First, and perhaps most tangibly, the Australian example highlights that the export of the European state system through colonization and, later, decolonization cannot be consigned to history. We can continue to observe the implications of unjust colonial practices in the present day. Secondly, colonialism was a process that was shaped through unequal power relations between colonizer and colonized. British colonizers claimed, through military might, the sovereign power to set laws and designate who were the legitimate citizens of the newly established colony. But this should not be taken as evidence of the absence of resistance. There was perpetual contestation of the policies of the Australian state and this took many forms, from organized political dissent to the struggles of children to free themselves of their state captors and return home – for a powerful recreation of such resistance see the 2002 film *Rabbit-Proof Fence*.[3] The eventual government apology highlights the ultimate success of these practices of resistance. Finally, colonization did not simply operate through material exploitation, such as the denial of land rights or the appropriation of natural resources. Practices of representation were also crucial to colonizers and served as the means through which their ideas and policies were accepted as legitimate actions. The power of *terra nullius*, for example, is its ability to convey the idea of land as empty and uninhabited rather than its basis in fact (as we have seen, it was not actually true). The ability to label and create knowledge, then, was closely connected to the ability to colonize space. The European colonizers therefore drew on the prestige of the newly emerging scientific disciplines, such as geography, to grant legitimacy to their colonial adventures. In this chapter, we explore the close connection between the creation of geographical knowledge and the practices of imperialism and colonialism.

OVERVIEW

In this chapter, we want to turn to another aspect of the geography of state formation: the relationship between those first 'modern states' of Europe and other parts of the world. Paralleling their formation through warfare, the connections of modern states with other places and peoples have often been violent and bloody. 'Imperialism' is the control by one state of other territories. 'Colonialism' refers to the establishment of permanent or extended settlement (colonies) in those territories. Imperialism may be military and political (direct, or formal, imperialism), in which the government of the territory concerned is taken over by the imperial power, or it may be economic (indirect, or informal, imperialism), in which the territory is formally independent but tied to the imperial power by (unequal) trading relations. In addition, it is now becoming increasingly common to identify cultural imperialism, in which existing or traditional ways of life and ways of thinking are subordinated to the culture of the imperialists.

The geographies of imperialism are geographies of political strategies of suppression, domination and exploitation; they are also geographies of resistance that continue to develop and change into the present day. We will begin by briefly outlining the development of European imperialism and then consider some of its formative links with academic geography. We will then turn to the political strategies of colonizers and colonized and see how these continue today through the theories and practices of 'postcolonialism'.

The expansion of Europe

Encounters with 'other' peoples

The reasons why a small number of European states were able to dominate and control such a huge proportion of the globe, in terms both of land area and people, are hotly disputed.[4] A range of explanations have been advanced, including relative levels of technological development in Europe and other places, political conflict between European states, the emergence of capitalism, Western Europe's maritime traditions and expertise, and so on. Each of these factors no doubt played its part, and it seems increasingly unconvincing to rely on a mono-causal explanation. What is also clear, though, is that there was nothing inevitable about European geopolitical superiority. Wherever the Europeans went they found other people, who were, more often than not, living in complex societies with high levels of technological sophistication, political organization and cultural development. One of the mistakes of early imperialists was to attempt to judge the cultures and peoples they encountered by European standards, and thereby to fail to recognize that in their own terms they were as sophisticated and 'advanced' as the supposedly superior European societies. The fact that these 'other' peoples did not set out to rule and dominate the rest of the world was not a product of their so-called 'primitive' condition or 'degenerate' social structures, but rather reflected very different combinations of historical circumstances and political, cultural and economic priorities and values.

Although the modern world, and particularly the relations between the rich industrialized countries of the 'North' and the poorer countries of the 'South' cannot be understood without the context of Western imperialism, it would be a mistake to give the impression that European control was ubiquitous, complete, or homogeneous. Parts of the globe escaped formal European control altogether, but even places which were part of formal European empires were never wholly subordinated, or subdued. First, there was the logistical problem of governing tracts of territory and populations that were larger than the compact countries of Europe and often a long way away. The practical difficulties of colonial administration meant that in many cases the imperial powers had to incorporate and buy-off local political leaders, and, to some extent, adjust to local political and social structures. To say this is not to lessen the horrors of the practices of imperialism, but it is to recognize the force of the points made in Chapter 1, that any sustained system of rule or governance depends on coalition and alliance formation, and the use of the resources that are to hand. Imperial rule was constituted through *engagements* between the strategies and institutions of rulers and ruled, albeit ones that were highly unequal and unjust.

Secondly, imperialism was always resisted. Resistance did not always take the form of organized political struggle (although it often did), but included everything from sabotage and military actions, through civil disobedience and strikes to minor non-co-operation, foot-dragging and grumbling. Not all of these strategies were equally successful, of course (nor were they all equally strategic). But wherever Europeans went and tried to govern, people resisted them.

The motives for expansion

If the underlying reasons for the relative success of European domination were complex, so too were the motives which prompted European expansion. Certainly, no account of imperialism can ignore trade. Mercantile capitalism, which was the mode of economic organization of Europe's cities in the later middle ages, was based on a simple principle: buy cheap and sell dear. Many goods could be produced within Europe from local raw materials, including linen and woollen cloth, wood and timber, leather goods, a variety of food-stuffs, and wine and beer.

With the growth of medieval cities and the consequent development of a market for luxury products there was an increasing demand for raw materials and goods which could not be produced at home, or which were in short supply. These included silk and cotton, spices, and precious metals and stones. Good sources of many luxuries in Asia were known to Europeans and by 1400, as Europe teetered on the brink of modernity, there were already long-established overland trade routes to the East. However, the land routes were insecure and subject to delays, loss of cargo and the whims of rulers along the way:

> Before the voyages of discovery and the opening of the oceans to trade, the Italian city-states, especially Genoa and Venice, grew wealthy ... on the strength of their strategic position between Europe and western terminuses of the Asian trade routes. Vigorously commercial and active developers of maritime technology, they were frequently at war with one another in the competition for shares of the Eurasian trade. Initially Islam had been a boon to these merchants because it inhibited Muslim merchants in the Levant from venturing into Christian territories. But when the Turks captured Constantinople in 1453, thus making the Byzantine capital a Muslim city, Genoa and Venice lost an important outpost in what was becoming an increasingly hostile world. The city-states were soon to enter a long period of decline as the maritime strength of the west passed first to southwest and then to northwest Europe.[5]

The development of an all-water route to Asia became a priority. Because he first encountered the lands we know today as America, Christopher Columbus is probably the best known of the merchant adventurers and seafarers of the so-called 'age of discovery'. Columbus is celebrated in his adopted home, Spain, and to the present day commemorations of his life and achievements can be found across the country (Figure 8.1 shows the Columbus monument erected in Barcelona harbour). However, Columbus's voyages westwards in 1492, 1493, 1498 and 1502 were less immediately significant commercially than that of Vasco da Gama, who in 1497 travelled south past the huge continent of Africa and then east reaching the southwestern coast of India on 22 May 1498.[6] For the first time it was possible for Western Europe to trade with Asia without risking the difficult overland routes through the Near East.

The other great motive for overseas expansion was religious. Early explorations by Spain and Portugal were impelled in part by the perceived threats to Catholic Christendom from Islam in the East and the Protestant reformation to

Figure 8.1   Columbus Monument, Barcelona, Spain

the North. Wherever Iberian explorers went, they claimed land for their monarchs, but also souls for the Church. Later, in the seventeenth century, it was Protestantism that sought salvation overseas, with the settlement of the Eastern seaboard of North America by the Puritans.

Iberia abroad

The new maritime trade routes to the East were dominated initially by Portugal, whose seafarers established trading posts around the coasts of Africa and South Asia and in the Far East. The Portuguese emphasis on trade and commercial activity meant that to begin with the Portuguese empire in Africa and the East was made up of many tiny possessions. Little attempt was made to acquire large areas of territory in the hinterlands of the trading posts.

In due course, the significance of Columbus's encounter became evident and the first extensive overseas European empires were those established in the New World by Spain and Portugal. The Spanish empire, in particular, expanded rapidly through the Caribbean, Central and South America and north through Mexico into present-day California, Arizona, New Mexico, Texas and beyond. The Portuguese were also active in South America after Cabral's landing in 1500, expanding into present-day Brazil.

The Iberian expansion generated vast wealth for the Spanish and Portuguese Crowns, which were united from 1580 to 1640. Precious metals, and particularly silver, were the sources of wealth. They were stripped from America by the tonne and shipped back to Europe. In the process, the Conquistadors, the soldier-adventurers responsible for the process of colonization, laid waste to great civilizations, such as the Mayas, the Incas and the Aztecs. This occurred both through military conquest and as a result of the arrival of European diseases, which were previously unknown and to which the local people thus had little resistance.[7]

The beginnings of the British Empire

Within only a few decades, however, the dominance of Spain and Portugal was under threat. By the second half of the sixteenth century, the British and French exploration of the north and east of the North American continent was well under way. British, French and Dutch colonies were established along the Atlantic seaboard. British explorers sought in vain for a northwest route to Asia which would bypass the Spanish, while the French were busy opening up the interior in Canada and eventually travelling down the Mississippi to the Gulf of Mexico to what became Louisiana. The French influence is still in evidence in the French place-names along the great river and in the local language of Louisiana and New Orleans.

Meanwhile, to the East, the Dutch (who gained independence from Spain in 1584) and the British were in gradual ascendance, challenging the Portuguese monopoly of trade. In 1599, the British East India Company was founded and, in the following year, was chartered by Queen Elizabeth. Its Dutch counterpart followed it in 1602. Contact between Europe and the East during the seventeenth century was largely a commercial affair. The Dutch headed for South East Asia and the spice islands, while the English struggled to develop trading links with the Mughal emperor in India. Gradually, the English gained in strength relative to the Portuguese, who had long-established trading posts in India. However, the East India Company was by no means equivalent to the military conquerors of South and Central America. In the Mughal empire they met a civilization which, on land, was significantly stronger and which expected to receive tribute and deference from these overseas visitors.

Though stronger than the tiny forces of the East India Company, the Mughal empire was coming to an end. During the first half of the eighteenth century it collapsed and a variety of would-be successors vied for supremacy. Both the British and the French sought to capitalize on the confusion, with the British eventually prevailing. When Robert Clive gained political power in

Bengal in 1757, he unleashed a tide of greed and exploitation in which the merchants of the East India Company plundered the local economy, destroying the sources of their wealth and bringing the Company to the verge of bankruptcy. This led in 1773 to action by the British government in London to bring the Company under state regulation. Warren Hastings was appointed as first Governor General of all the British possessions in India. As the British were losing their North American colonies in the War of Independence (1775–83), they were securing their hold over what was to become known as the 'jewel in the imperial crown'. However, although hegemonic throughout the subcontinent, the British came to control only about two-thirds of the land area directly, with the remainder under the nominal rule of local princes. Moreover, the process of empire building was a long and slow one, taking a good century to complete and involving military, economic and cultural struggles with local people and institutions. Over time the emphasis of the British activities in India shifted from trading as equals, or even subordinates, through the extension of trade and by political and military means, to an assumption that the British were in India to rule, with trade left to private individuals and companies. This process culminated with the Indian revolution of 1857, the resulting transfer of powers from the East India Company to the Crown in 1858 and the naming of Queen Victoria as Empress of India.

At this point, however, the final wave of imperialist expansion had hardly begun. Africa was a vital and bloody link in the 'triangular trade' which brought Africans to the Caribbean and the American South to be sold as slaves to work on the cotton, sugar and tobacco plantations. These raw materials were then exported to Europe and manufactured into goods for re-export to the colonies. All around the coast of Africa, Europeans had established small colonies and trading ports. In the early nineteenth century the interior of the continent was almost completely unknown to Europeans. However, in the 35 years between 1880 and the First World War, the entire continent, its people and resources, had been carved up between the European powers.

Finally, in the South Pacific, the search for the Great Southern Continent, which had been a presence in European mythology during the middle ages, was finally discovered to be an island following its circumnavigation in 1801–2. Until 1851 the British government used Australia as a penal colony, and for the next 50 years, particularly with the discovery of gold, it was the focus of considerable emigration, becoming, with New Zealand, a major exporter of agricultural products. As we discussed at the opening of the chapter, neither of the two was an empty land, however, and, as in other parts of the globe, local people found their cultures and livelihoods altered and often destroyed by the colonizing Europeans.

Geography's imperial roots

Imperialism and the role of geographical knowledge

In this process of imperial expansion and overseas colonization, knowledge was of vital importance. Not only did European expansion produce new knowledge at an ever-increasing rate, but it also depended upon that knowledge. This dependence was practical in the sense that the development of overseas possessions required specific kinds of information and skills, such as cartography, surveying, ship-building, astronomy and navigation, settlement construction, mining, agriculture, and so on. It was also dependent on particular ways of knowing *about* other places and people. The arrogance with which Europeans asserted their dominion over the globe and the ease with which they could bring themselves to destroy, kill and maim other people and disparage their cultures and achievements was based on certain preconditions. In order to make these acts do-able, it was necessary for Europeans to understand themselves as superior and others as inferior. The barbarities of colonialism rested on a set of assumptions, representations and discourses about the rights of Europeans in relation to the rest of the world. We will consider some of these discursive practices in the following section. First, though, we want to look briefly at the role played by geography in these processes.

The modern discipline of geography was, perhaps more than any other, the product of imperialism. First, European knowledge of the earth's surface – its land masses and seas, its plants and animals, its peoples and their ways of life – was gained very largely through the process of European expansion and formed the content of the emerging subject of geography. Secondly, many of the practical skills and knowledges through which exploration and settlement were practised are central to geography, from map-making to settlement planning. Thirdly, geography operated through particular ways of knowing the world that both enabled and legitimated the practice of imperialism.

As we mentioned in Chapter 1, the origins of the sub-discipline of *Political Geography* were entangled with imperialist rivalries between the European powers. Such entanglement was not limited, however, to just one sub-discipline of geography. As David Livingstone, and many others, has pointed out, the development of the academic subject of geography as a whole was both the product of, and implicated in, the expansionist policies of Europe throughout the age of empire.[8] One clue is provided by timing. As David Stoddart avers:

> what distinguishes geography as an intellectual activity from ... other branches of knowledge is a set of attitudes, methods, techniques and questions, all of them developed in Europe *towards the end of the eighteenth century.*[9]

For Stoddart, the new methods and techniques which gave modern geography its coherence were united by their stress on *direct observation*[10] and what he regards as a move away from interpretations of the world based on myths, legends and fantastic narratives. Other commentators, however, have suggested that the writings and works of modern geography, particularly in its nineteenth-century phase, were rather less than objective, and were saturated with European assumptions about the world and its contents. The narratives may have been different, but they were stories nonetheless, and closely connected to moral and cultural views about the relationship between the 'West' and its 'Others'.

The discourse of climate

Relating the climate to human development constitutes one of the earliest attempts to develop an overarching theory of the human geography of the earth's surface. This early work was presented by its protagonists as a scientific endeavour that drew on geography's burgeoning knowledge of the natural environment to explain and predict the progress of human societies. In this framework, the climatic features of the environment determined the history and geography of human distributions and socio-cultural development. This concept, entitled *environmental determinism*, became extremely popular in both Western Europe and North America. In the USA, Ellen Churchill Semple constituted a key figure in this field, in particular in her major work, *The Influences of Geographic Environment* (1911).[11] This text was indebted to the scholarship of Freidrich Ratzel (whom we discuss in Chapter 9), though Semple was keen to apply his theories of political geography to empirical contexts. In Figure 8.2, we see one such attempt in the case of the Philippines, where Semple sought to map the distributions of 'Wild', 'Civilised' and 'Negrito' peoples on to the topography of the islands. As we see from Semple's work, the climate and topography of a given environment was deemed to affect the entire population in uniform ways, leading geographers to feel confident in pronouncing on the racial characteristics of given populations.

David Livingstone places considerable stress on the relationships between geographers' interpretations of climate and climatic zones and the discourses of racial inferiority and superiority that were central to the imperial project. According to Livingstone, geographers' study of climate was far from the objective science that it was claimed to be. Rather, notions about climate became entangled with moral, religious and political judgements about people. The impact of climatic variation on humanity was thought to be highly significant and to condition not just agricultural production, but whole ways of life *and people's biological make-up*. What Livingstone calls the 'moral economy' of climate operated through linking climatic variation closely to the supposed division of the human species into different 'races'.

Nowadays social scientists are much more critical of the whole idea of 'race' as a biological distinction. Indeed, many argue that there are no satisfactory biological grounds for grouping people into 'races' at all, and there are certainly no inherent differences between the potential physical, mental and emotional characteristics of members of supposedly different 'races'. For many decades, however, it was widely, almost universally, assumed that the human species consisted of biologically distinct groups ('Caucasian', 'Negro', 'Asiatic', and so on). Indeed, some writers even believed that Africans were actually a separate species and represented an earlier evolutionary 'stage' in the development of modern *homo sapiens*.

The study of climate was significant because it was argued that different 'races' suited different types of climate, either because racial differences were produced by climatic ones, or because the different 'races' had been allocated 'by nature or God [to] climatically appropriate regimes'.[12] Thus it was thought that the bracing climates of northwest Europe were responsible for producing

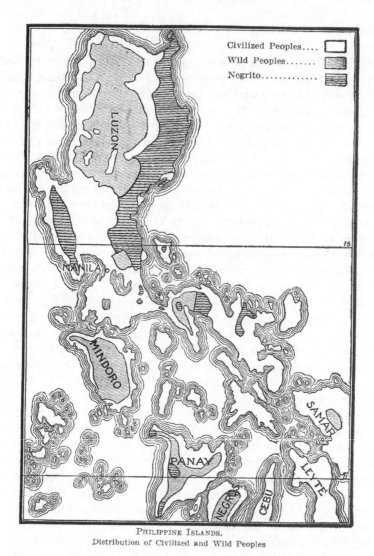

PHILIPPINE ISLANDS.
Distribution of Civilized and Wild Peoples

Figure 8.2   Ellen Churchill Semple's (1911) map of population distribution in the Philippines

a race of hard-working, intelligent and rational people, the warm Mediterranean climate generated the relaxed and emotional 'Latin temperament', while the hot climates of the tropics led to the moral and physical degeneracy and indolence thought to be characteristic of the Africans.

It is not possible to dismiss these ideas either as simple, if barbaric, racism, or as immature and underdeveloped science, for their significance was widespread. Not only did the discourse of 'climate's moral economy' underpin and provide scientific 'justification' for what became the routine practices of nineteenth-century imperialism (such as slavery), it also exerted a surprisingly long-lived influence on geography as an academic discipline:

The idea that climate had stamped its indelible mark on racial constitution, not just physiologically, but psychologically and morally, was a motif that was both deep and lasting in English-speaking geography. ... In Austin Miller's standard textbook on *Climatology*, first published in 1931, he explained that 'Psychologically, each climate tends to have its own mentality, innate in its inhabitants and grafted on its immigrants. ... The enervating monotonous climates of much of the tropical zone, together with the abundant and easily obtained food-supply, produce a lazy and indolent people, indisposed to labour for hire and therefore in the past subjected to coercion culminating in slavery'. What is remarkable here is the way moralistic terms – enervating, monotonous, lazy, indolent – were still presented as settled scientific maxims.[13]

Even as late as 1957, the following words of the renowned geographer Griffith Taylor were being republished: 'The writer believes that it is precisely because the Negro was thrust into the stagnant environment of the Tropics ... that he preserves so many primitive features ... Racial evolution' has left the Negro 'far behind'.[14]

Mapping and naming

As a subject, geography was also implicated in the imperial project in highly practical ways. Controlling and ruling distant lands and peoples required knowledge of the land as much as the people. Maps and charts were central to European strategies throughout the overseas empires. Mapping brought the land into sight and into Western frameworks of understanding. It allowed order and Western rationality to be imposed on human landscapes shaped through very different world views. In *The Road to Botany Bay* (1987), Paul Carter discusses the significance of the survey and the map for colonists in Australia:

> Maps were understood as ways of getting in. ... Exploring and surveying were ... two dimensions of a single strategy for possessing the country. The map was an instrument of interrogation, a form of spatial interview which made nature answer the invader's need for information.[15]

European colonialism also sought to possess the land through naming and labelling it either in familiar terms with English, French or Spanish words, or by using the words of local people. In either case, as Carter points out, the act of naming, of inscribing maps, and thus the land, linguistically, was another strategy through which the land could be made knowable, and thereby possessed. In Australia,

> the historical space of the white settlers emerged through the medium of language. But the language that brought it into cultural circulation was not the language of the dictionary: on the contrary, it was the language of

naming, the language of travelling. What was named was not something out there; rather it represented a mental orientation, an intention to travel. Naming words were forms of spatial punctuation, transforming space into an object of knowledge, something that could be explored and read.[16]

The close links between geography as a system of knowledge, geography as a practical activity and the expansion of European empires have been made increasingly clear in recent years.[17] An interest in imperialism among geographers continues to this day, albeit usually in a rather more critical vein. Until recently, this interest was largely in the political economy of imperialism. Although that perspective continues, contemporary writers have focused increasingly on imperialism as a way of thinking about and looking at the world, of constructing the identities of ourselves and of others, and of attempting to control not only the economic and political fates of other peoples and lands, but their cultural destinies as well. In this geographers have increasingly drawn on the writings and ideas of the so-called 'postcolonial' theorists such as Edward Said and Gayatri Chakravorty Spivak. We will return to these more recent attempts to write more critical geographies of imperialism later in the chapter. Now, though, we want to turn to the development of imperialism itself and examine its spatial practices in a little more detail, beginning with a discussion of one particular theory of the expansion of Europe overseas: world-systems theory.

World-systems theory

An outline

Interpreting and explaining the broad sweep of the expansion of Europe into the rest of the world is a complicated business, and has been the focus of much debate and academic dissent. One framework is 'world-systems analysis', which has been developed over many years by Immanuel Wallerstein.[18] It is a perspective which has been particularly influential within Political Geography through the work of Peter Taylor, and especially his *Political Geography: World-economy, Nation-state and Locality*. First published in 1985 as part of an upsurge of interest in Political Geography, this book was one of the first attempts to place the sub-discipline Political Geography comprehensively within a coherent theoretical framework. It is probably still the best-known example in this field of study, and at the time of writing it has already reached its fifth edition.

Wallerstein draws on the pioneering work of economic historians Fernand Braudel and Karl Polanyi. Central to Braudel's ideas was the concept of *longue durée,* which stresses the long timescale of social and economic change over decades or even centuries. Polanyi proposed that, historically, economic activity has always taken one of three forms. The first of these is the *reciprocal-lineage* system, which is characteristic of the traditional societies within which human life has been organized for most of its history. In this system, exchange between producers takes place on a mutual basis (hence 'reciprocal') and is organized through kinship groupings (hence 'lineage'). The second form is the *redistributive-tributary* form, in which there is a net 'upwards' redistribution of the products of human labour from producers to a dominant group, such as occurred during feudalism. The third form is *market exchange,* in which goods are exchanged 'freely' in a market. This form is typical of capitalism. Although, in principle, these forms can exist together in time and space, Polányi argues that one is likely to dominate the others and thus structure the overall character of the economy. In addition, over time, there has been a move from the reciprocal form through the redistributive form to the market form.

Wallerstein shares Braudel's stress on long-term shifts in economic and social relations. He argues that Polanyi's three forms of exchange correspond to three distinctive types of social system. Indeed, these three types are the only kinds of socio-economic system which have existed. They are *mini-systems*, in which exchange is reciprocal; *world-empires*, in which exchange is redistributive; and a *capitalist world-economy,* in which market exchange dominates. Historically, mini-systems have been by far the most numerous, although in the modern world we know of only a tiny proportion of them and today there are probably no remaining cases. They include, for example, the social systems of certain North American tribes prior to the expansion of European settlement. According to Wallerstein, there have been many world-empires, which have a large base of agricultural producers providing both subsistence for everyone and luxuries for a small elite group. They include the Roman Empire, the Chinese Empire, and the feudal system in medieval Europe. According to world-systems analysis, all mini-systems and world-empires have been eliminated or incorporated into the only remaining system: the capitalist world-economy. There have been previous examples of nascent world-economies, based on market exchange, but until the sixteenth century they were quickly incorporated into existing world-empires. From the sixteenth century onwards, however, the world came to be dominated by the European world-economy, which, Taylor suggests, became truly *global* in about 1900.

Following Taylor,[19] we can identify two important insights from Wallerstein which distinguish the world-systems approach from traditional conceptions of global economic change. The first of these is the 'one-society assumption'. Traditional social science has assumed that the world consists of many 'societies' which are normally seen as being the same as countries. Hence we speak of British, American or Chinese society. This, says Wallerstein, is mistaken. The integration of economic activity in the world-economy means that there is now just one, global, society. This insight is related to the second, which Taylor calls the 'error of developmentalism'. Traditionally, 'development' has been seen as a path along which the multiple societies (countries) pass from low levels of economic activity to more complex and wealthy ones. Walt Rostow's *The Stages of Economic Growth* (1960)[20] serves as an oft-cited example of such a vision of development. But Taylor argues that because there is only one world-economy, it is not possible for individual bits of it to pass independently up what he refers to as a 'ladder' of development. The economic activities going on in all countries are closely related to each other. The capacity of some countries to produce a great deal and to sustain high material standards of living depends upon the existence of other countries whose economies are actively 'underdeveloped' by the processes of the world-economy to promote wealth for the few at the top. These two insights are very important, particularly as they correct other, more conventional, assumptions about the relations between societies.

Wallerstein's approach, therefore, offers a broad framework within which the expansion of Europe, which we described above, may be understood. There are clear parallels with the stress we have placed on the emergence and development of the overseas empires as a historical process. The world-systems approach has attracted both fervent support and criticism from academics, and, as we have mentioned, it has had an important influence within Political Geography. Its existing stress on the *spatial* structure of the world-economy, which Wallerstein argues is divided into a core, a semi-periphery and a periphery, is highly geographical, and this aspect of world-systems theory has been carefully developed by Peter Taylor. Despite its attractive elements, however, it is not, in the end, compatible with the approach adopted in this book.

Critiques of the world-systems approach

There are a number of principal criticisms which have been made of Wallerstein's ideas. Here we will rely on Anthony Giddens' summary of them.[21] Giddens suggests that world-systems theory is flawed in two important ways. First, he argues, it suffers from *economic reductionism*. This does not mean that it only looks at economic processes, but it does imply that where politics and culture are examined, they tend to be explained in terms of the economy. Thus, the dynamic of state formation, which we examined in Chapter 2, and which seemed to be closely shaped by war and military strategy, is considered in Wallerstein's account as a feature of the development of the world-economy. In Giddens' view, and ours, the dynamics of the world-economy are crucial in explaining the changing world, but that changing world is also a product of the development of the international system of states, which cannot be accounted for entirely in economic terms. This also means that the 'one society assumption' in Wallerstein's approach needs to be modified. There may be only one capitalist world-economy, but British 'society', French 'society' and American 'society' do have meaning in other ways. Since each is a territorial state which accords, for example, citizenship to its population in different ways, being part of British 'society' is politically very different from being part of French 'society'. The same point could be made in terms of religious, national, linguistic or ethnic groupings, although these would not map neatly on to modern states in the way that citizenship does. In other words, the 'one society' perspective holds truer when 'society' is being thought of as a system of *economic* integration, and does not work so well when political or cultural relations are being considered.

The second difficulty that Giddens encounters with Wallerstein's ideas is the *functionalist* element within them. Functionalism, in the sense Giddens uses it, means explaining something in terms of its effects. This is common in the biological sciences. For example, we explain that fish have gills because the effect of possessing gills is to enable 'breathing' underwater. In thinking about social systems, an interpretation is functionalist if it explains one feature of a system in terms of the function it fulfils in helping to keep the system as a whole going. Giddens argues that Wallerstein's category of 'semi-periphery' is an example of his functionalist thinking because 'the existence of semi-peripheral regions is explained by reference to the "needs" of the world system'.[22] From Giddens' perspective, social systems can't have 'needs'; only people can have needs. Now, it may be true, as Wallerstein says, that the existence of a middle tier of semi-peripheral countries between the rich core and poor periphery helps to stabilize the world-economy. But this stabilizing function can't account for the initial emergence, or the continuing existence, of the semi-periphery.[23]

Strategies of colonial domination

The interpretative framework we outlined in Chapter 1 seeks to avoid both economic reductionism and functionalism. First, it avoids functionalism by stressing politics as the pursuit of strategies (whose outcomes are uncertain and which may be disruptive rather than functional to the integration of the social system). Thus investigating (and explaining) the pattern of imperialist expansion involves studying the strategies of both colonizers and colonized in a particular context. This also means that the integration of the world beyond Europe into the world-economy was (and remains) rather less complete and comprehensive than Wallerstein's account suggests. Secondly, it avoids economic reductionism by emphasizing that political strategies, and the resources on which political power depends, are not just economic but also cultural, military, patriarchal, racist, and so on. These other forms of power are qualitatively distinct from capitalist economic power and have different histories, geographies, preconditions and effects. In other words, imperialism was as much about strategies of cultural domination of the rest of the world as it was about strategies of economic exploitation and control.

Economic and military dimensions

The economic and military strategies through which Europe's overseas empires were put in place have been widely studied. In general, the opening-up of territory and the implementation of imperial government in Europe's overseas colonies was carried on by military, or quasi-military, means. Military strategies varied widely between different imperial powers. In the early phase of Iberian expansion in South America, the military campaigns were of crucial importance in wiping out existing forms of social and political organization. By contrast, in south Asia, the British exploited the *political* weakness of the Mughal state, and, while military activity was important at various times, the economic and administrative incorporation of local elites was also of crucial significance.

One of the standard accounts of European imperialism is provided by the historian D.K. Fieldhouse. Although it is clear that Europe gained massively in economic terms during the early phases of overseas expansion, Fieldhouse argues that Europe's later (nineteenth and early twentieth century) overseas empires were not subject to economic 'exploitation' by the imperial powers. While we do not entirely share this view, Fieldhouse is correct in suggesting that the later empires in tropical Africa and Asia were certainly not established initially *for the purpose* of economic profit-making:

> Modern empires were not artificially constructed economic machines. The second expansion of Europe was a complex historical process in which political, social and emotional forces in Europe and on the periphery were more influential than calculated imperialism. Individual colonies might serve an economic purpose; collectively no empire had any definable function, economic or otherwise. Empires represented only a particular phase in the ever-changing relationship of Europe with the rest of the world: analogies with industrial systems or investment in real estate were simply misleading.[24]

As he goes on to point out, however:

> though the colonial empires were undoubtedly functionless in origin, this is not to say that they did not later provide an economic return, a 'profit', to their owners. Certainly many colonial enthusiasts alleged that they could and did.[25]

Despite his doubts about the exploitative character of later imperial rule, Fieldhouse identifies six ways in which economic advantages can accrue from it, and these usefully summarize the economic strategies involved.[26]

(1) 'Looting' an occupied territory of its treasures. This occurred, for example, with the shipment of precious metals from Mexico and Peru.
(2) The transfer of colonial revenues to the metropolitan treasury.
(3) The transfer of money to the imperial metropolis in the form of 'interest on loans, payment for services rendered, the pensions and savings of colonial officials and the profits made by business firms'.[27]
(4) The imposition of unequal terms of trade on a colony.
(5) The exploitation of natural resources without corresponding compensation.
(6) The availability of higher rates of return on investments in the colonies than on investments at home.

This last aspect of imperial economics has been of particular significance because it was the focus of one of the earliest and most influential interpretations of imperialism: that of the Russian revolutionary leader, Vladimir Ilyich Lenin. Lenin defined imperialism in terms of a number of characteristics: (1) capital is exported from the imperial economies (instead of only finished manufactured goods); (2) production becomes concentrated in the hands of a group of large companies; (3) banking capital is merged with finance capital; (4) the world is divided between the imperial (capitalist) states; (5) imperialist expansion buys off social dissent at 'home'.[28] This formulation is interesting in the context of our framework because of the stress placed on strategic behaviour by state governments and capitalist enterprises. Imperialism is seen as a strategic response to particular problems faced by business in the wealthy 'core' countries. According to Lenin, these included the lack of markets for the output from increased production as well as social and political discontent.

According to Fieldhouse, the evidence relating to the existence or otherwise of these kinds of relationship is ambiguous. It is clear that the earlier period of imperialism, during the sixteenth, seventeenth and eighteenth-centuries, was much more significant economically than the later, nineteenth- and twentieth-century phase. Where profit-taking is in evidence, it is not clear, Fieldhouse suggests, whether it occurred because of imperialist government or in spite of it. In terms of political strategies, however, it is clear that overseas empires were supported by many politicians and industrialists 'at home' because of their perceived economic returns. It is also clear, however, that by the time formal imperialism reached its high point at the start of the twentieth century, the maintenance of elaborate colonial governments, administrations and security forces in Africa and Asia was rapidly becoming an economic drain on the European powers. This suggests that nineteenth-century expansion and the sustaining of imperial control involved a range of strategies other than purely economic ones.

Cultural and discursive dimensions

By contrast, *cultural* and *discursive* strategies of imperial domination have not been examined in the same detail until recently. This does not mean, however, that they were of any less consequence than those of a military or economic nature, not least because in many respects they continue to this day with the widespread stereotyping of the 'Third World' as degenerate, corrupt, incompetent and violent. Even the more humanitarian approaches to materially poor countries (such as those associated with some overseas aid) have the potential to be quite patronizing, as is exemplified in the often-used slogan 'helping them to help themselves'.

Discursive strategies are important because they embody particular understandings of the respective roles and natures of European and colonized people.[29] Such understandings can be necessary preconditions for military or economic exploitation. Thus it is considerably easier to kill someone if you have been brought up to see them as less than fully human, or as a member of an 'inferior' race. It may be easier to reorganize a system of production to appropriate profits 'back home' if local forms of industry are represented as less efficient or more primitive, regardless of their actual productivity.

However, the cultural relationship between 'the West and the rest'[30] was rather more ambiguous than this. It was not the case that the Europeans merely regarded themselves as 'superior' to other 'races'. The discursive strategies of imperialism depended on constructing 'the rest' as qualitatively different from 'the West', not only as inferior. One aspect of such strategies involved a discourse which contrasted a familiar, everyday 'West' with an exotic 'other'. Among other things, this involved sexual exoticism. For example, the 'Orient' is often represented as sexually degenerate, or the setting for exciting and exotic sexual encounters.

Anton Gill has charted the complex and ambiguous sexual discourses and practices of empire in his book *Ruling Passions* (1995), written to accompany a BBC television series of the same name. He writes of India:

> ... allure and repulsion sometimes went hand in hand. In the less hidebound eighteenth century, allure had the upper hand, and it maintained its supremacy for many – perhaps one could say for most – as long as the British were in India. For some it was a simple proposition. Edward Sellon, a British Indian Army officer of the 1840s, had no embarrassment about the joys of the east: 'I now commenced a regular course of fucking with native women. They understand in perfection all the arts and wiles of love, are capable of gratifying any tastes, and in face and figure they are unsurpassed by any women in the world ... It is impossible to describe the enjoyment I have had in the arms of these syrens ...'[31]

In these discourses, Western men were presented as the very embodiment of virile, upright manhood. In the early 1920s, a small book appeared called *The Romance of Empire*. Aimed at British schoolboys, it seems to have been popular, as the edition Joe found in a second-hand bookshop shows that 24,000 copies had been printed. The book opens with a Preface in which the author, Philip Gibbs, claims that the 'making of the British Empire has been a great adventure of which we may well be proud'. It was, he continues:

> an adventure in which the manhood of the race has proved its mettle, time and time again, through many centuries and in many lands; an adventure in which men have spilt their blood freely, with a genial courage, with a really rollicking spirit of gallantry, and with a fine carelessness of danger and death. ... Not yet has the time come when the audacity of a brave man in a tight place, the steady nerve of a strong man in a dangerous encounter, the quick wit of a gallant fellow in a difficult enterprise, shall not be honoured and admired.[32]

By contrast, the world beyond Europe was often presented in feminized forms. Early images depicting the initial encounters between the West and the New World, for example, often showed America as a woman. For the West, which prided itself on its Enlightened, masculine reason, this

symbolism not only made the New World seem inferior, socially and culturally to the West, but also served to emphasize the exoticism, fertility and
unknowability with which European accounts of the colonial world were
often saturated.

It was through the discursive elements of imperialist strategies that imperialist practices were justified and legitimated to the colonizers as well as to the
colonized. However, the strategies were far from being all one way, and wherever imperialism went, resistance followed.

Anti-colonial strategies and the end of the formal empires

Western imperialism was thus produced through a diversity of strategies,
some military, some economic, some discursive. Appropriately enough, it was
opposed and challenged by a similarly wide range of strategies and tactics on
the part of colonized peoples. Since they were undertaken, by definition, by
groups and individuals who occupied subordinate positions in the social hierarchy, and who did not always have any need or wish to document their activities, our knowledge of the forms of opposition to colonial rule is less detailed
than that of the strategies of the rulers.

For the most part, therefore, the accounts we are left to work with tend to
be told from the perspective of the colonizing power. Even where this gives
due weight to the process and practices of anti-colonial resistance, the
episodes referred to tend inevitably to be those which loomed largest in the
minds and lives of the colonizers, such as those in which violence was
involved, for example. Hence the armed Indian rebellion of 1857 (referred to
as the Indian 'Mutiny' by British imperialists) gained an especially prominent
place in the official history of the British Empire. We do not mean to down-
play the significance of such events, and armed revolutions were central to the
ending of many cases of colonial rule. The fact that they dominate the history
books, however, obscures other more mundane and everyday, but often
potent, forms of resistance to imperial rule.

In the case of Kenya, in East Africa, Anton Gill documents the following
story from 1907, retold by the daughter of the President of the Kenyan
Colonists' Association:

> I think it was my mother and her sister-in-law – my father's oldest sister –
> who were trying to take a couple of rickshaws from the centre of Nairobi
> to go back to their houses in Muthaiga, and my rather tiresome aunt obvi-
> ously said something that upset a rickshaw boy and he let go of his han-
> dles, with the result that my aunt was thrown out of the rickshaw
> backwards, and of course in those days that was an absolutely unthink-
> able thing to do.[33]

The brutality of the subsequent punishment meted out to the 'offender', and
to thousands like him in similar circumstances, helps to explain the resentment in Kenya which later led to the violent uprisings of the so-called

'Mau-Mau' rebellions. Even an otherwise sympathetic commentator such as Victor Kiernan recoils at the anti-colonial strategies of Mau-Mau:

> Because the fighters came mostly from the poorest, most illiterate strata, with scarcely any leadership of more modern outlook, the rising took on the aspect, like many earlier ones in Afro-Asia, of a religious or magical cult. 'Mau-Mau' had some grotesque features which made it easy to denigrate the whole movement as a relapse into an abysmal past. Rebel weapons were at first not much more up to date, a few home-made guns the best of them. Nothing like a regular force emerged from the guerrilla bands.[34]

Yet, from the point of view of the participants, the Mau-Mau uprisings, and the rituals and oath-taking surrounding them, seemed very different. According to one of those involved, they reflected everyday aspects of Kikuyu life:

> The *Muma wa Thenge* (the he-goat oath) is a prominent feature of our social life, an integral part of the ceremonies uniting partners in marriages, in the exchange or sale of land (before the Europeans came, when land was plentiful, the sale of land was almost unknown), or in transactions involving cattle or goats. The warriors also took an oath, known as *Muma wa Aanake* (the oath of the warriors), to bind them before going on a raid. The purpose of all these oaths was to give those participating a feeling of mutual respect, unity, shared love, to strengthen their relationship, to keep away any bad feelings, and to prevent disputes.[35]

In due course, African demands for independence, supported by more or less violent campaigns of resistance, began to be met. India had already gained its independence in 1947, following a prolonged campaign of civil disobedience and unrest, which was largely, although not wholly non-violent, in line with the philosophy (drawn from Indian religious teaching) of Mahatma Gandhi (see Figure 9.3). France lost her major overseas possessions in wars during the 1940s and 1950s.[36] Portugal, with the longest-standing imperial territories in Africa, held out the longest, and with great bitterness. However, by the mid-1970s, Africa had seen the back of Portugal too. With the ending of white minority rule in South Africa in the early 1990s, five centuries of formal white domination of Africa came to an end. According to D.K. Fieldhouse:

> Nothing in the history of the modern colonial empires was more remarkable than the speed with which they disappeared. In 1939 they were at their peak: by 1981 they had practically ceased to exist.[37]

Postcolonialism

A dilemma

The ending of formal political control is only part of the picture, however. Other commentators have remarked on the process of informal imperialism

Figure 8.3   Statue of Mahatma Gandhi, Tavistock Square, London
© Matthew Bolton, 2005

in which economic advantages continue to accrue to the metropolitan power in the absence of direct rule.[38] Here we want to focus once more on the issue of the discursive construction of colonial relations and conclude the chapter by considering the comparatively recent development of postcolonialism as an intellectual and political position.[39]

In writing the previous section, we found that one of the difficulties with trying to identify 'anti-colonial strategies' is that they tend to involve forcing the histories and geographies of colonized peoples into the story as told by the West. This problem has been considered in detail by Partha Chatterjee, an Indian political philosopher. Chatterjee argues that in a situation of imperial domination, even discourses of resistance and nationalist dissent are caught up in the Western world view which they seek to repudiate.[40] Derek Gregory makes a similar point:

As I understand it, Indian historiography has been dominated by two (not one) 'imperial histories'. On the one side is the modern, secular history that the British brought to the subcontinent, through which India is ushered from brigandage and feudalism into capitalist modernity under the tutelage of the Raj. On the other side is a nationalist historiography, which casts a native Indian elite in an heroic role, wresting the state apparatus from the imperialists and completing the political trajectory inaugurated by the British.[41]

Although the two versions of history are opposed to one another, argues Gregory, from a broader perspective they are both telling the same story – of the movement of India towards a modern, ordered future. Neither, therefore, has much room for alternative ways of being and becoming, which fall outside the imperial story altogether.

Postcolonialism and geography

We referred above to the cultural practices of the Kikuyu people of Kenya. It is clear from the first-hand account of oath-taking that one of the things which made such resistance effective was a refusal to assimilate to the European world view, which regarded such activities as barbaric. It is this difficult and complicated relationship between the ways of being, doing, thinking and speaking of the West, on the one hand, and of the people of its former colonies on the other, which is the focus of postcolonialism.

Postcolonial writers and thinkers argue, among other things, that formal decolonization is not enough in itself. They suggest that there was much more to imperialism than political and military control, and that the domination of much of the world by Europe was also a domination by European ways of thinking and of understanding that world. As the historical geographer Stephen Legg neatly argues, the end of formal occupation 'has not signalled the withdrawal of colonial categories, procedures and technologies of rule, nor has it beheaded Europe as the sovereign subject to which many postcolonial histories and geographies are constructed'.[42] One postcolonial writer, the novelist Ngugi wa Thiong'o, captures this postcolonial perspective in the title of his book, *Decolonizing the Mind*.[43]

Jonathan Crush suggests that there are four elements to current attempts to write geography from a postcolonial standpoint:

> the aims of a post-colonial geography might be defined as: the unveiling of geographical complicity in colonial dominion over space; the character of geographical representation in colonial discourse; the de-linking of local geographical enterprise from metropolitan theory and its totalizing systems of representation; and the recovery of those hidden spaces occupied, and invested with their own meaning, by the colonial underclasses.[44]

Let us briefly unpack each of these in turn. The injunction to examine 'geographical complicity in colonial dominion over space' implies that geographers should critically consider the ways in which geographical knowledge and skills have been (and continue to be) used to implant colonialism and imperialism in practice. Exposing 'geographical representation in colonial discourse' means showing how the discourses of colonialism involved a particular understanding of geography and particular depictions of places and regions. This has been an especially fertile area of research for geographers who have drawn on postcolonial theorists such as Edward Said and Gayatri Chakravorty Spivak to chart the systemematic spatial inclusions and exclusions of colonial rule. In his text *The Colonial Present*, Derek Gregory explores the ongoing implications of colonial imaginary geographies as they have shaped recent military incursions in Afghanistan, Iraq and Palestine.[45] Through rich historical and geopolitical narratives, Gregory argues that what he terms 'colonial couplets' of 'us' and 'them', 'civilization' and 'barbarism', are not 'mirrors of the world',[46] but rather performative acts, as they make the world through a series of representations. Gregory's work therefore draws our attention to the persistent and productive nature of colonial discourses, as they continue to shape the world in the twenty-first century.

Crush's third element is the 'de-linking of local geographical enterprise from metropolitan theory and its totalizing systems of representation'. The proposal here challenges the ways in which geography itself has been subject to colonialism. Perspectives, theories and frameworks developed in the West are widely adopted by geographers working throughout the world. Postcolonialism suggests that geographical knowledge developed in different local contexts should not be based on the assumption that Western frameworks of understanding are the only, or the best, ways of describing and understanding the world. For example, Crush states that in South Africa, until recently, even radical geographers have tended to adopt theoretical ideas, such as world-systems theory and structural Marxism, which were developed in Europe and North America. Lately, he suggests that this situation has improved with geographers at three universities in particular shaking off some of these 'colonial' theories.[47] The asymmetry of knowledge production between the so-called core and periphery was further developed in the historian Dipesh Chakrabarty's *Provincializing Europe: Postcolonial Thought and Historical Difference* (2000).[48] Chakrabarty critiques the assumed universalism of European academic practices, in contrast to the supposedly provincial and backward nature of knowledge production in former colonies. Referring to European scholars, he suggests:

'They' produce their work in relative ignorance of non-Western histories, and this does not seem to affect the quality of their work. This is a gesture, however, that 'we' cannot return. We cannot even afford an equality of symmetry of ignorance at this level without appearing 'old-fashioned' or 'outdated.'[49]

According to Crush, the fourth component of postcolonialism in geography is the 'recovery of those hidden spaces occupied, and invested with their own meaning, by the colonial underclasses'. What are involved here are attempts to write geography in ways which give full weight to the experience of those who suffered under colonialism and to the places in which they live and work. This might involve, for example, considering the lives, places and political strategies of Kikuyu people on their own terms, rather than from the perspective of the imperial rulers. Crush reports that in South Africa, geographers' moves away from Euro-American theoretical perspectives has been accompanied by an increased interest in, and involvement with, local people and local political struggles.[50]

Conclusion

This chapter has highlighted the historical roots of past European imperial practices, but the point of this discussion is not to reproduce the notion that colonialism and imperialism should be understood as an historical relic. Rather, we have sought to identify the significant legacies and continuities in colonial relationships, knowledges and practices of rule. We would highlight two points in particular that are emerging from recent postcolonial scholarship. First, colonialism was not simply a form of territorial domination. If it were understood in these terms, then the practice of decolonization would simply involve the removal of colonial state bureaucracies. Rather, colonization also involved the domination of forms of knowledge production – the writing of history and geography has been from the perspective of the colonizer rather than the colonized. Scholars of postcolonialism have traced the mechanisms, rules and tacit understandings that have served to reproduce these colonial forms of domination through to the present. As Ngugi wa Thiong'o suggests, the challenge for Western forms of knowledge production is the decolonization of the mind. The secondly, and closely related, legacy of the colonial past is the continuing imperial practices of powerful state actors in the present day. In the current political moment, we hear renewed talk of 'Empire'. The US-led military intervention in Iraq in 2003 was explained by many observers an act of US imperialism.[51] As Derek Gregory[52] has identified, these practices are reliant upon colonial categories of thought: of 'friend of freedom' and 'terrorist'; 'either you are with us or against us'. In dividing the world spatially into friend and enemy, the administration of George W. Bush has drawn on the power of *geopolitics* to legitimize its military strategy. In the following and final chapter, we explore the production of (and resistance to) this form of knowledge production and the inherently spatial nature of its operation.

Notes

1. 'Indigenous people' is used as a collective term for Australian Aborigines (indigenous peoples who live on the Australian landmass) and Torres Strait Islanders (indigenous peoples who live on the Torres Strait Islands between Australia and Papua New Guinea).
2. National Inquiry into the Separation of Aboriginal and Torres Strait Islander Children from Their Families (1997) *Bringing Them Home*. Available at: www.humanrights.gov.au/social_justice/bth_report/index.html (accessed 18/07/08).

3. Noyce, Phillip (2002) *Rabbit-Proof Fence*. New York: Miramax Films.
4. Elson, Diane (1984) 'Imperialism', in Gregor McLennan, David Held and Stuart Hall (eds), *The Idea of the Modern State*. Milton Keynes: Open University Press. pp. 154–82.
5. De Schweinitz Jr, Karl (1983) *The Rise and Fall of British India: Imperialism as Inequality*. London: Methuen. p. 39.
6. Boorstin, Daniel J. (1986) *The Discoverers*. Harmondsworth: Penguin. p. 175.
7. Wolf, Eric R. (1982) *Europe and the People without History*. Berkeley, CA: University of California Press. pp. 131–57.
8. Livingstone, David (1992) *The Geographical Tradition: Episodes in the History of a Contested Enterprise*. Oxford: Blackwell. pp. 216–59.
9. Stoddart, David (1986) *On Geography and Its History*. Oxford: Blackwell. p. 29. Emphasis added.
10. Stoddart, *On Geography*. p. 33.
11. Semple, Ellen Churchill (1911) *The Influences of Geographic Environment, on the Basis of Ratzel's System of Anthropo-geography*. London: Constable.
12. Livingstone, *The Geographical Tradition*. p. 222.
13. Livingstone, *The Geographical Tradition*. pp. 224–5. Livingstone is quoting from A. Austin Miller (1931) *Climatology*. London: Methuen. p. 2.
14. Griffith Taylor, T. (1957) 'Racial geography', in T. Griffith Taylor (ed.), *Geography in the Twentieth Century*. New York: Philosophical Library. pp. 455, 454. (Quoted in Livingstone, *The Geographical Tradition*. p. 230.)
15. Carter, Paul (1987) *The Road to Botany Bay*. London: Faber & Faber. p. 113.
16. Carter, *The Road to Botany Bay*. p. 67.
17. Driver, Felix (1992) 'Geography's empire: histories of geographical knowledge', *Environment and Planning D: Society and Space,* 10: 23–40; Godlewska, Anne and Smith, Neil (eds) (1994), *Geography and Empire*. Oxford: Blackwell.
18. See Wallerstein, Immanuel (2004) *World-Systems Analysis: An Introduction*. Durham, NC: Duke University Press.
19. Taylor, Peter (1989b) 'The error of developmentalism in human geography', in Derek Gregory and Rex Walford (eds), *Horizons in Human Geography*. Basingstoke: Macmillan. pp. 303–19.
20. Rostow, Walt Whitman (1960) *The Stages of Economic Growth*. Cambridge: Cambridge University Press.
21. Giddens, Anthony (1985) *The Nation-state and Violence*. Cambridge: Polity Press. pp. 161–71.
22. Giddens, *The Nation-state*. pp. 167–8.
23. Peter Taylor couches his account of world-systems analysis in a way which avoids functionalist phrasing. For example, in the second edition (1989a) of *Political Geography* he writes that the three-tier systems helps to stabilize the system and prevents confrontation, and that therefore 'those at the top will always manoeuvre for the "creation" of a three-tier structure whereas those at the bottom will emphasize the two tiers of "them and us"' (p. 10). However, while such 'divide and rule' strategies are undoubtedly pursued by powerful groups, it is difficult to see how they could work at the scale of the world-economy which, by definition, is marked by the fragmentation and distribution of political power among a plethora of states.
24. Fieldhouse, D.K. (1981) *The Colonial Empires: A Comparative Survey from the Eighteenth Century*. Basingstoke: Macmillan. p. 381.
25. Fieldhouse, *The Colonial Empires*. p. 381.
26. Fieldhouse, *The Colonial Empires*. pp. 382–6.
27. Fieldhouse, *The Colonial Empires*. p. 382.
28. Lenin, V.I. (1915) *Imperialism: The Highest Form of Capitalism*. Moscow: Foreign Languages Publishing House.
29. Mangan, J.A. (ed.) (1990) *Making Imperial Mentalities: Socialisation and British Imperialism*. Manchester: Manchester University Press.
30. Hall, Stuart (1992) 'The West and the rest: discourse and power', in Stuart Hall and Bram Gieben (eds), *Formations of Modernity*. Cambridge: Polity Press. pp. 275–331.
31. Gill, Anton (1995) *Ruling Passions: Sex, Race and Empire*. London: BBC Books. p. 37.

32. Gibbs, Philip (undated) *The Romance of Empire*. London: Hutchinson. p. 5.

33. Quoted in Gill, *Ruling Passions*. p. 114.

34. Kiernan, V.G. (1982) *European Empires from Conquest to Collapse, 1815–1960*. Leicester: Leicester University Press. p. 221.

35. Mwangi Kariuki, Josiah (1970) 'The "Mau-Mau" oath', in Elie Kedourie (ed.), *Nationalism in Asia and Africa*. London: Weidenfeld & Nicolson. pp. 462–71. p. 469.

36. Clayton, Anthony (1994) *The Wars of French Decolonization*. London: Longman.

37. Fieldhouse, *The Colonial Empires*, p. 395.

38. See, for example, Frank, A.G. (1969) *Capitalism and Underdevelopment in Latin America*. New York: Monthly Review Press.

39. Corbridge, Stuart (1993) 'Marxisms, modernities, and moralities: development praxis and the claims of distant strangers', *Environment and Planning D: Society and Space*, 11: 449–72; Gregory, Derek (1994) *Geographical Imaginations*. Oxford: Blackwell. pp. 133–205; Mitchell, Timothy (1988) *Colonizing Egypt*. Cambridge: Cambridge University Press; Said, Edward (1978) *Orientalism: Western Conceptions of the Orient*. Harmondsworth: Penguin, and (1993) *Culture and Imperialism*. London: Chatto & Windus; Spivak, Gayatri Chakravorty (1988) 'Can the subaltern speak?', in Cary Nelson and Lawrence Grossberg (eds), *Marxism and the Interpretation of Culture*. Chicago: University of Illinois Press. pp. 271–313; Young, Robert (1990) *White Mythologies: Writing History and the West*. London: Routledge.

40. Chatterjee, Partha (1986) *Nationalist Thought and the Colonial World: A Derivative Discourse?* London: Zed Books.

41. Gregory, *Geographical Imaginations*. p. 183.

42. Legg, S. (2007) 'Beyond the European province: Foucault and postcolonialism', in Jeremy Crampton and Stuart Elden (eds), *Space, Knowledge and Power: Foucault and Geography*. Aldershot: Ashgate. pp. 265–70. p. 265.

43. Ngugi wa Thiong'o (1986) *Decolonizing the Mind*. London: James Currey.

44. Crush, Jonathan (1994) 'Postcolonialism, de-colonization, and geography', in Anne Godlewska and Neil Smith (eds), *Geography and Empire*. Oxford: Blackwell. pp. 333–50. p. 336–7.

45. Gregory, Derek (2004) *The Colonial Present*. Oxford: Blackwell.

46. Gregory, *The Colonial Present*. p. 121.

47. Crush, 'Postcolonialism, de-colonization, and geography'. p. 340.

48. Chakrabarty, Dipesh (2000) *Provincializing Europe: Postcolonial Thought and Historical Difference*. Princeton, NJ: Princeton University Press.

49. Chakrabarty, *Provincializing Europe*. p. 28.

50. Crush, 'Postcolonialism, de-colonization, and geography'. p. 341.

51. See Harvey, D. (2003) *The New Imperialism*. Oxford: Oxford University Press; Retort (2005) *Afflicted Powers Capital and Spectacle in a New Age of War*. London: Verso; Smith, Neil (2005) *The Endgame of Globalization*. New York: Routledge.

52. Gregory, *The Colonial Present*.

Further reading

The nature of geography's imperial past intersects with the historical, political, economic and cultural sub-disciplines of geography. This broad canvas has been captured in a number of authoritative texts. We would highlight two in particular:

Godlewska, Anne and Smith, Neil (eds) (1994) *Geography and Empire*. Oxford: Blackwell.

Livingstone, David (1992) *The Geographical Tradition: Episodes in the History of a Contested Enterprise*. Oxford: Blackwell.

Inquiry into the geographies of postcolonialism has grown significantly in recent years. A number of special journal issues provide helpful syntheses of these empirical and theoretical developments. For example, in 2003, James Sidaway, Tim Bunnell and Brenda Yeoh edited a special issue of the *Singapore Journal of Tropical Geography* (volume 24, issue 3) and in 2006 Joanne Sharp and John Briggs edited a special issue exploring new dialogues between postcolonialism and development geographies in *The Geographical Journal* (volume 172, issue 1).

In addition, it will be important to consult the key research monographs that have stimulated much of this renewed reflection:

Chakrabarty, Dipesh (2000) *Provincializing Europe: Postcolonial Thought and Historical Difference.* **Princeton, NJ: Princeton University Press.**

Gregory, Derek (2004) *The Colonial Present.* **Oxford: Blackwell.**

Finally, there has been a wealth of recent books attempting to trace and critique the role of the USA in the world today. Many have depicted its foreign policy as a new example of imperialist practice. The following books provide a succinct and provocative account of this position:

Harvey, D. (2003) *The New Imperialism.* **Oxford: Oxford University Press.**

Retort (2005) *Afflicted Powers Capital and Spectacle in a New Age of War.* **London: Verso.**

NINE

Geopolitics and Anti-geopolitics

In March 2003 one of the authors of this book (Alex) was in a dentist's waiting room and flicked through the pages of men's magazine *Esquire*. Alongside articles on the film stars Benicio Del Toro and Connie Nielsen there was an article entitled *The Pentagon's New Map*[1] by Thomas Barnett, a Senior Strategic Researcher in the Center for Naval Warfare Studies, US Naval War College, Newport, Rhode Island. Barnett's article was a rallying cry for military intervention in Iraq (which had started around the middle of this month but after the article would have already been in print) and a celebration of the USA's opportunity to reorganize global security in an era of globalization. The article argued that the world is divided into a *Functioning Core* (USA, Canada, parts of South America, Oceania, Western Europe, China and India) and a *Non-Integrating Gap* (Africa, Central America, the Middle East and South East Asia). The task, according to Barnett, is for the USA to use its security expertise and military might to 'shrink the Gap'. The article was accompanied by high-quality maps detailing the specific territorialization of the Core and the Gap, and the subsequent military interventions that are scattered on the line that intersects the two. It is a testament to the rapidly changing times that much of Barnett's argument now seems naive or misjudged. For example, on America's capacity to export security, Barnett suggests that the USA is 'the only nation on earth capable of exporting security in a sustained fashion, and we have a very good track record of doing it'.

But we do not open with Barnett's essay in order to provide a critique (many excellent examples of such an activity already exist[2], but rather to reflect on the significance of this essay as an object for popular consumption. Barnett's thesis is indicative of a broader set of popular narratives of globalization that attempt to make sense of contemporary politics through simply cartographic stories. In an era of US anxiety over perceived terrorist threats and its position within a mythical international community, such stories provide reassuring clarity concerning the international system. But Barnett's essay is not written to simply reassure law-makers or elites in government. The location of the essay in a magazine such as *Esquire* speaks of the public appetite for uncomplicated ideas that clarify the position of states. Consequently, the positioning of Barnett's essay points to renewed interest in *geopolitics,* or the geographical dimensions of state power. In addition, the essay highlights the importance of *ideas* to geopolitics; it is a sphere of political geography that has thrived on the imagination of the world as divided in often creative and contested ways.

OVERVIEW

This chapter explores the concepts of geopolitics and anti-geopolitics. Our critical analysis explores how geopolitical ideas are produced, why they endure and how they are resisted. Over the era of the 'War on Terror' and the associated military interventions in Afghanistan and Iraq, this is a topic that has risen to prominence. Articles examining the geopolitical imaginations and performances of political leaders are regular features in the pages of journals such as *Political Geography* and *Geopolitics.* But the concept of geopolitics has a far longer lineage, emerging as a term in Scandinavian political geography in the late nineteenth century, and further popularized after the First World War through the work of German political scientist Karl Haushofer. Following a brief introduction, we use the first section of the chapter to explore these historical antecedents. Through this historical narrative it becomes clear that geopolitical ideas are grounded in the political and geographical contexts within which they emerge. This attention to the situated nature of geopolitical ideas is explored in greater detail in the second section through the concept of *critical geopolitics,* a perspective that emerged in the 1980s and 1990s and is concerned with exposing the power/knowledge relationships within which geopolitical ideas are embedded. Rather than natural descriptions of the world, scholars of this critical school have identified geopolitical ideas as partial, parochial and grounded in self-interest. We explore this viewpoint through empirical examples of the Cold War and international intervention in Yugoslavia. In the final section, we examine scholarship concerned with anti-geopolitics, or a perspective that challenges established geopolitical scripts from subaltern or disempowered positions.

Introduction

'I have an idea.' These words seem so familiar as to be banal. We all have ideas, thoughts regarding how to proceed in the world, how to respond to particular problems or alternatives to prevailing conditions. It is an initial idea of what would improve her or his life that leads a candidate to apply for a job; suddenly deciding to go to the cinema on a particular evening can be classed as an idea on the 'spur of a moment'. These examples locate ideas as central to practice: ideas are ways of narrating and interpreting the world, of predicting the future on account of past and present circumstances. But we do not simply generate ideas; we are also shaped by the ideas of others. They are the frameworks upon which strategies are formed, policies are resolved, and interventions are made. This book has argued for the importance of social and cultural theory to the workings of political geography. In doing so, we are promoting the importance of the ideas of scholars and intellectuals to our understandings of the relationship between space and politics. As we saw in Chapter 1, politics is occupied with the tension and negotiation between different ideas on and different attitudes to how the world is divided, distributed and organized. Ideas form the framework for political action. People often adjudicate 'good' or 'bad' ideas. But we must be sensitive to such apparently universal adjudications of the quality of an idea. There is no neutral standpoint at which an idea may be judged; there are no natural criteria for what constitutes a good or bad idea. Instead, we need to be attentive to the unequal power of the production of ideas. Ideas emerge from different people and institutions to suit their interests and, depending on their position in hierarchies of authority, their persuasiveness, their ability to communicate their idea and their similarity to the ideas of others, some ideas will be successful and will change the world while others will be forgotten.

This chapter is concerned with ideas about world politics. Geopolitics has, over the last century or so, risen to prominence as a term indicating ideas about the ordering, arrangement and division of the surface of the earth. While in some uses the emphasis of geopolitics seems to focus on practices – the invasion of a country or a diplomatic standoff – these actions are only justified or interpreted through geopolitical ideas. We are constantly engaging in geopolitics: when we talk of the 'Third World' as a space in need of aid or humanitarian relief, when we discuss the enlargement of the European Union as an ongoing political project, or when we refer to other states as 'allies' or 'enemies'. In so doing, we are ordering the world, making it meaningful through a practice of labelling and communication. As these examples suggest, and considering the prominence of the state as the primary territorialization of political space (see Chapter 2), this process of ordering has often emphasized state competition and the geographical dimensions of state power.[3]

Geopolitical ideas therefore involve numerous metaphors of space, of heartlands and rims, cores and peripheries, buffers and barriers. The terms of geopolitics are so common that we often take them for granted, but each conveys a particular idea about how the world is or should be organized. It is our task as scholars of Political Geography to investigate the production of these ideas and how they reflect prevailing structures of power. In rejecting taken-for-granted assumptions concerning geopolitical labels, we are adopting a *critical geopolitics* perspective, a position popularized in the 1980s and early 1990s by political geographers such as John Agnew, Gearoid Ó Tuathail and Simon Dalby. As we discussed in Chapter 1, this approach was animated by the 'cultural turn' experienced in the wider geographical discipline, where the influence of postmodernism had widened the methodological and theoretical scope of geographical inquiry. Specifically, the work of continental philosophers such as Friedrich Nietzsche, Michel Foucault and Jacques Derrida had led to the questioning of essential truths and the rejection of grand historical or theoretical narratives. One clear postmodern objective was to deconstruct texts to expose the underlying power/knowledge relationships. Thus *critical geopolitics* perspectives view geopolitics as a discursive practice by which intellectuals and politicians '"spatialize" international politics and present it as a "world" characterized by particular types of places, people and dramas'.[4] In taking seriously the discourses of geopolitics, scholars have been interested in questions of representation: critiquing the practices and images through which individuals and groups convey particular ideas about the world.

As with all the terms confronted in this book, geopolitics has its own history and geography, though perhaps, more than others, geopolitics is intricately entwined in the political contexts in which it has emerged. As we will see, one formative moment in the history of geopolitics was its connection to the expansionist policies of Nazi Germany through the work of Karl Haushofer. Similarly, the geopolitical imagination of American geographer Isaiah Bowman was shaped by his concern for America's national interest in the early part of the twentieth century. Consequently, Bowman's ideas influenced the outcome of the Versailles Peace Treaty following the First World War and contributed to the establishment of the League of Nations. We should also note that the close correspondence between ideas and real-world events is also reflected in the rise of critical geopolitics. This field of inquiry increased markedly around the time of the end of the Cold War in 1989–91, a period when the established divisions of the world were changing and a new era of uncertainty and reappraisal was taking place. Similarly, recent interest in geopolitics in both the media and academy can be traced to the terrorist attacks of 11 September 2001, events that were interpreted by US President George W. Bush as ushering in 'a different world ... where freedom itself is under attack'.[5] We seem to be living through an era of both heightened geopolitical sloganeering and increased inquiry into the production of geopolitical visions. Geopolitics, then, may be about ideas, but these are ideas that are grounded in real-world events.

Classical foundations

The term 'geopolitics' entered the scholarly lexicon through the work of the Swedish political scientist Rudolf Kjellen in 1899. For Kjellen, the elision of geography and politics in the term 'geopolitics' was a useful means of indicating the geographical base of the state, in particular its natural endowment and resources.[6] In Kjellen's thought, the physical geography of the state reflected its power potential. This language tapped into a wider European school of political geography that was growing in influence and stature at this time. In particular, Kjellen's ideas draw on the scholarship of German political geographer Friedrich Ratzel (1844–1904), whose text *Politishe Geographie* (1897)[7] applied the theory of evolution to the behaviour of states. Though similar to Darwin's *On the Origin of Species* (1859)[8], this approach can be more correctly identified as Neo-Lamarckian. In place of the randomness of the natural selection process in Darwin's work, Lamarckian biology stresses the direct influence of the environment over the evolutionary process. Ratzel suggested that the state can be understood as a living organism, striving with and against others to grow and develop. In doing so, Ratzel described the state's imperative for *lebensraum* (living space), arguing that stronger states should expand territorially into areas that were not exploited efficiently by their current residents.[9]

Three points can be made regarding this early scholarship. First, Kjellen's work draws attention to the centrality of the state to geopolitical analysis.

Early geopoliticians were interested in the threats and opportunities facing states, a point that emphasizes the dominance of the state as the primary unit of political territory at the end of the nineteenth century. More specifically, this focus on the threats and opportunities facing states should be understood as a specific response to growing anxieties in Western Europe at the end of an era of territorial expansion through colonization. The growing uncertainty over the future relationships between states in Western Europe promoted scholarly study of the nature of international relations. As we see later in the chapter, it has been argued that this focus on the antagonistic relationships between states reflects the underlying realist philosophy of early work in geopolitics, where international relations are characterized by the struggle between competing sovereign states.

Secondly, this early geopolitics linked the natural environment with political potential. The possibilities for the future of a state were closely connected to its resources, space for growth and climate. The neo-Lamarckian perspective served to emphasize the role of environmental factors in shaping the evolutionary process, a relationship we discussed in Chapter 8. This connection between climate and human development was further developed through the work of environmental determinists, who argued that climate and environmental factors are the key determinants to human history and geography. Central figures in the field of environmental determinism, such as Ellen Churchill Semple (1863–1932), attempted to develop Ratzel's theories through empirical studies of the relationship between climate and race. This work was heralded at the time for providing a scientific justification for the supremacy of white European races and the naturalness of imperialism. It has subsequently been strongly criticized for legitimizing colonialism, overt racism and ethnocentrism.

Thirdly, while interested in the nature of states, early geopolitical texts exhibited an ambitious commitment to theorizing at a global scale. These early texts sought to reject the subjective and particular, and instead develop a *science* of international relations. This is a reflection of two interconnected aspects of the historical period in which geopolitical ideas emerged. First, this was a key moment in the expansion of universities and the institutionalization of geography as a discipline. Geographers Sara O'Hara and Mike Heffernan argue that the emergence of geopolitics as a discrete body of knowledge is a reflection of the academic colonization of pre-existing activities conducted in the fields of government and commerce.[10] Secondly, the late nineteenth century was a high-point for modernity. Though subject to almost infinite interpretations, modernity can be classified as an era that celebrated the triumph of the human mind over the chaos of nature. Modernist theory focused on totality and synthesis, the ability for the social scientist to cast her or his (though it was more often his) expert gaze over the world and theorize accordingly. It is perhaps this technological and epistemological self-confidence that allowed the concept of geopolitics to emerge as a field of knowledge production.

We can witness these three aspects of the classical foundations of geopolitics in the work of three scholars from the early twentieth century, Sir Halford Mackinder (1861–1947), Karl Haushofer (1869–1948) and Isaiah Bowman (1878–1950).

Sir Halford Mackinder

Sir Halford Mackinder was a key figure in the institutionalization of geography in the UK and a central figure in the history of geopolitics (though he did not use the term himself). Mackinder was the first dedicated scholar of geography at a UK university when he was appointed as a Reader at Oxford University in 1887. His published work is concerned with attempting to map the opportunities and threats facing Britain in what he termed a 'post-Columbian era' – a reference to the end of the 'Colombian age' of European exploration and expansion lasting from the voyages of Columbus in the fifteenth century to the scramble for Africa in the late nineteenth century. In these new historical circumstances, he saw geographical knowledge as a powerful tool in maintaining Britain's pre-eminent role in the world.

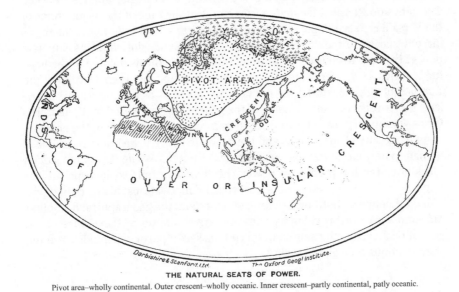

THE NATURAL SEATS OF POWER.

Pivot area–wholly continental. Outer crescent–wholly oceanic. Inner crescent–partly continental, patly oceanic.

Figure 9.1   The Natural Seats of Power by Halford Mackinder. Reproduced with permission of the Royal Geographical Society (with IBG)

Mackinder is best known for his heartland thesis. This work, originally published in 1904 as 'The geographical pivot of history', argued that the world could be divided into three regions that reflected their differential power potential: the pivot area (renamed in later work 'the heartland'); the inner crescent; and the outer or insular crescent (see Figure 9.1).[11] Though subject to alteration over his lifetime, Mackinder first identified the Eurasian landmass as the 'geographical pivot', an area that was inaccessible to the naval might of the British Empire and consequently posed a threat to its pre-eminence. The potential of the pivot/heartland lay in its resources. Once covered by a network of railways, Mackinder felt that this region will wield unparalleled military and economic power. Mackinder's vision thus posed a clear warning to the powerful states and empires of the early twentieth century, such as Britain. Refining his thoughts in his major work, *Democratic Ideals and Reality* (1919), he condensed his thesis of threat:

> Who rules East Europe commands the Heartland;
> Who rules the Heartland commands the world-island;
> Who rules the World-Island commands the world.[12]

This may strike the reader as a simplistic invocation of the relationship between geography and power, but we must place Mackinder's thoughts in context. Mackinder was a strong advocate for sustaining the power of the British Empire (he would go on to fight for this cause as a British MP and later as the chairman of the Imperial Economic Committee), and consequently his ideas must be seen as attempts to simplify the complexity of state competition to address what he felt was the key threat: a strategic alliance between Germany and Russia. Mackinder was writing at the time of the negotiations of the Versailles Peace Treaty at the end of the First World War, hence his thesis directly speaks to the wider danger of German expansion and Russian state power. In order to counter this threat, Mackinder's thesis pointed to the need for a series of 'buffer states' occupying a position between Germany and Russia. Though Mackinder did not describe his work as geopolitics, his heartland thesis reflects many aspects of the geopolitics pioneered by Kjellen. His thesis was underpinned by an interest in interstate competition, the environmental capacity of such states and the desire to construct a grand narrative of human potential based on geographical factors. While we can criticize Mackinder for his predictive power (he famously fails to incorporate the implications of air power) or his imperialistic motivations, his work had profound influence on both British foreign policy and the geographical discipline. Mackinder's work provides us with an early example of the nature of the geopolitical gaze – the self-confidence to assert a particular model of interstate relations on a global scale.

Karl Haushofer

The work of German scholar Karl Haushofer built on the work of Mackinder to cultivate a body of work under the banner of *Geopolitik*. Haushofer spent an early part of his career as an officer in the German army but following the First World War he took a lectureship in political geography at Munich University, rising to a professor in 1933. In 1924 he established *Zeitschrift für Geopolitik* (*Journal of Geopolitics*), a journal whose pages were devoted to developing the work of Kjellen, Ratzel and Mackinder (among others) towards a consideration of the threats facing the German state. Again, Haushofer's work must be placed in context. The Versailles Peace Treaty significantly reduced Germany's territory, both in terms of the confiscation of its overseas colonies and in the reorganization of its national boundaries, for example granting Alsace-Lorraine to France and Upper Silesia to Poland. Haushofer looked to Ratzel's concepts to explain how Germany needed greater *lebensraum* and, subsequently, to justify expanding its borders into surrounding smaller and less populous states. Haushofer's *Geopolitik* therefore involved the incorporation of Ratzel's theorizations of the state as a living organism with Mackinder's ideas of state territorial strategy.

Haushofer's *Geopolitik* may have remained an obscure scholastic endeavour were it not for two points. First, it tapped into a popular imagination of Germany's territorial loss – the image of Germany as a (wounded) organism echoed popular German sentiments. Secondly, and perhaps more importantly, Rudolf Hess, the future deputy to Adolf Hitler, was Haushofer's student. Historians have noted that Hess served just over seven months in Landsberg prison (1923–24) at the same time as Hitler, another inmate, was writing *Mein Kampf*. Through this link, and Hess's later Nazi Party connections, Haushofer's ideas and concepts were incorporated into Nazi Party strategy. This connection between geopolitics and German expansionism has provoked numerous 'hysterical and paranoid' readings of Haushofer's influence over German expansionism.[13] As political geographer John Agnew cautions, we must be careful that we do not overstate the role of Haushofer, or geography more broadly, in the violent crimes enacted by the Nazi regime.[14] We cannot easily conflate Haushofer's *Geopolitik* with the pernicious combination of anti-Semitism and racial purity that the Nazi Party used to pursue violent action against domestic and, later, neighbouring populations. What we can trace quite clearly is the implication of geography's entanglement in the violence of Nazi philosophies: that the discipline retreated away from normative theorizations following the Second World War towards more rational and scientific approaches that used positivist approaches.

Isaiah Bowman

But we need to be wary of drawing a clear division between normative and rational/scientific approaches. In this respect, the career of Isaiah Bowman is instructive. Bowman was a key figure in the institutionalization of geography in the USA over the early part of the twentieth century, serving as the President of the American Geographical Society and as President of Johns Hopkins University (1933–48). Like Mackinder and Haushofer, Bowman was not solely an academic but was also involved in practical politics. He was an important member of Woodrow Wilson's Inquiry, an early example of a foreign policy think-tank comprising around 150 members and established prior to the Versailles Peace Treaty. Woodrow Wilson wanted a 'scientific peace', to study closely the geography of the world and to explore how a rational reorganization of territories, particularly in Europe, could take place after the First World War.[15] The geographer Neil Smith describes Bowman as a 'policy entrepreneur' who understood and capitalized on 'the necessity and limitations of specific geographical solutions to the hurdles of American globalism as well as the shifting importance of geography'.[16]

Bowman was trained in geomorphology by Mark Jefferson, a student of the renowned physical geographer William Morris Davis, and his initial field trips to South America were concerned with mapping the nature of river erosion. Through these experiences Bowman became interested in human development, in particular the role of economic relations with the USA on the development of South American states. Unlike his contemporaries, Bowman shifted his thinking away from environmental determinism (though this body of work certainly influenced his early teaching and research) towards a more grounded and empirically verifiable approach. He was influenced by the work of Ratzel and argued for US economic *lebensraum*, referring to the need to look beyond previous colonial forms of territorial expansion and focus instead on the development of economic relations that advanced US national interest. This adoption of Ratzel's terminology extended to his work in the Inquiry, where he lobbied for the creation of strong states in East and Central Europe at the Versailles negotiations. He was therefore concerned that the subsequent creation of small states with little room for expansion would fuel imperial rivalries. Bowman capitalized on his experience in Versailles through the publication *The New World* in 1921.[17] This book encapsulated an era of American internationalism, developing and expanding the geographical and diplomatic strategy that Wilson had introduced through the Versailles negotiations to provide a sweeping review of the nature of the political, economic and social geography of the world.

Bowman studiously avoided attaching the label 'geopolitics' to his own work, a consequence of the association of this perspective with Nazi Germany's expansionism. In the 1942 paper 'Geography vs. geopolitics',[18] Bowman set his own scholarship in sharp contrast to the work conducted in Germany:

> Geopolitics presents a distorted view of the historical, political, and geographical relations of the world and its parts. It identifies no universal force or process like gravity. It is relative to the state to which it is applied. ... Its arguments as developed in Germany are only made up to suit the case for German aggression. It contains, therefore, a self-destroying principle: when international interests conflict or overlap *might* alone shall decide the issue.[19]

In the remainder of the paper Bowman constructed a rigid binary between his own scientific geography, based around empiricism, and a wider humanism, in relation to the imperialistic, militaristic and superstitious nature of German *Geopolitik*. Of course, such a strict division does not stand up to close scrutiny. Bowman's scholarship and diplomacy was closely bound to the interests of the US state, despite claims of the universal benefit of its outcomes or the scientific nature of its approach. For example, Bowman stated that his motivations in South America were 'cultural exchange, trade and general economic improvement'.[20] However philanthropic this may sound, his cartography served US corporate interests and did not improve the economic outcomes for the region's rubber producers. Like other scholars in the field of geopolitics, Bowman makes a case for the objectivity of his own world view while criticizing the subjectivity of others. And like others, we must understand his world vision as a situated and partial account that serves as an important reflection on the practice of knowledge production, as it was shaped by the personal and collective interests within which it was embedded.

We would make three points by way of summary. First, Mackinder, Haushofer and Bowman all developed the work of Freidrich Ratzel and, specifically, his biological framework for understanding the practice of states. This lens viewed states as organisms locked in a struggle for survival shaped by their physical environment. Secondly, these early geopolitical visions attempted to provide a scientific rationale for the behaviour of states. Each gestured at the partial and unscientific nature of competing theorizations, while defending the cold, scientific rationality of their own approaches. Thirdly, this work highlights the entanglement of geopolitical practice with the interests of the state. The work of Mackinder, Haushofer and Bowman was practical knowledge designed to serve the state within which it was produced. In each case it is difficult to discern the distance between scholar and state, bound as they were within institutional and personal networks with those in power.

Critical geopolitics

The limitations of the early work in geopolitics could lead us to reject this style of envisioning the world and turn to alternative intellectual activities. Indeed, this was the response of political geographers following the Second World War, when the supposed connections between geopolitical ideas and German expansionism promoted increased work on quantitative and technical studies, an avowed shift away from theorizing or offering a political perspective. As John Agnew reports, through an association of theory with 'speculation' and the politicization of the field, political geography 'sank into irrelevance and political obscurity'.[21] Geopolitics had placed geographical knowledge at the heart of imperial politics, and while this afforded the discipline funding and acclaim, it also served to question the independent nature of political geography and connect this field of knowledge with militaristic and undemocratic practices.

While political geographers may not have studied geopolitics in the post-Second World War era, this did not stop politicians and their advisers using geopolitical ideas. As we will see, the language of geopolitics was still deployed by powerful states, though geographers were no longer at the heart of its creation. By the 1980s there was a renaissance in interest in geopolitics within political geography, but with a markedly different perspective from the classical foundations discussed above. This new approach was entitled *critical geopolitics*, since it was directed towards refuting and questioning the traditions of the classical foundations of geopolitics. Specifically, critical geopolitics served to reintroduce questions of power into the analysis of geopolitical texts. Geopolitics was not a neutral exercise, but was rather a reflection of the power of the geopolitician to describe and divide the world in particular ways.

At the root of critical geopolitics is a rejection of geography as a descriptive enterprise of an external world that exists beyond the analysis of the inquirer.

In contrast, critical geopoliticians argue that geography is not earth description but *earth writing* (literally *geo-graphing*). For example, the critical geopolitician does not see in Mackinder's heartland thesis a description of an external reality, but the creation of a world invented to correspond to the national interests of a declining British imperial state. Mackinder's map erases geographical and historical differences and imposes a simplistic division of the world as seen from the eyes of an agent of the British state. This insight draws on the work of French social theorist Michel Foucault, who argued that power and knowledge are inextricably connected. He famously suggested that there is 'no power relation without the correlative constitution of a field of knowledge, nor any knowledge that does not presuppose and constitute at the same time relations of power'.[22] Using Foucault's terminology, the critical perspective treats geopolitics as a *discourse*, or set of representations that perform the function of organizing knowledge and shaping practice. Therefore, critical geopolitics forces us to reject geopolitical ideas as natural or neutral representations of the world, and consider them as discursive practices bound into existing structures of power and privilege.

In order to understand the discursive production of geopolitical ideas, scholars have turned to the work of postcolonial theorist Edward Said (discussed in Chapter 8). Influenced by Foucault, Said was interested in the power of representations and their ability to shape the production of knowledge. In his classic 1978 text *Orientalism*, he critiqued Western (predominantly British and French) literary representations of the Middle East (Orient). He felt that such cultural enterprises presented an imaginative geography of the Orient as a site of threat and danger to Western culture. In doing so, Said suggests a clear binary was produced in such texts between a modern, virtuous and progressive West (or Occident) and a backward, deviant and retrogressive Orient. Said explains this complex production:

> The Orient is not only adjacent to Europe; it is also the place of Europe's greatest and richest and oldest colonies, the source of its civilizations and languages, its cultural constant, and one of the deepest and recurring images of the Other.[23]

This distinction between 'self' and 'other' has been a key reference point for scholars of critical geopolitics, who see similar practices of identity formation in geopolitical texts.

Gearóid Ó Tuathail, a leading figure in the study of critical geopolitics, uses the insights of Foucault and Said (among others) to draw attention to an irony that lies behind the workings of geopolitics. Despite its name, geopolitics has functioned through the *suppression* of geography and politics. To highlight this point, Ó Tuathail draws our attention to two manoeuvres within the operation of classical geopolitics.[24] First, geopolitics involves the systematic erasure of geography. Within geopolitical ideas, places are not evoked through their heterogeneous histories and geographies; they become labelled and categorized within a homogeneous world of objects, attributes and patterns. Entire continents and landmasses are redefined by their relations to the centres of power, rather than by the conflicts, contestations and world views of their inhabitants. According to Ó Tuathail, geopolitics *depluralizes* the surface of the earth by organizing it into essential zones, identities and perspectives. This process of classification within Western forms of knowledge thereby promotes the geopolitician as the only individual with the correct credentials to narrate the complexity of a dangerous and divided earth.

The second manoeuvre of geopolitics is the depoliticization of political processes by presenting interstate conflict as an inevitable and eternal process of nature. We saw this process of depoliticization in the use of neo-Lamarckian evolutionary language – within this framework, conflict is not the outcome of complex economic and social processes but an inevitable natural consequence of the physical environment of states. Geopolitics therefore drains the agency out of social conflict and replaces this with grand narratives of struggles between states.

Critical geopolitics provides us with a toolkit with which we can analyze a range of practices of geopolitics and illuminate how they have erased geography and served to depoliticize conflict. In order to do this, scholars have looked beyond the traditional sites of the classical foundations of geopolitics, to look to the plural sites of geopolitical knowledge production. Critical scholars have identified three sites in particular:

- Formal geopolitics
- Practical geopolitics
- Popular geopolitics.

Formal geopolitics

This label refers to what we have associated with the classical foundations of geopolitics – the production of geopolitical theory by self-identified geopoliticians. While Mackinder, Kjellen and Haushofer may be readily identified under this heading, we should not restrict this group to pre-Second World War social scientists. The example of Thomas Barnett's 'Pentagon's new map', the article with which we opened this chapter, would serve as a contemporary example of formal geopolitics. The political geographer Virginie Mamadouh identifies such current examples of formal geopolitics as *neoclassical geopolitics*.[25] While both classical and neoclassical approaches may be grouped under the formal banner, for Mamadouh the neoclassical work does not conceive the state as an organism in the classical mould since its borders are considered fixed and given. Despite this difference, a glance at Barnett's work will illustrate that the neoclassical approach continues to use phrases such as 'the national interest' and 'national security' as if the state were a single person and strategized accordingly.

Practical geopolitics

This label refers to geopolitical ideas used by policy-makers and politicians in the activity of government and foreign policy. We see practical geopolitics all around us, in the speeches and addresses of political leaders, in official policy statements and in the interview responses of politicians. An example that has been heavily cited in recent years is US President George W. Bush's 2002 State of the Union Address where he described Iran, Iraq and North Korea and their 'terrorist allies' as an 'axis of evil'. In doing so, President Bush was using geopolitics to provide a simple geographical template of the world that would connect the attacks on 11 September 2001 to Saddam Hussein's regime in Iraq.[26] The use of the axis device serves to erase the significant historical and geographical differences between the three states and bring them together as a single terrorist entity. But the enactment of practical geopolitics is not always so explicit or dramatic. The power of practical geopolitics is in its banality. Geopolitical ideas often appear so ordinary as to be invisible, and this is one of the crucial points. The repetition of geopolitical ideas within the practical performance of politics serves to naturalize certain categorizations of the world: for example, developed/less developed, core/periphery, or simply 'us' and 'them'. These phrases may seem innocuous, but they are affirming particular political perspectives and legitimizing foreign policy decisions.

Popular geopolitics

This label refers to the communication of geopolitical ideas through the popular culture of the state, its cinema, cartoons, books and magazines. Through this lens, geopolitics is no longer the preserve of key elite intellectuals or politicians, but is formulated and transmitted through everyday cultural practices. To highlight the significance of popular geopolitics, scholars have drawn on the theorizations of Italian Marxist theorist Antonio Gramsci and, in particular, on his concept of *hegemony*. For Gramsci, hegemony forms the basis of strong governments and indicates their ability to rule the population through consensus as opposed to coercion. The political geographer Joanne Sharp explains the role of popular culture in the production of consensus:

> hegemony is constructed not only through political ideologies but also, more immediately, through detailed scripting of some of the most ordinary and mundane aspects of everyday life. Gramsci's concept of hegemony posits a significant place for popular culture in any attempt to understand the workings of society because of the very everydayness and apparently nonconflictual nature of such productions.[27]

Critical studies of popular geopolitics have explored the role of a range of cultural practices in the moulding of public perceptions of political events. For example, the political geographer Jason Dittmer examines the communication of US national identity and security post-9/11 through the lens of *Captain America* comic books. This fascinating work draws attention to the ability of *Captain America* 'to connect the political projects of American nationalism, internal order, and foreign policy (all formulated at the national or global scale) with the scale of the individual, or the body'.[28] By literally embodying

American identity, Dittmer argues that *Captain America* presents its readers with 'a hero both of, and for, the nation'.[29] In addition to cartoons, films have also been a productive terrain for critical analysis.[30] For example, the political geographer Klaus Dodds analyzes the geopolitical ideas communicated in James Bond films.[31] Dodds argues that part of the success of the James Bond franchise is its ability to communicate contemporary geopolitical anxieties of Western states, from the Cold War narratives of *From Russia with Love* (1963) through to the threat posed by Central Asia in *The World is Not Enough* (1999). Therefore, just as grand theoretical schemes and political speeches can conjure geopolitical ideas, instruments of popular culture can be working to build what are portrayed as 'commonsense' understandings of the geography of world politics.

Critical geopolitics in practice

Examples of formal, practical and popular geopolitics have proved an extremely fertile area of political geography over the last 15 years. Utilizing the tools of critical geopolitics, this work has drawn attention to the role of geopolitics in suppressing geographical difference and depoliticizing conflicts and struggles. In doing so, geopolitical discourses have shaped policy responses. But echoing the recent work of political geographer Merje Kuus, we must be careful not to simply assume that geopolitical discourses 'cause' particular policy responses. Instead, they frame political debate in such a way as to make 'certain policies seem reasonable or feasible while marginalizing other policies as unreasonable and unfeasible'.[32] In what follows, we look at two spheres where the techniques of critical geopolitics have been applied to practices of geopolitical knowledge production: the Cold War and the fragmentation of Yugoslavia.

Cold War geopolitics

The Cold War is the term given to the era of diplomatic and proxy military confrontations between the USA and the Soviet Union from 1947 to 1991. The image of a clash between the free-market democratic ideology of the USA and the communist authoritarian Soviet Union has become a trusted backdrop to the global politics of the second half of the twentieth century. But we should not read the ubiquity of Cold War narratives as an indication of their inevitability or truth. By examining USA policy statements, critical scholars have drawn on the conceptions of Edward Said to argue that the Cold War was constructed through particular policy iterations that depended upon binary distinctions between a good/free/capitalist world (centred on the USA) and an evil/enslaved/communist world (centred on the Soviet Union). Numerous global conflicts that occurred over the period of the Cold War were read through the lens of this abstract and simplistic binary. Scholars have identified the foundations of this framework in an influential communiqué sent by

US *chargé d'affaires* in Moscow George Kennan to Washington in February 1946. This document, known as the Long Telegram, expounded the dangers of the Soviet Union as an expanding geographical entity, a consequence of the essential desire of the Soviet Union to claim greater territory. Keenan's thoughts proved influential to the US administration of Harry Truman. In a speech in 1947 that would become known as the Truman Doctrine, the US President articulated the importance of confronting an expansionist Soviet Union. Echoed in the geopolitical narratives of the current 'War on Terror', Truman suggested that we have a choice in a worldwide struggle between freedom and totalitarianism. In doing so, the complexity of global politics was reduced to abstract absolutes, where the USA claimed to stand as the exemplar of universal human values of freedom and democracy.

Expanding this binary template, the geographer John Agnew isolates three geopolitical concepts that played a central function in US narratives of the Cold War: containment, the domino theory and hegemonic stability.[33] Emerging first in Keenan's Long Telegram, the containment thesis presented the Soviet Union as an expanding geographical entity that posed a risk to the world order by 'infecting' neighbouring states with communist ideology. This containment myth presented the Soviet Union as a potential seducer and rapist, with repressed instincts that could burst forth at any point along its boundary unless there was constant pressure to keep it contained. The second (and related) geopolitical concept was that of the domino effect. The domino theory suggests that threats to the world order could have 'knock on' consequences in neighbouring states, and thus, one by one, states could fall to the peril of communism. This metaphor proved a valuable explanation for the USA military engagement in Vietnam, where the domino theory collapsed the distance between the USA and South East Asia and brought this conflict into the moral consciousness of the US public. We can see in both the containment and domino geopolitical texts the use of epidemiology as political explanation, the globe is presented as a sick body that could be overcome at any moment without the correct surgical military process. The third geopolitical concept that Agnew identifies from the Cold War texts is that of the USA as a benevolent hegemon. Drawing again on Gramscian concepts, this image presents America as a central global power capable of mediating the chaos and division of the Cold War world. In a narrative that seems familiar in our present age, the successful working of the global political and economic system was presented as dependent upon US leadership.

Fragmentation of Yugoslavia

The fragmentation of Yugoslavia from the secession of Slovenia and Croatia in 1991 through to the independence of Kosovo in 2007 serves as a second example of how the practice of geopolitics has been critically assessed by political geographers. Comprising six separate republics (Slovenia, Croatia, Bosnia and Herzegovina, Serbia, Montenegro and Macedonia), Yugoslavia was a communist state that lay outside the Soviet Union after a split with Stalin in

1948. Between 1945 and 1980 it was led by Josep Broz 'Tito', a charismatic though often ruthless dictator who unified the republics under the banner of Yugoslav 'brotherhood and unity'. Over the course of the 1980s, Slovene, Croat and Serb nationalist movements rose to the forefront of Yugoslav political life, each arguing that national security could only be secured through exclusive national territories. For Slovenia and Croatia, this led to declarations of independence in 1991, moves that were violently resisted by the Serb-dominated Yugoslav army. Despite this military resistance, Slovenia and Croatia gained their independence, the latter involving the expulsion of substantial numbers of Serb citizens. In Bosnia and Herzegovina, the fragmentation of Yugoslavia prompted acute political confrontation. The republic exhibited the most heterogeneous population of the former Yugoslav territories, mixed between Bosnian Muslims (also called Bosniaks), Serbs and Croats. Bosnian Muslims and Croats feared minority status in a Serb-dominated Yugoslavia and, consequently, Bosnia and Herzegovina claimed its own independence following a referendum in March 1992. This move agitated the large Serb minority in Bosnia (around 31% of the population in the 1991 Yugoslav census), who sought to establish an exclusive Serb territory in Bosnia: the Republika Srspka. This move sparked violent conflict which lasted for nearly four years. Over this period a series of war crimes were committed, including the Serb siege of Sarajevo (see Figure 9.2) and the Srebrenica Massacre, where Serb military and paramilitary groups killed around 6,000 Bosnian Muslim men and boys.

The work of critical scholars has focused on how the fragmentation of Yugoslavia, and particularly the Bosnian war, were interpreted and

Figure 9.2   Sarajevo, February 2007 © Alex Jeffrey, 2007

represented in the speeches, interviews and policy reports of Western political elites. Studying this practical geopolitics serves to illustrate how particular policy positions were justified and alternatives discredited. The predominant geopolitical framing of the Bosnian conflict by Western political leaders was that it was a consequence of 'ancient ethnic hatreds'. That this explanation for the violence may seem rather straightforward illustrates the power of geopolitical ideas to naturalize particular explanatory narratives. The work of scholars of critical geopolitics has argued that we should explore the assumptions that underpin this explanation for the conflict and its implications in terms of international policy on the Bosnian war. Below, we draw out two points from the recent critical examination of the 'ancient ethnic hatreds' discourse: that it is depoliticizing and erases the geographical specificity of the conflict.

First, blaming the conflict on 'ancient ethnic hatreds' suggests that violence is pre-programmed into the Bosnian population and it erupted for irrational and inexplicable reasons. Rather than viewing nationalist political programmes as opportunistic political sloganeering built on tangible economic and social concerns among the Bosnian population, this response validates their political message: that pluralist democracy is impossible in Bosnia on the basis of the presence of antagonistic political identities. Consequently, this representation of the violence assumes that there are no clear aggressors or victims, but rather that the entire population is condemned to a status as aggressors *and* victims. On account of this image of the violence, international intervention was enacted in Bosnia through humanitarian relief rather than as an attempt to assist militarily the political objectives of any single group or community. As a recent United Nations report has confirmed, this approach was grounded in a position of *moral equivalency*, where all sides were viewed as equally responsible for the violence.

Secondly, the 'ancient ethnic hatreds' label contributed to the effacement of place in Bosnia. The rich social history of the country, documented by anthropologists such as Tone Bringa,[34] was reduced to an image of the past mired in conflict and aggression. Scholars have noted the establishment of a self/other dichotomy within these geopolitical narratives, between a rational and peaceful Europe and an irrational and deviant Bosnia. This relationship echoed a longer historical tradition within Western literature and thought that relied upon a binary relationship between a civilized Europe with a barbaric Balkans. Reflecting its roots in Edward Said's critique of *Orientalism*, this binary representation has been labelled as *Balkanism*. As the literary theorist Maria Todorova has noted, the Balkans has served as a repository of negative characteristics against which a self-congratulatory image of a civilized and progressive Western Europe has been constructed.[35] In critiquing this binary, a series of studies have explored the representation of the Balkans within imaginary geographies of Western European travel writers, novelists, scholars and politicians. Vesna Goldsworthy's *Inventing Ruritania* (1998) serves as a key example of this literature, where she suggests that authors such as Bram Stoker, Anthony Hope and George Bernard Shaw locate their narratives in the Balkans as a means of 'subverting a variety of taboos and satisfying hidden desires'.[36]

These imaginaries are often dismissed as irrelevant to the more tangible politics of international affairs. But we would draw attention to two ways in which they are important. First, reflecting the discussion on popular geopolitics (see above), these cultural performances build public consensus over particular geographical imaginations and identity formations. As Merje Kuus has argued, such practices render certain policy responses feasible or reasonable. Hegemonic ideas – in this case of Balkan deviance – are consequently naturalized through their repetition. When these ideas are enrolled into the services of foreign policy, we find it easier to accept them as truths. Secondly, there are direct connections between popular and practical geopolitics. US President Bill Clinton, incumbent towards the end of the Bosnian conflict, was reportedly influenced in his policy towards the Bosnia war by reading Robert Kaplan's *Balkan Ghosts: A Journey Through History*.[37] This travel book revels in a Balkanistic reading of Yugoslavian history that foregrounds the 'unfathomable' hatred between different ethnic groups and its roots in histories of violence.[38] Here we see a rare direct connection between Balkanistic imaginaries and the formation of geopolitical scripts by elites of statecraft.

Anti-geopolitics

Research in the field of critical geopolitics has scrutinized the significant power relations within which geopolitical knowledge is constructed. This work has highlighted that the dominance of a particular territorial vision of the world is not a consequence of its inherent truth, but rather is an effect of the political, economic or cultural power of the vision's author. While this perspective has drawn welcome attention to the constructed nature of geopolitical visions, it has remained focused on the practices and pronouncements of state elites. In recent years, a new perspective has emerged which has drawn on feminist theorizations to construct an *anti-geopolitics*. This term reworks the dissident Hungarian scholar George Konrad's concept of anti-politics, which he defined as the political activities 'of those who don't want to be politicians and refuse to share power'.[39] The anti-geopolitical perspective highlights a number of silences within both the classical and critical canons of geopolitics. The first is the absence of resistance to geopolitical scripts. As feminist political geographers Lorraine Dowler and Joanne Sharp have suggested, critical geopolitics may offer 'eloquent deconstructions of dominant political discourse', but 'there is often little sense of alternative possibilities'.[40] Keeping with our examples, dominant narratives of the Cold War or the fragmentation of Yugoslavia were not accepted uncritically by the audiences for which they were designed. Rather, they have been resisted and reconfigured by individuals and institutions outside the spheres of state power. Secondly, geopolitics has been a masculinist activity that has erased the role of women in both the production of geopolitical ideas and in practices of resistance. This criticism is not reserved for classical geopolitics alone. Dowler and Sharp identify similar gender-blindness in critical perspectives, which they claim have reflected 'a genealogy of heroic men'.[41] Let us now examine these two emerging areas of geopolitical thought in greater detail.

Resistance

The recent work under the banner of anti-geopolitics draws attention to the practices of individuals and institutions that resist the hegemonic narratives of geopolitics that originate within state bureaucracies. The political geographer Paul Routledge, whose work on the Clandestine Insurgent Rebel Clown Army we examined in Chapter 6, has suggested that the term 'anti-geopolitics' refers to an 'ambiguous, political and cultural force within civil society'.[42] Routledge's reference to civil society highlights that anti-geopolitical knowledge is produced by organizations that exist outside the state or corporate interests. These are not the grand historical and geographical stories told by Sir Halford Mackinder or Thomas Barnett, but rather constitute alternative visions that challenge the *status quo*. For Routledge, this alternative vision is posed in two ways. First, anti-geopolitics challenges the *material* geopolitical power of states or global institutions, thereby resisting the dominant model of global capitalist production. Secondly, anti-geopolitics resists the geopolitical *representations* imposed by state elites that are constructed and reproduced to serve their interests. Anti-geopolitics is therefore a diverse field of knowledge production that connects a wide range of groups struggling against the dominant geopolitical ideas of the state. We could group social movements, journalists, critical intellectuals and terrorists all under the anti-geopolitics banner. While these groups and individuals differ in their methods, they share a commitment to dissenting from geopolitical discourses.

Gearóid Ó Tuathail illustrates the production of anti-geopolitical visions using the case of the output of journalist Maggie O'Kane during the Bosnian war (1992–5).[43] Drawing on feminist arguments developed within political geography since the 1980s, Ó Tuathail highlights the embodied nature of geopolitical ideas; they are not neutral designations but representations from a distinct vantage point. Highlighting the importance of perspective, Ó Tuathail labels this situated account 'the anti-geopolitical eye'. Maggie O'Kane's articles, posted from besieged Sarajevo comprised vivid accounts of the violence and brutality of the conflict, describing the civilian casualties, the distress of the city's population and the improvised coping mechanisms that characterized everyday life. These were stories of outrage, evoking the 'starved cities, overflowing hospitals, blockaded roads, teeming refugee centers and vile concentration camps'.[44] Ó Tuathail argues that O'Kane's 'anti-geopolitical eye' provides a perspective that counters the dominant geopolitical scripts of the Bosnian war. As we have seen, the conflict was framed by Western leaders as a consequence of 'ancient ethnic hatreds'. This label distanced Bosnia, placing it outside the moral concerns of the Western public. In contrast, O'Kane's stories 'cut through the frameworks wrapping Bosnia'[45] and drew the Bosnian conflict into the moral responsibility of her audience.

Building on Ó Tuathail's analysis, similar anti-geopolitical perspectives may be identified in the blogs that emerged during the US-led invasion of Iraq in 2003. These accounts brought Iraq into the moral universe of the West and countered the dominant narratives that stressed the inherent deviance of Saddam Hussein's country and the subsequent virtue of the US-led liberation.

Bloggers such as Salam Pax situated the conflict in terms of the security challenges of everyday life in Iraq.[46] Through Pax's blog, Iraq became a place, rather than a target.

Significantly, such grounded accounts highlight the need for detailed ethnographic work in the sphere of geopolitics, research that takes seriously localized subversions of dominant territorial narratives. The political geographer Nick Megoran has undertaken such research, examining boundary disputes in the Fergana Valley.[47] In Figure 9.3, Megoran is undertaking ethnographic fieldwork on what popular and media accounts often termed a 'geopolitical fault line': the trees in the immediate background mark the border between Kyrgyzstan and Uzbekistan. Though he does not use the term *anti-geopolitics*, Megoran's ethnographic accounts highlight the resistance of local residents to a state-led boundary demarcation (often through everyday practices such as drinking tea – see Figure 9.3). Megoran concludes that '[e]lite visions of the importance of tightly controlled boundaries ... were not only not shared by borderland dwellers, but actively contested'.[48] To understand resistance to geopolitical discourse we need to expand research into such localized narratives of space and power.

Figure 9.3   Nick Megoran conducting Ethnography on the Kyrgyz–Uzbek border
© Nick Megoran, 2008

Gendering geopolitics

As we have seen, research into 'anti-geopolitics' has drawn upon feminist critical perspectives. But this does not present an adequate gender critique of the production of geopolitical knowledge. In two important ways, recent work by feminist political geographers has attempted to gender geopolitics. First, feminist political geographers have highlighted the notable absence of women from both classical and critical geopolitics. Geopolitics has been a process of knowledge creation by men, about men and, in the main, for men. The disembodied nature of geopolitical knowledge production supposes a detached objectivity, but this masks the inherently gendered nature of its ideas and concepts. Secondly, feminist approaches have offered alternative geopolitical visions that move beyond traditional preoccupations with state security. Bringing the advances in feminist thought into the field of Political Geography, such alternative visions move beyond simple binary logics to construct 'a more accountable and embodied notion of politics that analyzes the intersection of power and space at multiple scales, one that eschews violence as a legitimate means to political ends'.[49] We explore these two approaches to gendering geopolitics below.

There is a marked absence of women in both classical and critical perspectives on geopolitics. In the classical tradition, this can be explained through the patriarchal nature of imperial geographical knowledge production at the end of the nineteenth century. For example, when Sir Halford Mackinder presented his paper 'The geographical pivot of history' to the Royal Geographical Society (RGS) in 1904 women were still barred from membership. It was not until 1913 that membership to the RGS was extended to women.[50] But we should not dismiss gender inequality as a century-old phenomenon. A glance at the formal and practical geopolitical texts from the last decade attests to the continued male dominance of geopolitical knowledge production. As Dowler and Sharp suggest, '[w]omen's places in international politics tend not to be those of decision makers, but of international labourers and migrants, as images in international advertising and as "victims" to be protected by international peacekeepers'.[51] The focus of geopolitics on the formal politics of international foreign policy has therefore erased informal arenas of political participation, where women often play an active and central role.[52] But feminist critiques are not restricted to the elite geopolitics of classical traditions; they also question the gender politics of critical geopolitics. Joanne Sharp has suggested that Ó Tuathail's account of critical geopolitics has reproduced geopolitics as a masculinist practice by focusing on the history of 'Big Men' such as Mackinder, Haushofer and Bowman.[53] Feminist scholars have argued that critical geopoliticians must be more attentive to the situated nature of their own knowledge production within the Western male-dominated academy.

Feminist interventions are not limited to critical observations of gender bias; they have also offered alternative geopolitical visions. This work has served to question the location of geopolitics and, in doing so, unsettled the assumption that geopolitics takes place in the formal institutions of state foreign policy. In particular, feminist political geographers have drawn attention to the (geo)political nature of everyday life, highlighting the role of localized practices and identities in sustaining and contesting geopolitical discourse. This perspective reflects the position of feminist theorizations at the heart of research examining 'anti-geopolitics'. As political geographer Anna Secor emphasizes through her work on the role of women in Islamist practices and discourses in Turkey, the feminist perspective does not simply replace the global with the local as the authoritative scale of analysis. Instead, 'feminist approaches show

how the (imminently political) categories of public and private, global and local, formal and informal, ultimately blur, overlap and collapse into one another in the making of political life'.[54] In doing so, feminist perspectives offer an alternative vision of political life that rejects the scalar logic of dominant narratives and in place offers a situated set of accounts that illuminate the multiple scales and spaces of geopolitical knowledge production.

Conclusion

Geopolitics concerns ideas about the world. This chapter has explored the production of these ideas, from their roots in the emergence of the geographical discipline in the nineteenth-century age of empire, through to their relevance today in the so-called 'War on Terror'. Throughout this chronology, geopoliticians have declared themselves in a privileged position to pronounce on the divisions, hierarchies and organization of global space. But like all ideas, these ideas about the world have a point of origin. They are not views from nowhere and everywhere, but are situated accounts that present the world in a fashion that is advantageous to the author. Critical geopolitics, a perspective that emerged in the 1980s, has sought to draw on a range of social and cultural theorists to explore and expose the power/knowledge relations that underpin the production of geopolitical ideas. But recent scholarship, particularly engaging with the theoretical traditions of feminist thought, has sought to critique critical geopolitics in two ways. First, scholars have questioned whether critical geopoliticians have sufficiently scrutinized their own privileged position and gender bias. Secondly, recent methodological reflections have questioned whether critical geopoliticians have focused on texts and discourses at the expense of practices and materiality. There is certainly corrective work taking place in this field, as political geographers have embraced ethnographic methodologies as useful techniques for understanding the everyday reproduction and contestation of geopolitical ideas.[55]

Notes

1. Barnett, Thomas P.M. (2003) 'The Pentagon's new map', *Esquire*. Available at: www.thomaspmbarnett.com/published/pentagonsnewmap.htm (accessed 13/02/08).
2. See Roberts, Susan, Secor, Anna and Sparke, Matthew (2003) 'Neoliberal geopolitics', *Antipode*, 25(5): 886–97; Bialasiewicz, Luiza, Campbell, David, Elden, Stuart, Graham, Stephen, Jeffrey, Alex and Williams, Alison (2007) 'Performing security: the imaginative geographies of current US strategy', *Political Geography*, 26: 405–22.
3. Ó Tuathail, Gearóid (2006) 'General introduction: thinking critically about geopolitics', in Gearóid, Ó Tuathail, Simon, Dalby and Paul Routledge (eds), *The Geopolitics Reader*. Abingdon: Routledge. pp. 1–14.
4. Ó Tuathail, Gearóid and Agnew, John (1992) 'Geopolitics and discourse: practical geopolitical reasoning in American foreign policy', *Political Geography*, 11: 190–204. p. 190.
5. See Bush, George W. (2001) Address to a Joint Session of Congress and the American People. Available at: www.whitehouse.gov/news/releases/2001/09/20010920-8.html (accessed 13/02/08).

6. Ó Tuathail, 'General introduction'. p. 1; see also Kjellen, R. (1899) 'Studier ofver Sueriges Politiska granser', *Ymer* 19: 283–331.

7. Ratzel, Freidrich (1897 [1923]) *Politische Geographie*. Munich and Berlin: R. Oldenbourg.

8. Darwin, Charles (1859) *On the Origin of Species by Means of Natural Selection, or, The Preservation of Favoured Races in the Struggle for Life*. London: J. Murray.

9. Agnew, John (2002) *Making Political Geography*. London: Arnold. pp. 58–60.

10. O'Hara, Sarah and Heffernan, Michael (2006) 'From geo-strategy to geo-economics: the 'heartland' and British imperialism before and after Mackinder', *Geopolitics*, 11(1): 54–73.

11. Mackinder, Halford J. (1904) 'The geographical pivot of history', *The Geographical Journal*, 23(4): 421–37. Map located on p. 435.

12. Mackinder, H. (1919) *Democratic Ideals and Reality: A Study in the Politics of Reconstruction*. London: Constable and Company. p. 150.

13. Ó Tuathail, Gearóid (1996a) *Critical Geopolitics*. London: Routledge. pp. 53–4.

14. Agnew, J. (2002) *Making Political Geography*. London: Arnold. p. 78.

15. Smith, Neil (2003) *American Empire: Roosevelt's Geographer and the Prelude to Globalization*. Berkeley, CA: University of California Press. pp. 118–19.

16. Smith, *American Empire*. p. 27.

17. Bowman, I. (1921) *The New World: Problems in Political Geography*. New York: World Book Company.

18. Bowman, Isaiah (1942) 'Geography vs. geopolitics', *Geographical Review*, 32(4): 646–58.

19. Bowman, 'Geography vs. geopolitics'. p. 646.

20. Bowman, 'Geography vs. geopolitics'. p. 649.

21. Agnew, *Making Political Geography*. p. 85.

22. Foucault, Michel (1979) *Discipline and Punish*. New York: Vintage. p. 27, cited in Gearóid Ó Tuathail (1996a) *Critical Geopolitics*. London: Routledge. p. 10.

23. Said, Edward (1978) *Orientalism: Western Conceptions of the Orient*. Harmondsworth: Penguin. p. 1.

24. Ó Tuathail, *Critical Geopolitics*. pp. 53–4.

25. Mamadouh, Virginie D. (1998) 'Geopolitics in the nineties: one flag, many meanings', *GeoJournal*, 46: 237–53.

26. For a discussion of this point, see Dodds, Klaus (2007) *A Very Short Introduction to Geopolitics*. Oxford: Oxford University Press. p. 13.

27. Sharp, Joanne (2000a) *Condensing the Cold War: Reader's Digest and American Identity*. Minneapolis, MN: University of Minnesota Press. p. 31.

28. Dittmer, Jason (2005) '*Captain America*'s empire: reflections on identity, popular culture, and post-9/11 geopolitics', *Annals of the Association of American Geographers*, 95(2): 626–43. p. 267.

29. Dittmar, '*Captain America*'s empire'. p. 267.

30. See, in particular, Power, Marcus and Crampton, Andrew (2005) 'Reel geopolitics: cinematographing political space', *Geopolitics*, 10(2): 193–203.

31. See Dodds, Klaus (2005) 'Licensed to stereotype: geopolitics, James Bond and the spectre of Balkanism', *Geopolitics*, 8(2): 125–56.

32. Kuus, Merje (2007) *Geopolitics Reframed: Security and Identity in Europe's Eastern Enlargement*. New York and Basingstoke: Palgrave Macmillan. p. 10.

33. Agnew, John (2003) *Geopolitics Re-visioning World Politics*. London: Routledge. pp. 109–12.

34. Bringa, T. (1995) *Being Muslim the Bosnian Way: Identity and Community in a Central Bosnian Village*. Princeton N.J.: Princeton University Press.

35. See Todorova, Maria (1997) *Imagining the Balkans*. New York: Oxford University Press.

36. Goldsworthy, Vesna (1998) *Inventing Ruritania: The Imperialism of the Imagination*. New Haven, CT and London: Yale University Press. p. 126.

37. See Kaplan, Robert D. (1994) *Balkan Ghosts: A Journey through History*. New York: Vintage. For a critical discussion, see Ó Tuathail, *Critical Geopolitics*. p. 212.

38. Kaplan, *Balkan Ghosts*. p. 70.

39. See Konrad, George (2006 [1984]) 'Antipolitics: a moral force', in Gearóid, Ó Tuathail, Simon Dalby and Paul Routledge (eds), *The Geopolitics Reader*. Abingdon: Routledge. pp. 259–61. p. 260.

40. Dowler, Lorraine and Sharp, Joanne (2001) 'A feminist geopolitics?', *Space and Polity*, 5(3): 165–76. p. 167.

41. Dowler and Sharp, 'A feminist geopolitics?' p. 167.
42. Routledge, Paul (2006a) 'Introduction to Part Five', in Gearóid Ó Tuathail, Simon Dalby and Paul Routledge (eds), *The Geopolitics Reader*. Abingdon: Routledge. pp. 233–48. p. 233.
43. See Ó Tuathail, Gearóid (1996b) 'An anti-geopolitical eye: Maggie O'Kane in Bosnia 1992–1993', *Gender, Place and Culture*, 3(2): 171–85.
44. Ó Tuathail, 'An anti-geopolitical eye'. p. 175.
45. Ó Tuathail, 'An anti-geopolitical eye'. p. 182.
46. For Salam Pax's latest blog, see www.dear_raed.blogspot.com/ (accessed 13/03/08).
47. See Megoran, Nick (2006) 'For ethnography in Political Geography: experiencing and re-imagining Ferghana Valley boundary closures', *Political Geography*, 25(6): 622–40.
48. Megoran, 'For ethnography in Political Geography'. p. 637.
49. Hyndman, Jennifer (2003) 'Beyond either/or: a feminist analysis of September 11th', *Acme*, 2: 1–13. p. 3.
50. See Bell, Morag and McEwan, Cheryl (1996) 'The admission of women fellows to the Royal Geographical Society, 1892–1914: the controversy and the outcome', *The Geographical Journal*, 162(3): 295–312.
51. Dowler and Sharp, 'A feminist geopolitics?' p. 168.
52. See Secor, Anna (2001) 'Towards a feminist counter-geopolitics: gender, space and Islamist politics in Istanbul', *Space and Polity*, 5(3): 191–211.
53. Sharp, Joanne (2000b) 'Remasculinising geo-politics? Comments on Gearóid Ó Tuathail's *Critical Geopolitics*', *Political Geography*, 19: 361–4.
54. Secor, 'Towards a feminist counter-geopolitics'. p. 193.
55. See Kuus, *Geopolitics Reframed*; Megoran, 'For ethnography in Political Geography'; Navaro-Yashin, Yael (2002) *Faces of the State: Secularism and Public Life in Turkey*. Princeton, NJ: Princeton University Press; Ferguson, James and Gupta, Akhil (2002) 'Spatializing states: toward an ethnography of neoliberal governmentality', *American Ethnologist*, 29(4): 981–1002.

Further reading

Those interested in studying geopolitics should first return to some of the original texts produced by the classical geopoliticians, such as:

Bowman, Isaiah (1928) *The New World*, London: Harrap.

Mackinder, Halford J. (1904) 'The geographical pivot of history', *The Geographical Journal*, 23(4): 421–37.

The recent second edition of the ***Geopolitics Reader*** provides a very helpful collation of these foundation texts (and much more besides):

Ó Tuathail, Gearóid, Gerard, Dalby, Simon and Routledge, Paul (eds) (2006) *The Geopolitics Reader* (2nd edition). Abingdon: Routledge.

Following this work, there have been a number of helpful historical analyses of these scholars. We would particularly draw attention to Neil Smith's magisterial exploration of the life, politics and geographies of Isaiah Bowman:

Smith, Neil (2003) *American Empire: Roosevelt's Geographer and the Prelude to Globalization*. Berkeley, CA: University of California Press.

The field of critical geopolitics has stimulated a wide body of theoretical and empirical studies. We would urge students to engage with the following key texts:

Dowler, Lorraine and Sharp, Joanne (2001) 'A feminist geopolitics?', *Space and Polity*, 5(3): 165–76.

Ó Tuathail, Gearóid (1996) *Critical Geopolitics*. London: Routledge.

Ó Tuathail, Gearóid and Agnew, John (1992) 'Geopolitics and discourse: practical geopolitical reasoning in American foreign policy', *Political Geography*, 11: 190–204.

The study of popular geopolitics has expanded in recent years. We would draw particular attention to:

Power, Marcus and Crampton, Andrew (2005) 'Red geopolitics: cinematographing political space', *Geopolitics*, 10(2): 193–203.

In addition, the following texts have advanced recent thinking in the field of popular geopolitics:

Dittmer, Jason (2005) '*Captain America's* empire: reflections on identity, popular culture, and post-9/11 geopolitics', *Annals of the Association of American Geographers*, 95(2): 626–43.

Sharp, Joanne (2000) *Condensing the Cold War: Reader's Digest and American Identity*. Minneapolis, MN: University of Minnesota Press.

Finally, Klaus Dodds' recent contribution to the ***Very Short Introduction*** series provides an essential overview of the history and politics of geopolitics:

Dodds, Klaus (2007) *A Very Short Introduction to Geopolitics*. Oxford: Oxford University Press.

References

Agnew, John (1996) 'Mapping politics: how context counts in electoral geography', *Political Geography*, 15(2): 129–46.

Agnew, John (2002) *Making Political Geography*. London: Arnold.

Agnew, John (2003) *Geopolitics: Re-visioning World Politics*. London: Routledge.

Allen, John (2003) *Lost Geographies of Power*. Oxford: Blackwell.

Allen, John (2004) 'The whereabouts of power: politics, government and space', *Geografiska Annaler*, 86B(1): 19–32.

Amin, Ash (2002) 'Ethnicity and the multicultural city: living with diversity', *Environment and Planning A*, 34: 959–80.

Amin, Ash and Graham, Stephen (1997) 'The ordinary city', *Transactions of the Institute of British Geographers*, 22: 411–29.

Anderson, Benedict (1991) *Imagined Communities*. London: Verso.

Archer, J. Clark (1981) 'Public choice paradigms in political geography', in Alan D. Burnett and Peter J. Taylor (eds), *Political Studies from Spatial Perspectives*. New York: John Wiley. pp. 73–90.

Archibugi, D. (2003) 'Cosmopolitical democracy', in D. Archibugi (ed.), *Debating Cosmopolitics*. London: Verso. pp. 1–15.

Atkinson, Rowland (2003) 'Misunderstood saviour or vengeful wrecker: the many meanings and problems of gentrification', *Urban Studies*, 40(12): 2343–50.

Bacon, Roger and Eltis, Walter (1978) *Britain's Economic Problem: Too Few Producers*. London: Macmillan.

Barnett, Thomas, P.M. (2003) 'The Pentagon's new map', *Esquire*. Available at: www.thomaspmbarnett.com/published/pentagonsnewmap.htm (accessed 13/02/08).

Barry, Andrew (2001) *Political Machines: Governing a Technological Society*. London: Athlone.

Bayart, J.-F. (1993) *The State in Africa: The Politics of the Belly*. London and New York: Longman.

BBC News (2007) 'Viewpoint: Belgian crisis', *BBC News*. Available at: www.news.bbc.co.uk/1/hi/world/europe/6995511.stm (accessed 08/03/08).

Bell, James (1999) 'Redefining national identity in Uzbekistan: symbolic tensions in Tashkent's official public landscape', *Ecumene*, 6(2): 183–213.

Bell, James and Staeheli, Lynn (2001) 'Discourses of diffusion and democratization', *Political Geography*, 20(2): 175–95.

Bell, Morag and McEwan, Cheryl (1996) 'The admission of women fellows to the Royal Geographical Society, 1892–1914; the controversy and the outcome', *The Geographical Journal*, 162(3): 295–312.

Bennett, Robert (1980) *The Geography of Public Finance*. London: Methuen.

Berman, Marshall (1982) *All That is Solid Melts into Air*. London: Verso.

Beveridge, William (1942) *Social Insurance and Allied Services*. London: HMSO.

Beveridge, William (1944) *Full Employment in a Free Society*. London: Allen and Unwin.

Bialasiewicz, Luiza, Campbell, David, Elden, Stuart, Graham, Stephen, Jeffrey, Alex and Williams, Alison (2007) 'Performing security: the imaginative geographies of current US strategy', *Political Geography*, 26: 405–22.

Billig, Michael (1995) *Banal Nationalism*. London: Sage.

Blumer, Herbert (1951) 'Collective behaviour', in Alfred M. Lee (ed.), *Principles of Sociology*. New York: Barnes and Noble. pp. 167–222.

Bojicic, Vesna (1996) 'The disintegration of Yugoslavia: causes and consequences of dynamic inefficiency in semi-command economies', in David A. Dyker and I. Vejvoda (eds), *Yugoslavia and After: A Study in Fragmentation, Despair and Rebirth*. Harlow: Longman. pp. 28–47.

Boorstin, Daniel, J. (1986) *The Discoverers*. Harmondsworth: Penguin.

Bowman, Isaiah (1921) *The New World: Problems in Political Geography*. New York: World Book Company.

Bowman, Isaiah (1942) 'Geography vs. geopolitics', *Geographical Review*, 32(4): 646–58.

Bratton, M. (1994) 'Civil society and political transitions in Africa', in J. Harbeson, D. Rothchild and N. Chazan (eds), *Civil Society and the State in Africa*. Boulder, CO: Lynne Rienner.

Bremner, C. (2008) 'Champagne region expanded to meet world demand', *The Times Online*, 14 March, www.timesonline.co.uk/tol/life_and_style/food_and_drink/wine/article3548465.ece (accessed 16/03/08).

Bringa, T. (1995) *Being Muslim the Bosnian Way: Identity and Community in a Central Bosnian Village*. Princeton, N.J.: Princeton University Press.

Burrows, Roger and Loader, Brian (eds) (1994) *Towards a Post-Fordist Welfare State?* London: Routledge.

Bush, George, W. (2001) Address to a Joint Session of Congress and the American People. Available at: www.whitehouse.gov/news/releases/2001/09/ 20010920-8.html (accessed 13/02/08).

Camilleri, Joseph and Falk, Jim (1992) *The End of Sovereignty?* Aldershot: Edward Elgar.

Carter, Paul (1987) *The Road to Botany Bay*. London: Faber & Faber.

Castells, Manuel (1977) *The Urban Question: A Marxist Approach*. London: Edward Arnold.

Castells, Manuel (1983) *The City and the Grassroots: A Cross-cultural Theory of Urban Social Movements*. London: Edward Arnold.

Chakrabarty, Dipesh (2000) *Provincializing Europe: Postcolonial Thought and Historical Difference*. Princeton, NJ: Princeton University Press.

Chatterjee, Partha (1986) *Nationalist Thought and the Colonial World: A Derivative Discourse?* London: Zed Books.

Chatterton, Paul (2006) '"Give up activism" and change the world in unknown ways: or, learning to walk with others on uncommon ground', *Antipode*, 38(2): 259–81.

Clarke, John, Cochrane, Allan and Smart, Carol (1987) *Ideologies of Welfare: From Dreams to Disillusionment*. London: Hutchinson.

Clayton, Anthony (1994) *The Wars of French Decolonization*. London: Longman.

Coppieters, Bruno, Emerson, Michael, Huysseune, Michel, Kovzidre, Tamara, Noutcheva, Gergana, Tocci, Nathalie and Vahl, Marius (2004) *Europeanization and Conflict Resolution: Case Studies from the European Periphery*. Gent: Academia Press.

Corbridge, Stuart (1993) 'Marxisms, modernities, and moralities: development praxis and the claims of distant strangers', *Environment and Planning D: Society and Space,* 11: 449–72.

Cornwall, A. (2002) 'Locating citizen participation', *IDS Bulletin,* 33(2): 49–58.

Corrigan, Philip and Sayer, Derek (1985) *The Great Arch: English State Formation as Cultural Revolution.* Oxford: Blackwell.

Cresswell, Tim (1994) 'Putting women in their place: the carnival at Greenham Common', *Antipode: A Radical Journal of Geography,* 26: 35–58.

Crush, Jonathan (1994) 'Post-colonialism, de-colonization, and geography', in Anne Godlewska and Neil Smith (eds), *Geography and Empire.* Oxford: Blackwell. pp. 333–50.

Curtis, Sarah (1989) *The Geography of Public Welfare Provision.* London: Routledge.

Dandeker, Christopher (1990) *Surveillance, Power and Modernity: Bureaucracy and Discipline from 1700 to the Present Day.* Cambridge: Polity Press.

Darwin, Charles (1859) *On the Origin of Species by Means of Natural Selection, or, The Preservation of Favoured Races in the Struggle for Life.* London: J. Murray.

Day, Graham and Thompson, Andrew (2004) *Theorizing Nationalism.* Basingstoke: Palgrave Macmillan.

de Schweinitz Jr, Karl (1983) *The Rise and Fall of British India: Imperialism as Inequality.* London: Methuen.

Dear, Michael, J. (1988) 'The postmodern challenge: reconstructing human geography', *Transactions of the Institute of British Geographers,* 13: 262–74.

Department for Constitutional Affairs (2006) *Voting Rights of Convicted Prisoners Detained within the United Kingdom.* Available at: http://www.Dca.Gov.Uk/Consult/Voting-Rights/Cp2906.pdf (accsseed 04/02/08).

Dietz, M. (1985) 'Citizenship with a feminist face: the problem of maternal thinging', *Political Theory,* 13(1): 19–37.

Dittmer, Jason (2005) '*Captain America*'s empire: reflections on identity, popular culture, and post-9/11 geopolitics', *Annals of the Association of American Geographers,* 95(2): 626–43.

Dodds, Klaus (2005) 'Licensed to stereotype: geopolitics, James Bond and the spectre of Balkanism', *Geopolitics,* 8(2): 125–56.

Dodds, Klaus (2007) *A Very Short Introduction to Geopolitics.* Oxford: Oxford University Press.

Dolhinow, Rebecca (2005) 'Caught in the middle: the state, NGOs, and the limits to grassroots organizing along the US–Mexico border', *Antipode,* 37(3): 558–80.

Domosh, Mona (1991) 'Towards a feminist historiography of geography', *Transactions of the Institute of British Geographers,* 16: 95–104.

Dowler, Lorraine and Sharp, Joanne (2001) 'A feminist geopolitics?', *Space and Polity,* 5(3): 165–76.

Driver, Felix (1992) 'Geography's empire: histories of geographical knowledge', *Environment and Planning D: Society and Space,* 10: 23–40.

Drover, Glenn and Kerans, Patrick (eds) (1993) *New Approaches to Welfare.* Aldershot: Edward Elgar.

Elson, Diane (1984) 'Imperialism', in Gregor McLennan, David Held and Stuart Hall (eds), *The Idea of the Modern State.* Milton Keynes: Open University Press. pp. 154–82.

Esping-Andersen, Gøsta (1990) *The Three Worlds of Welfare Capitalism.* Cambridge: Polity Press.

Featherstone, Mike (1991) *Consumer Culture and Postmodernism.* London: Sage.

Ferguson, James and Gupta, Akhil (2002) 'Spatializing states: toward an ethnography of neoliberal governmentality', *American Ethnologist,* 29(4): 981–1002.

Fieldhouse, D.K. (1981) *The Colonial Empires: A Comparative Survey from the Eighteenth Century*. Basingstoke: Macmillan.

Flint, C. (2000) 'Electoral geography and the social construction of space: the example of the Nazi Party in Baden, 1924–32, *Geojournal*, 51: 145–56.

Foucault, Michel (1979) 'On governmentality', *Ideology & Consciousness*, 6: 5–21.

Foucault, Michel (1979) *Discipline and Punish*. New York: Vintage.

Frank, A.G. (1969) *Capitalism and Underdevelopment in Latin America*. New York: Monthly Review Press.

Fraser, Nancy (2005) 'Mapping the feminist imagination: from redistribution to recognition to representation', *Constellations*, 12(3): 295–307.

Fukuyama, F. (1992) *The End of History and the Last Man*. London: Penguin.

Gellner, Ernest (1983) *Nations and Nationalism*. Oxford: Blackwell.

Gellner, Ernest (1994) 'Nationalism and modernization', in J. Hutchinson and Anthony D. Smith (eds), *Nationalism*. Oxford: Oxford University Press. pp. 52–62.

Gibbs, Philip (undated) *The Romance of Empire*. London: Hutchinson.

Giddens, Anthony (1984) *The Constitution of Society*. Cambridge: Polity Press.

Giddens, Anthony (1985) *The Nation-state and Violence*. Cambridge: Polity Press.

Giddens, Anthony (1986) *Modernity and Self Identity*. Cambridge: Polity Press.

Gill, Anton (1995) *Ruling Passions: Sex, Race and Empire*. London: BBC Books.

Glassner, Martin and Fahrer, Chuck (2004) *Political Geography*. New York: John Wiley.

Godlewska, Anne and Smith, Neil (eds) (1994) *Geography and Empire*. Oxford: Blackwell.

Goldsworthy, Vesna (1998) *Inventing Ruritania: The Imperialism of the Imagination*. New Haven, CT and London: Yale University Press.

Gray, John (1986) *Liberalism*. Milton Keynes: Open University Press.

Gregory, Derek (1994) *Geographical Imaginations*. Oxford: Blackwell.

Gregory, Derek (2004) *The Colonial Present*. Oxford: Blackwell.

Griffith Taylor, T. (1957) 'Racial geography', in T. Griffith Taylor (ed.), *Geography in the Twentieth Century*. New York: Philosophical Library.

Habermas, Jürgen (1976) *Legitimation Crisis*. London: Heinemann.

Habermas, Jürgen (2001) 'Why Europe needs a constitution', *New Left Review*, 11: 5–26.

Hale, Angela and Wills, Jane (eds) (2005) *Threads of Labour: Garment Industry Supply Chains from the Workers' Perspective*. Oxford: Blackwell.

Halford, Susan (1988) 'Women's initiatives in local government: where do they come from and where are they going?', *Policy and Politics*, 16(4): 251–9.

Hall, Stuart (1992) 'The West and the rest: discourse and power', in Stuart Hall and Bram Gieben (eds), *Formations of Modernity*. Cambridge: Polity Press. pp. 275–331.

Harvey, David (1982) *The Limits to Capital*. Oxford: Blackwell.

Harvey, David (1989) *The Urban Experience*. Oxford: Blackwell.

Harvey, David (2003) *The New Imperialism*. Oxford: Oxford University Press.

Hawton, Nick (2008) 'Serbian fury erupts in Belgrade', *BBC News*. Available at: www.news.bbc.co.uk/2/hi/europe/7258373.stm (accessed 08/03/08).

Hepple, Leslie (1989) 'Destroying local Leviathans and designing landscapes of liberty? Public choice theory and the Poll Tax', *Transactions of the Institute of British Geographers*, 14: 387–99.

Herod, Andrew (2001) *Labor Geographies: Workers and the Landscapes of Capitalism*. New York: Guilford Press.

Herod, Andrew (ed.) (1998) *Organizing the Landscape: Geographical Perspectives on Labor Unionism*. Minneapolis, MN: University of Minnesota Press.

Hobsbawm, Eric (1990) *Nations and Nationalism since 1780*. Cambridge: Cambridge University Press.

Hobsbawm, Eric and Ranger, Terrence (eds) (1983a) *The Invention of Tradition*. Cambridge: Cambridge University Press.

Hobsbawm, Eric and Ranger, Terrence (1983b) 'Introduction: inventing traditions' in Eric Hobsbawn and Terrence Ranger (eds), *The Invention of Tradition*. Cambridge: Cambridge University Press. pp. 1–14.

Holmes, D. (2000) *Integral Europe: Fast-Capitalism Multiculturalism, Neofascism*. Princeton, N.J.: Princeton University Press.

hooks, bell (1981) *Ain't I a Woman: Black Women and Feminism*. Boston, MA: South End Press.

hooks, bell (1984) *Feminist Theory: From Margin to Centre*. Boston, MA: South End Press.

Huntington, S. (1991) *The Third Wave: Democratization in the Twentieth Century*. London: University of Oklahoma Press.

Hutton, Will (1995) *The State We're In*. London: Jonathan Cape.

Hyndman, Jennifer (2003) 'Beyond either/or: a feminist analysis of September 11th', *ACME: An International E-Journal for Critical Geography*, 2: 1–13.

Ingham, Geoffrey (1984) *Capitalism Divided: The City and Industry in British Social Development*. London: Macmillan.

Isaac, J. (1996) 'The meanings of 1989', *Social Research*, 63(2): 291–344.

Isin, E. (2002) *Being Political: Genealogies of Citizenship*. Minneapolis, MN: University of Minnesota Press.

Itzigsohn, J. (2000) 'Immigration and the boundaries of citizenship: the institutions of immigrants' political transnationalism', *International Migration Review*, 34(4): 1126–54.

Iveson, Kurt (2007) *Publics and the City*. Oxford: Blackwell.

Jeffrey, Alex (2007) 'The geopolitical framing of localized struggles: NGOs in Bosnia and Herzegovina', *Development and Change*, 38(2): 251–74.

Jessop, Bob (1990) *State Theory: Putting Capitalist States in Their Place*. Cambridge: Polity Press.

Johnston, R.J. (1993) 'The rise and decline of the corporate welfare state: a comparative analysis in global context', in P. Taylor (ed.), *Political Geography of the Twentieth Century*. London: Belhaven, pp. 115–70.

Johnston, R.J. (2000) 'Manipulating maps and winning elections: measuring the impact of malapportionment and gerrymandering', *Political Geography*, 21(1): 1–31.

Johnston, R.J. (2002) 'If it isn't a gerrymander, what is it?', *Political Geography*, 21: 55–65.

Johnston, R.J., Shelley, F.M. and Taylor, P.J. (1990) *Developments in Electoral Geography*. London: Routledge.

Jones, Rhys and Desforges, Luke (2003) 'Localities and the production of Welsh nationalism', *Political Geography*, 22(3): 271–92.

Judd, Dennis, R. and Swanstrom, Todd (1994) *City Politics: Private Power and Public Policy*. New York: HarperCollins.

Kaldor, M. (2003) *Global Civil Society*. London: Polity Press.

Kaplan, Robert D. (1994) *Balkan Ghosts: A Journey through History*. New York: Vintage.

Keating, Michael (1998) *The New Regionalism in Western Europe*. Cheltenham: Edward Elgar.

Keynes, John Maynard (1936) *The General Theory of Employment, Interest and Money*. London: Macmillan.

Kiernan, V.G. (1982) *European Empires from Conquest to Collapse, 1815–1960*. Leicester: Leicester University Press.

Konrad, George (2006 [1984]) 'Antipolitics: a moral force', in Gearóid Ó Tuathail, Simon Dalby and Paul Routledge (eds), *The Geopolitics Reader*. Abingdon: Routledge. pp. 259–61.

Kjellen, R. (1899) 'Studier ofver Sueriges Politistic granser', *Ymer* 19: 283–331.

Kurtz, Hilda (2007) 'Gender and environmental justice in Louisiana: blurring the boundaries of public and private spheres', *Gender, Place and Culture*, 14(4): 409–26.

Kuus, Merje (2004) 'Europe's eastern expansion and the inscription of Otherness in East–Central Europe', *Progress in Human Geography*, 28(4): 472–89.

Kuus, Merje (2007) *Geopolitics Reframed: Security and Identity in Europe's Eastern Enlargement*. New York and Basingstoke: Palgrave Macmillan.

Lampe, John R. (1996) *Yugoslavia as History: Twice There was a Country*. Cambridge: Cambridge University Press.

Lees, Loretta, Slater, Tom and Wyly, Elvin (2008) *Gentrification*. London: Routledge.

Legg, S. (2007) Beyond the European Province: Foucault and Postcolonalism,' in Jeremy Crampton and Stuart Elden (eds), *Space, Knowledge and Power: Foucault and Geography*. Aldershot: Ashgate.

Lenin, V.I. (1915) *Imperialism: the Highest Form of Capitalism*. Moscow: Foreign Languages Publishing House.

Lewis, Jane (ed.) (1993) *Women and Social Policies in Europe: Work, Family and the State*. Aldershot: Edward Elgar.

Ley, David (1996) *The New Middle Class and the Remaking of the Central City*. Oxford: Blackwell.

Lister, R. (1997) 'Citizenship: towards a feminist synthesis', *Feminist Review*, 57: 28–48.

Livingstone, David (1992) *The Geographical Tradition: Episodes in the History of a Contested Enterprise*. Oxford: Blackwell.

Locke, Geoffrey (2002) *The Serbian Epic Ballads: An Anthology*. London: The Association of Serbian Writers Abroad.

Lowe, Stuart (1986) *Urban Social Movements: The City after Castells*. London: Macmillan.

MacAllister, I., Johnston, R.J., Pattie, C.J., Tunstall, H., Dorling, D.F.L. and Rossiter, D.J. (2001) 'Class dealignment and the neighbourhood effect: Miller revisited', *British Journal of Political Science*, 31: 41–59.

Mackinder, Halford J. (1904) 'The geographical pivot of history', *The Geographical Journal*, 23(4): 421–37.

Mackinder, Halford J. (1919) *Democratic Ideal and Reality: A Study in the Politics of Reconstruction*. London: Constable and Company.

Mamadouh, Virginie, D. (1998) 'Geopolitics in the nineties: one flag, many meanings', *GeoJournal*, 46: 237–53.

Mangan, J.A. (ed.) (1990) *Making Imperial Mentalities: Socialisation and British Imperialism*. Manchester: Manchester University Press.

Mann, Michael (1988) *States, War and Capitalism*. Oxford: Blackwell.

Mansvelt Beck, Jan (2005) *Territory and Terror: Conflicting Nationalisms in the Basque Country*. Abingdon: Routledge.

Marshall, T.H. (1950) *Citizenship and Social Class*. Cambridge: Cambridge University Press.

Marshall, T.H. (1991) 'Citizenship and social class', in T.H. Marshall and Tom Bottomore, *Citizenship and Social Class*. London: Pluto Press. pp. 3–51.

Martin, Ron, Sunley, Peter and Wills, Jane (1996) *Union Retreat and the Regions: The Shrinking Landscape of Organised Labour*. London: Jessica Kingsley/RSA.

Massey, Doreen (2005) *For Space*. London: Sage.

Massey, Doreen and Painter, Joe (1989) 'The changing geography of trade unions', in J. Mohan (ed.), *The Political Geography of Contemporary Britain*. Basingstoke: Macmillan. pp. 130–50.

McCarthy, J. (1996) 'Mobilizing structures: constraints and opportunities in adopting, adapting, and inventing', in D. McAdam, J. McCarthy and M. Zald (eds), *Comparative Perspectives on Social Movements*. Cambridge: Cambridge University Press. pp. 141–51.

McDowell, Linda (1999) *Gender, Identity and Place: Understanding Feminist Geographies*. Minneapolis, MN: University of Minnesota Press.

McFarlane, Colin (2008) 'Sanitation in Mumbai's informal settlements: state, "slum", and infrastructure', *Environment and Planning A*, 40: 88–107.

Megoran, Nick (2006) 'For ethnography in Political Geography: experiencing and re-imagining Ferghana Valley boundary closures', *Political Geography*, 25(6): 622–40.

Mercer, Claire (2002) 'NGOs, civil society and democratization: a critical review of the literature', *Progress in Development Studies*, 2(1): 5–22.

Miller, A. Austin (1931) *Climatology*. London: Methuen.

Milosevic, Slobodan (1989) 'St. Vitus Day speech'. Available at: www. slobodan-milosevic. org/spch-kosovo1989.htm (accessed 10/03/08).

Miraftab, Faranak and Wills, Shana (2005) 'Insurgency and spaces of active citizenship: the story of Western Cape Anti-eviction Campaign in South Africa', *Journal of Planning Education and Research*, 25: 200–17.

Mitchell, Timothy (1988) *Colonizing Egypt*. Cambridge: Cambridge University Press.

Mitchell, Timothy (1991) 'The limits of the state: beyond statist approaches and their critics', *American Political Science Review*, 85(1): 77–96.

Moore, D. (2006) *Suffering for Territory: Race, Place and Power in Zimbabwe*. Durham N.C.: Duke University Press.

Moss, Pamela (ed.) (2002) *Feminist Geography in Practice: Research and Methods*. Oxford: Blackwell.

Mulgan, Geoff (1994) *Politics in an Antipolitical Age*. Cambridge: Polity Press.

Mwangi Kariuki, Josiah (1970) 'The "Mau-Mau" oath', in Elie Kedourie (ed.), *Nationalism in Asia and Africa*. London: Weidenfeld & Nicolson.

Nairn, Tom (1975) 'The modern Janus', *New Left Review*, 94: 3–29.

National Inquiry into the Separation of Aboriginal and Torres Strait Islander Children from Their Families (1997) *Bringing Them Home*. Available at: www.humanrights.gov.au/social_justice/bth_report/index.html (accessed 18/07/08).

Navaro-Yashin, Yael (2002) *Faces of the State Secularism and Public Life in Turkey*. Princeton, NJ: Princeton University Press.

Nelson, Lise and Seager, Joni (eds) (2004) *A Companion to Feminist Geography*. Oxford: Blackwell.

Neocleous, Mark (2003) *Imagining the State*. Maidenhead: Open University Press.

Ngugi wa Thiong'o (1986) *Decolonizing the Mind*. London: James Currey.

Nicholls, Walter J. (2007) 'The geographies of social movements', *Geography Compass*, 1(3): 607–22.

Noyce, Phillip (2002) *Rabbit-proof Fence*. New York: Miramax Films.

Ó Tuathail, Gearóid (1996a) *Critical Geopolitics*. London: Routledge.

Ó Tuathail, Gearóid (1996b) 'An anti-geopolitical eye: Maggie O'Kane in Bosnia 1992–1993', *Gender, Place and Culture*, 3(2): 171–85.

Ó Tuathail, Gearóid (2006) 'General introduction: thinking critically about Geopolitics', in Gearóid Ó Tuathail, Simon Dalby and Paul Routledge (eds), *The Geopolitics Reader*. Abingdon: Routledge. pp. 1–14.

Ó Tuathail, Gearóid and Agnew, John (1992) 'Geopolitics and discourse: practical geopolitical reasoning in American foreign policy', *Political Geography*, 11: 190–204.

O'Connor, James (1973) *The Fiscal Crisis of the State*. New York: St Martin's Press.

O'Connor, James (1987) *The Meaning of Crisis*. Oxford: Blackwell.

O'Hara, Sarah and Heffernan, Michael (2006) 'From geo-strategy to geo-economics: the 'Heartland' and British Imperialism before and after Mackinder', *Geopolitics*, 11(1): 54–73.

Offe, Claus (1984) *Contradictions of the Welfare State*. London: Hutchinson.

Omhae, Kenichi (1993) 'The rise of the regional state', *Foreign Affairs*, 72(2): 78–87.

OSCE (2007) *OSCE Election Observation Mission: The Kyrgyz Republic Statement of Preliminary Findings and Conclusions*. Available at: www.osce.org/documents/odihr/2007/12/28916_en.pdf (accessed 10/01/08).

Painter, Joe (1991) 'The geography of trade union responses to local government privatization', *Transactions of the Institute of British Geographers*, 16(2): 214–26.

Painter, Joe (1995) *Politics, Geography and 'Political Geography': A Critical Perspective*. London: Edward Arnold.

Painter, Joe (2006) 'Prosaic geographies of stateness', *Political Geography*, 25(7): 752–74.

Paasi, Anssi (2002) 'Place and region: regional worlds and words', *Progress in Human Geography*, 26(6): 802–11.

Peck, Jamie (2001) *Workfare States*. New York: Guilford Press.

Pierson, Christopher (1991) *Beyond the Welfare State: the New Political Economy of Welfare*. Cambridge: Polity Press.

Pierson, Christopher (2006) *Beyond the Welfare State: The New Political Economy of Welfare* (3rd edition). Cambridge: Polity Press.

Pinch, Steven (1980) *Cities and Services*. London: Routledge and Kegan Paul.

Power, Marcus and Crampton, Andrew (2005) 'Reel geopolitics: cinematographing political space', *Geopolitics*, 10(2): 193–203.

Ratzel, Freidrich (1897 [1923]) *Politische Geographie*. Munich and Berlin: R. Oldenbourg.

Renan, Ernest (1882 [1996]) *'Qu-est-ce qu'une nation?'*, in Geoff Eley and Ronald Grigor Suny (eds), *Becoming National: A Reader*. New York and Oxford: Oxford University Press. pp. 41–55.

Retort (2005) *Afflicted Powers: Capital and Spectacle in a New Age of War*. London: Verso.

Roberts, Susan, Secor, Anna and Sparke, Matthew (2003) 'Neoliberal geopolitics', *Antipode*, 25(5): 886–97.

Robinson, Jennifer (2006) *Ordinary Cities: Between Modernity and Development*. London: Routledge.

Rose, Gillian (1993) *Feminism and Geography: The Limits of Geographical Knowledge*. Cambridge: Polity Press.

Rostow, Walt Whitman (1960) *The Stages of Economic Growth*. Cambridge: Cambridge University Press.

Routledge, Paul (2005) 'Reflections on the G8: an interview with General Unrest of the Clandestine Insurgent Rebel Clown Army (CIRCA)', *ACME: An International E-Journal for Critical Geography*, 3(2): 112–20.

Routledge, Paul (2006a) 'Introduction to Part Five', in Gearóid Ó Tuathail, Simon Dalby and Paul Routledge (eds), *The Geopolitics Reader*. Abingdon: Routledge. pp. 233–48.

Routledge, Paul (2006b) 'Protesting and empowering: alternative responses to global forces', in Ian Douglas, Richard J. Hugget and Chris Perkins (eds), *Companion Encyclopaedia of Geography: From Local to Global*. London: Routledge, pp. 927–40.

Routledge, Paul, Cumbers, Andrew and Nativel, Corinne (2007) 'Grassrooting network imaginaries: relationality, power, and mutual solidarity in global justice networks', *Environment and Planning A*, 39(11): 2575–92.

Rush, M. (2000) 'Redistricting and partisan fluidity: do we really know a gerrymander when we see one?', *Political Geography*, 19: 249–60.

Sadler, David (2000) 'Organizing European labour: governance, production, trade unions and the question of scale', *Transactions of the Institute of British Geographers*, 25(2): 135–52.

Sadler, David and Fagan, Bob (2004) 'Australian trade unions and the politics of scale: reconstructing the spatiality of industrial relations', *Economic Geography*, 80(1): 23–43.

Said, Edward (1978) *Orientalism: Western Conceptions of the Orient.* Harmondsworth: Penguin.

Said, Edward (1993) *Culture and Imperialism.* London: Chatto & Windus.

Savage, Mike and Witz, Anne (eds) (1992) *Gender and Bureaucracy.* Oxford: Blackwell.

Secor, Anna (2001) 'Towards a feminist counter-geopolitics: gender, space and Islamist politics in Istanbul', *Space and Polity*, 5(3): 191–211.

Semple, Ellen Churchill (1911) *The Influences of Geographic Environment, on the Basis of Ratzel's System of Anthropo-geography.* London: Constable.

Sharp, Joanne (2000a) *Condensing the Cold War: Reader's Digest and American Identity.* Minneapolis, MN: University of Minnesota Press.

Sharp, Joanne (2000b) 'Remasculinising geo-politics? Comments on Gearóid Ó Tuathail's *Critical Geopolitics*', *Political Geography*, 19: 361–4.

Shaw, Wendy S. (2007) *Cities of Whiteness.* Oxford: Blackwell.

Siegfried, A. (1913) *Tableau Politique de la France L'Ouest.* Paris Colin.

Smith, Anthony D. (1989) 'The origins of nations', *Ethnic and Racial Studies*, 12(3): 340–67.

Smith, Anthony, D. (1998) *Nationalism and Modernism.* London: Routledge.

Smith, David, M. (1994) *Geography and Social Justice.* Oxford: Blackwell.

Smith, G., Law, V., Wilson, A. Bohr, A. and Allworth, E. (1998) *Nation-building in the Post-Soviet Borderlands.* Cambridge: Cambridge University Press.

Smith, Neil (1984) *Uneven Development.* Oxford: Blackwell.

Smith, Neil (1996) *The New Urban Frontier: Gentrification and the Revanchist City.* London: Routledge.

Smith, Neil (2003) *American Empire: Roosevelt's Geographer and the Prelude to Globalization.* Berkeley, CA: University of California Press.

Smith, Neil (2005) *The Endgame of Globalization.* New York:

Soja, Edward, W. (1968) 'Communications and territorial integration in East Africa: an introduction to transaction flow analysis', *East Lakes Geographer*, 4: 39–57.

Soja, Edward, W. (1989) *Postmodern Geographies: The Reassertion of Space in Critical Social Theory.* London: Verso.

Soja, Edward, W. (2000) *Postmetropolis: Critical Studies of Cities and Regions.* Oxford: Blackwell.

Spivak, Gayatri Chakravorty (1988) 'Can the subaltern speak?', in Cary Nelson and Lawrence Grossberg (eds), *Marxism and the Interpretation of Culture.* Chicago: University of Illinois Press. pp. 271–313.

Stoddart, David (1986) *On Geography and Its History.* Oxford: Blackwell.

Sunley, Peter, Martin, Ron and Nativel, Corinne (2006) *Putting Workfare in Place: Local Labour Markets and the New Deal.* Oxford: Blackwell.

Tarrow, Sydney (1998) *Power in Movement: Social Movements and Contentious Politics.* Cambridge: Cambridge University Press.

Taylor, Peter (1989a [1985]) *Political Geography: World-economy, Nation-state and Locality* (2nd edition). Harlow: Longman.

Taylor, Peter (1989b) 'The error of developmentalism in human geography', in Derek Gregory and Rex Walford (eds), *Horizons in Human Geography*. Basingstoke: Macmillan. pp. 303–19.

Tiebout, Charles, M. (1956) 'A pure theory of local expenditures', *The Journal of Political Economy*, 64(5): 416–24.

Tilly, Charles (1990) *Coercion, Capital and European States: AD 990–1990*. Oxford: Blackwell.

Todorova, Maria (1997) *Imagining the Balkans*. New York: Oxford University Press.

Trevor-Roper, Hugh (1983) 'The invention of tradition: the Highland tradition of Scotland', in Eric Hobsbawm and Terrence Ranger (eds), *The Invention of Tradition*. Cambridge: Cambridge University Press. pp. 15–42.

United Nations (2008) *World Urbanization Prospects*. New York: United Nations.

United Nations Development Programme (2007) *Human Development Report 2007/2008*. Basingstoke: Palgrave Macmillan.

Urban Task Force (1999) *Towards an Urban Renaissance*. London: Department of Environment, Transport and the Regions.

Valentine, Gill and Skelton, Tracey (2007) 'The right to be heard: citizenship and language', *Political Geography*, 26(2): 121–40.

Velek, J. (2004) 'Jürgen Habermas and the utopia of perpetual peace', *Filosoficky Casopis*, 52(2): 231–56.

Wallerstein, Immanuel (2004) *World-Systems Analysis: An Introduction*. Durham, NC: Duke University Press.

Whatmore, Sarah (1997) 'Dissecting the autonomous self: hybrid cartographies for a relational ethics', *Environment and Planning D: Society and Space*, 15: 37–53.

White House (2002) 'The national security strategy of the United States of America'. Washington, DC: The White House. Available at: www.whitehouse.gov/nsc/nss.html (accessed 03/02/08).

Willetts, P. (2002) *What is a Non-Governmental Organization?* Available at: www.staff.city.ac.uk/p.willetts/CS-NTWKS/NGO-ART.HTM (accessed 13/01/08).

Williams, Fiona (1989) *Social Policy: A Critical Introduction*. Cambridge: Polity Press.

Wolch, Jennifer, R. (1989) 'The shadow state: transformations in the voluntary sector', in Jennifer R. Wolch and Michael Dear (eds), *The Power of Geography: How Territory Shapes Social Life*. Boston, MA: Unwin Hyman. pp. 197–221.

Wolf, Eric, R. (1982) *Europe and the People without History*. Berkeley, CA: University of California Press.

Wollstonecraft, Mary (2004) *A Vindication of the Rights of Woman*. London: Penguin.

Young, Iris Marion (1990) *Justice and the Politics of Difference*. Princeton, NJ: Princeton University Press.

Young, Robert (1990) *White Mythologies: Writing History and the West*. London: Routledge.

Index

Research Methods Books from SAGE

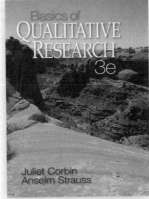

Basics of QUALITATIVE RESEARCH 3e

Juliet Corbin
Anselm Strauss

The Mixed Methods Reader

Vicki L. Plano Clark • John W. Creswell

DOING QUALITATIVE RESEARCH USING YOUR COMPUTER

A PRACTICAL GUIDE

CHRIS HAHN

SECOND EDITION
INTERVIEWS
Learning the Craft of Qualitative Research Interviewing

Steinar Kvale
Svend Brinkmann

DISCOVERING STATISTICS USING SPSS THIRD EDITION

ANDY FIELD

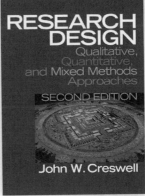

RESEARCH DESIGN
Qualitative, Quantitative, and Mixed Methods Approaches
SECOND EDITION

John W. Creswell

www.sagepub.co.uk

Supporting researchers for more than forty years

Research methods have always been at the core of SAGE's publishing. Sara Miller McCune founded SAGE in 1965 and soon after, she published SAGE's first methods book, Public Policy Evaluation. A few years later, she launched the Quantitative Applications in the Social Sciences series – affectionately known as the "little green books".

Always at the forefront of developing and supporting new approaches in methods, SAGE published early groundbreaking texts and journals in the fields of qualitative methods and evaluation.

Today, more than forty years and two million little green books later, SAGE continues to push the boundaries with a growing list of more than 1,200 research methods books, journals, and reference works across the social, behavioral, and health sciences.

From qualitative, quantitative, mixed methods to evaluation, SAGE is the essential resource for academics and practitioners looking for the latest methods by leading scholars.

www.sagepublications.com